The
HIDDEN INNS
of
THE WELSH BORDERS

Edited by
Barbara Vesey

Published by:
Travel Publishing Ltd
7a Apollo House, Calleva Park
Aldermaston, Berks, RG7 8TN
ISBN 1-902-00762-X
© Travel Publishing Ltd

First Published: *2000*

Regional Titles in the Hidden Inns Series:

Central & Southern Scotland	Southeast England
South of England	Wales
Welsh Borders	West Country

Regional Titles in the Hidden Places Series:

Cambridgeshire & Lincolnshire	Chilterns
Cornwall	Derbyshire
Devon	Dorset, Hants & Isle of Wight
East Anglia	Gloucestershire & Wiltshire
Heart of England	Hereford, Worcs & Shropshire
Highlands & Islands	Kent
Lake District & Cumbria	Lancashire and Cheshire
Lincolnshire	Northumberland & Durham
Somerset	Sussex
Thames Valley	Yorkshire

National Titles in the Hidden Places Series:

England	Ireland
Scotland	Wales

Printing by: Ashford Colour Press, Gosport
Maps by: © MAPS IN MINUTES ™ (2000)
Line Drawings: Sarah Bird
Editor: Barbara Vesey
Cover Design: Lines & Words, Aldermaston
Cover Photographs: The Plaisterers Arms, Winchcombe, Gloucestershire;
The Black Horse, Maesbrook, Shropshire;
The Hollow Bottom, Guiting Power, Gloucestershire

FOREWORD

The **Hidden Inns** series originates from the enthusiastic suggestions of readers of the popular **Hidden Places** guides. They want to be directed to traditional inns "off the beaten track" with atmosphere and character which are so much a part of our British heritage. But they also want information on the many places of interest and activities to be found in the vicinity of the inn.

The inns or pubs reviewed in the **Hidden Inns** may have been coaching inns but have invariably been a part of the history of the village or town in which they are located. All the inns included in this guide serve food and drink and many offer the visitor overnight accommodation. A full page is devoted to each inn which contains a line drawing of the inn, full name, address and telephone number, directions on how to get there, a full description of the inn and its facilities and a wide range of useful information such as opening hours, food served, accommodation provided, credit cards taken and details of entertainment. **Hidden Inns** guides however are not simply pub guides. They provide the reader with helpful information on the many places of interest to visit and activities to pursue in the area in which the inn is based. This ensures that your visit to the area will not only allow you to enjoy the atmosphere of the inn but also to take in the beautiful countryside which surrounds it.

The **Hidden Inns** guides have been expertly designed for ease of use. **The Hidden Inns of the Welsh Borders** is divided into 8 regionally based chapters, each of which is laid out in the same way. To identify your preferred geographical region refer to the contents page overleaf. To find a pub or inn simply use the index and locator map at the beginning of each chapter which refers you, via a page number reference, to a full page dedicated to the specific establishment. To find a place of interest again use the index and locator map found at the beginning of each chapter which will guide you to a descriptive summary of the area followed by details of each place of interest.

We do hope that you will get plenty of enjoyment from visiting the inns and places of interest contained in this guide. We are always interested in what our readers think of the inns or places covered (or not covered) in our guides so please do not hesitate to write to us. This is a vital way of helping us ensure that we maintain a high standard of entry and that we are providing the right sort of information for our readers. Finally if you are planning to visit any other corner of the British Isles we would like to refer you to the list of Hidden Inns and Hidden Places guides to be found at the rear of the book.

Travel Publishing

LOCATOR MAP

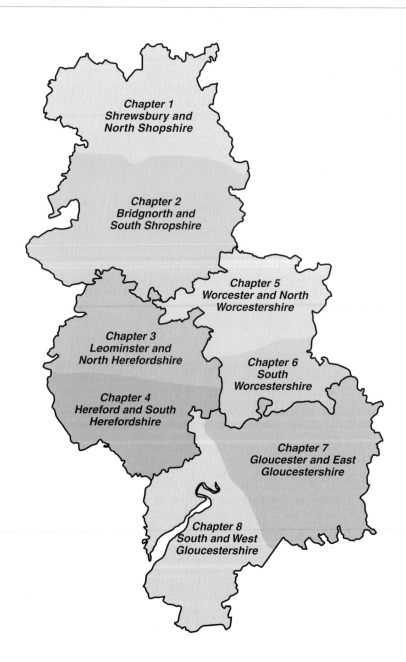

Chapter 1
Shrewsbury and
North Shopshire

Chapter 2
Bridgnorth and
South Shropshire

Chapter 5
Worcester and North
Worcestershire

Chapter 3
Leominster and
North Herefordshire

Chapter 6
South
Worcestershire

Chapter 4
Hereford and South
Herefordshire

Chapter 7
Gloucester and East
Gloucestershire

Chapter 8
South and West
Gloucestershire

CONTENTS

TITLE PAGE   *i*

FOREWORD   *iii*

LOCATOR MAP   *iv*

CONTENTS   *v*

GEOGRAPHICAL AREAS:

Chapter 1: Shrewsbury and North Shopshire   1
Chapter 2: Bridgnorth and South Shropshire   21
Chapter 3: Leominster and North Herefordshire   47
Chapter 4: Hereford and South Herefordshire   67
Chapter 5: Worcester and North Worcestershire   87
Chapter 6: South Worcestershire   109
Chapter 7: Gloucester and East Gloucestershire   125
Chapter 8: South and West Gloucestershire   151

INDEXES AND LISTS:

Alphabetic List of Pubs and Inns   181
Special Interest Lists of Pubs and Inns:
    With accommodation   184
    Opening all day   186
    With childrens facilities   188
    Accepting credit cards   189
    With garden, patio or terrace   191
    With occasional or regular live entertainment   193
    With a separate restaurant or dining area   195

Index of Towns, Villages and Places of Interest   197

ADDITIONAL INFORMATION

Reader Reaction Forms   199
Order Form   201

1 Shrewsbury and North Shropshire

PLACES OF INTEREST:

Boscobel 3
Colehurst 3
Ellesmere 3
Hodnet 4
Llanymynech 4
Maesbury 4
Marchamley 4
Market Drayton 4
Melverley 5
Montford 5
Moreton Corbet 5

Nesscliffe 5
Newport 5
Oswestry 6
Shrewsbury 6
Tong 8
Wem 8
Weston-under-Lizard 8
Whitchurch 8
Whittington 9
Wollaston 9

PUBS AND INNS:

The Admiral Duncan, Baschurch 10
The Admiral Rodney, Criggion 11
The Black Bear, Whitchurch 12
The Black Horse Inn, Maesbrook 13
The Bradford Arms, Knockin 14
The Bradford Arms, Llanymynech 15
The Cleveland Arms, High Ercall 16
The Horse and Jockey, Whitchurch 17
The Horseshoes, Tilstock 18
The Narrowboat Inn, Whittington 19
The Penrhos Arms, Whittington 20

The Hidden Inns of the Welsh Borders

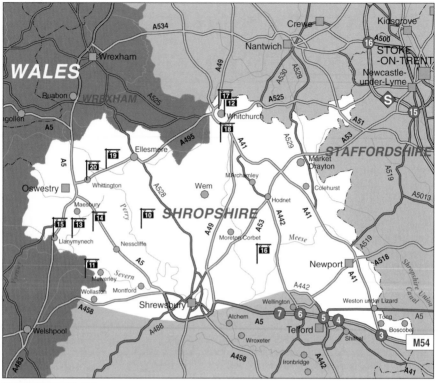

© MAPS IN MINUTES ™ (2000)

10	The Admiral Duncan, **Baschurch**	**16**	The Cleveland Arms, **High Ercall**
11	The Admiral Rodney, **Criggion**	**17**	The Horse and Jockey, **Whitchurch**
12	The Black Bear, **Whitchurch**	**18**	The Horseshoes, **Tilstock**
13	The Black Horse Inn, **Maesbrook**	**19**	The Narrowboat Inn, **Whittington**
14	The Bradford Arms, **Knockin**	**20**	The Penrhos Arms, **Whittington**
15	The Bradford Arms, **Llanymynech**		

Please note all cross references refer to page numbers

Shrewsbury and North Shropshire

Shropshire was recently accorded the title of "The Most Romantic County in Britain". A tranquil face hides an often turbulent past that is revealed at scores of sites by the remains of dykes and ramparts and hill forts, and by the castles of the Marcher Lords, who seem to have divided their time between fighting the Welsh and fighting each other. North Shropshire offers many delights: the lakes and canals of the northwest - including the county's own Lake District around Ellesmere - the rich farming plains around Oswestry and, of course, the historic town of Shrewsbury, the county capital located right in the middle of the county. Shrewsbury houses some of the most fascinating and evocative museums in the nation.

PLACES OF INTEREST

BOSCOBEL

After Charles II was defeated by the Roundheads at the Battle of Worcester in 1651, he fled for his life and was advised to seek refuge in a remote hunting lodge called **Boscobel House**, already known as a safe house for royals on the run. By day the King hid in the branches of an old oak tree, while at night he would creep into the house and hide in secret rooms with one of his trusty officers. He eventually escaped, of course, and nine years later was restored to the throne. The house has changed considerably since Charles' time, but it's still full of atmosphere and interest, with an exhibition giving a vivid account of the King's adventures. Every visitor naturally wants to see the famous oak in which he hid, but it is no longer standing, destroyed by souvenir-hunting loyalists. Today there stands a descendant of the original, itself now more than 300 years old.

COLEHURST

In a beautiful and relatively unknown part of England stands an old manor house trapped in a time warp. Visitors describe **Old Colehurst Manor** as 'a journey back through time to the real 16th century'. The tranquil grounds include walled, rose, herb and knot gardens. The manor and grounds are open for day visits from the beginning of April to the end of September.

ELLESMERE

The centre of Shropshire's Lakeland, Ellesmere is a pretty market town with Tudor, Georgian and Victorian buildings. The **Old Town Hall** and the **Old Railway Station** are two of the most impressive buildings, but nothing except the mound remains of the castle. The most impressive of all is the parish church of **St Mary the Virgin**, built by the Knights of St John. It is particularly beautiful inside, with an exceptional 15th-century carved roof in the chapel.

The church overlooks **The Mere**, largest of several lakes that are an equal delight to boating enthusiasts, anglers and birdwatchers. Herons, Canada geese and swans are among the

The Mere

4

inhabitants of The Mere.

A mile or so east of Ellesmere, on the A495, is **Welshampton**, whose church was built by Sir George Gilbert Scott in 1863. One of its memorial windows is dedicated to a Basuto chieftain; he had been a student of theology at Canterbury and part of his studies brought him to Welshampton, where he lodged with the vicar. Unfortunately he fell ill and died in the same year that saw the completion of the church.

HODNET

The sizeable village of Hodnet is overlooked by the church of St Luke from its hilltop position. The church is Norman, with some unusual features including a christening gate and wedding steps, and it has a very distinctive octagonal tower. There are some ornate carvings around the 17th-century font, and a chapel is dedicated to the Heber-Percy family, owners of **Hodnet Hall**. The most illustrious member of the family was Bishop Heber, who wrote, among many other hymns, *From Greenland's Icy Mountains*. Hodnet Hall is an Elizabethan-style mansion built in the 1870s, but the real reason for a visit

Hodnet Hall and Gardens

here is the wonderful gardens, which extend over 60 acres and were carefully planted (Brigadier Heber-Percy masterminded the transformation) to provide a show of colour throughout the seasons.

LLANYMYNECH

A small diversion is well worth while to visit Llanymynech, once a town of some standing, with a major canal and a thriving industry based on limestone. It was also a railway junction. The **Llanymynech Hills**, which include

a section of **Offa's Dyke**, make for good walking, with the old limestone workings to add interest - you can still see the old bottle lime kilns and an unusual Hoffman rotary kiln. The quarried limestone was taken to the kilns on a tramway and, after processing, to the nearby canalside wharf. Part of the quarry is now a designated nature reserve and supports abundant bird life. On top of the hill are traces of an ancient hill fort.

The **Montgomery Canal** was built at the end of the 18th century mainly for the transportation of limestone from the Llanymynech quarries. Large sections of it are now unnavigable, indeed dry, but a restoration project is under way with the aim of opening 35 miles of waterway from Oswestry through Welshpool to Newtown. Until the boats return there are some delightful walks along the towpath, as well as fishing where it is possible.

MAESBURY

This village was one of the main transit points on the Montgomery Canal, and many of the canal buildings at Maesbury Marsh are still standing, along with some boatmen's cottages.

Immediately south of Maesbury Marsh is the village of **Woolston**, where St Winifred's Well is said to have been a resting place for saints' bones being carried to their final destinations.

MARCHAMLEY

The beautiful Georgian mansion **Hawkestone Hall** was the ancestral home of the Hill family from 1556 until 1906. The Hall is now the seat of a religious order, but the principal rooms, including the splendid Venetian Saloon, are open for a short time in the summer. **The Pleasure Gardens** comprise terraces, lily pond, herbaceous borders and extensive woodland. On the same estate, at Weston-under-Lizard, is **Hawkestone Park**, a woodland fantasy of caves and follies and grottoes, of tunnels and secret pathways. The Hills built this extraordinary park, which if it were built today would probably be called a theme park.

MARKET DRAYTON

Market Drayton was mentioned in the Domesday Book as Magna Draitune. It changed its name when Abbot Simon Combermere obtained a Royal Market Charter in 1245:

"Know that we have granted and by this our

present charter confirmed to Brother Simon Abbot of Combermere and the minks serving God there that they and their successors forever shall have a weekly market in their manor of Drayton on Wednesday."

And so they have, every Wednesday.

The fire of 1651 raised most of the town, so there is now quite a diversity of styles among the buildings. One of the most interesting is the **Buttercross**, built in 1842 to enable farmers' wives to display their wares protected from the weather. The crest it carries is of the Corbet family, Lords of the Manor since 1650.

Market Drayton is often referred to as "The Home of the Gingerbread". Gingerbread has been baked here for 200 years and is made in all shapes and sizes, the best known being the Gingerbread Man. Traditionally dunked in port, it's also very good to nibble on the **Discovery Trail** that takes in the sights of the town. Gingerbread dates back far more than 200 years, of course, and Shakespeare had a good word for it:

> *"An' I had but one penny in the world thou shouldst have it to buy gingerbread."*

Market Drayton's most famous son (actually born just outside) was Clive of India, whose childhood escapades in the town included climbing the church tower and sitting on one of the gargoyles, and building a dam to flood a shop whose owner was unwilling to pay protection money.

MELVERLEY

Country lanes lead to the remarkable **Church of St Peter**, which stands serenely, if somewhat precariously, on the banks of the River Vyrnwy. This is a most unusual church: built in 1406 after the original was destroyed by Owen Glendower, it is timber-framed and painted black and white inside and out.

MONTFORD

It's worth pausing at Montford to look at the church where Charles Darwin was buried for a time. His body was subsequently moved to Westminster Abbey, showing that the furore caused by his theories had largely died down soon after his death - but not entirely, as *The Origin of Species* and *The Descent of Man* can still arouse fierce debate. Just beyond Montford are the ruins of Shrawardine Castle.

MORETON CORBET

5

Take the A53 to Shawbury and turn left on to the B5063 and you'll soon come across the splendid ruins of **Moreton Corbet Castle**, seat of the local bigwig family. Its stark greystone walls are an entrancing and moving sight, and not at all like a castle. In fact, what remains is the

Moreton Corbet Castle

shell of a grand Italian-influenced mansion which was never completed (Corbet funds ran out) and was severely damaged in the Civil War.

NESSCLIFFE

Near the village of Nesscliffe, which lies halfway between Shrewsbury and Oswestry, is **Nesscliffe Hill Country Park**, where paths lead up through woodland to the summit and fine views over Shropshire. The Hill is a sandstone escarpment, popular for walking and rock climbing; cut into the face of an abandoned quarry are caves, one of them reputedly the lair of the 16th-century worthy-turned-highwayman Humphrey Kynaston. The whole area southwest of Oswestry, including Nesscliffe, Knockin, Ruyton and Melverley, is known as Kynaston Country.

A short distance north of Nesscliffe, on the B4397, is the village of **Ruyton-XI-Towns**, which acquired its unusual name in medieval times when 11 communities were united into the borough of Ruyton.

NEWPORT

Newport is a handsome town which sadly lost many of its buildings in a fire in 1665. Most of the buildings on the broad main street are Georgian or early Victorian. There's plenty to keep the visitor active in the area, including the

6

Lilleshall National Sports Centre and the ruins of Lilleshall Abbey, the extensive and evocative remains of an Augustinian abbey.

OSWESTRY

Close to the Welsh border, Oswestry is an important market town whose look is mainly Georgian and Victorian, due in part to the fires which regularly ravaged timber-framed buildings. The town grew up around **St Oswald's Well**. Oswald was a Saxon king who was killed in a battle in 642 against a rival Saxon king, Penda of Mercia. Oswald's body was dismembered and hung on the branches of a tree. An eagle swooped and carried off one of his arms and where the limb fell to the ground a spring bubbled up to mark the spot. Thus St Oswald's Well came into being, soon to become a place of pilgrimage renowned for its healing powers.

There are many fine old buildings in Oswestry, none finer than the **Church of St Oswald**. It played an important part in the Civil War, when it was used as an observation point during the siege of the town by the Parliamentarians. The oldest section is the tower, which dates back to around 1200. The interior is beautiful, and among the treasures are a font presented by Colonel Lloyd of Llanforda as a thanksgiving for the restoration of the monarchy, a Gilbert Scott war memorial and a memorial to Hugh Yale, a member of the family that founded Yale University.

Standing in the grounds of the church is the 15th-century **Holbache House**. Once a grammar school, this handsome building now houses the Tourist Information Centre and the **Heritage Centre**, with displays of local interest and exhibitions of arts and crafts. Ferrequinologists (railway buffs) will make tracks for the **Cambrian Museum of Transport** on Oswald Road. Oswestry was the headquarters of the Cambrian Railway Company until it amalgamated with the GWR in 1922, and as late as the 1960s there were over 1,000 railwaymen in the area. Locomotives, carriages and wagons have been built and repaired in Oswestry for over 100 years, and the maintenance of 300 miles of track was directed from offices in the station building. One of the old engine sheds now houses a small museum with a collection of railway memorabilia and also some old bicycles and motorbikes. One of the

locomotives is regularly steamed up by the volunteers of the Cambrian Railway Society.

In 1559 a plague killed almost a third of the town's population. **The Croeswylan Stone** commemorates this disaster, marking the spot to which the market was moved during the plague. It is sometimes referred to as the Cross of Weeping.

On the northern edge of town, **Old Oswestry** is an impressive example of an Iron Age fortress, first occupied in about 300BC. It was on the border of the territory held by the Cornovii and is one of several in the region. At the southwest corner of the fort can be seen **Wat's Dyke**, built at the same time and for the same purpose - delineating the border between Saxon Mercia and the Welsh - as the better-known Offa's Dyke. Who was Wat? We know not, but he could have been one of Offa's officers.

SHREWSBURY

The River Severn winds round the lovely county town in a horseshoe bend, making it almost an island site, and it was on two hills within this protected site that the Saxon town developed. The Normans under Roger de Montgomery took over after the conquest, building the castle and the great Benedictine abbey. In the 15th and 16th centuries Shrewsbury prospered through the wool trade, and evidence of its affluence shows in the many black-and-white timbered buildings that still line the streets. In Victorian times steam made Shrewsbury an important railway centre whilst at the same time Darwin, born and educated in the town, was rocking the world with his theories. Everywhere there is a sense of history, and the Museums do a particularly fine job of bringing the past to life, in terms of both human and natural history. **Rowley's House** is a glorious timber-framed building of the late 16th century, with an adjoining brick and stone mansion of 1618. The

Shrewsbury Castle

home of William Rowley, 17th-century draper, brewer and leading citizen, now contains an impressive collection of pieces from *Viroconium*, along with spectacular displays of costumes, natural history and geology.

A short walk away is **Clive House**, in the Georgian area of the town. Clive of India lived here in 1762 while he was Mayor, and one or two mementoes can be seen. The major displays are of Shropshire ceramics and the life of Charles Darwin, whose statue stands opposite the Castle. The Castle, dating from 1083, was built by the Norman Earl Roger de Montgomery and last saw action in the Civil War. It was converted by Thomas Telford into a private residence and now houses the **Shropshire Regimental Museum** with the collections of the Kings Shropshire Yeomanry Cavalry and the Shropshire Royal Horse Artillery.

A museum with a difference is **Coleham Pumping Station** at Longden Coleham, which houses the splendid Renshaw pumping engines that powered Shrewsbury's sewerage system until 1970.

The Abbey, like the Castle, was founded by Roger de Montgomery, on the site of a Saxon wooden church. In 1283 a parliament met in the Chapter House, the first national assembly in which the Commons were involved. The Abbey Church remains a place of worship, and

in 1997 a stained glass window depicting St Benedict was dedicated to the memory of Edith Pargeter.

This lady, writing under the name of Ellis Peters, created the character of Brother Cadfael, who lived at the Abbey and became one of the country's best-loved fictional characters when portrayed by Derek Jacobi in the television series. Hard by the Abbey, **The Shrewsbury Quest** presents the sights and sounds of medieval Shrewsbury. Visitors can see Brother Cadfael's workshop, solve mysteries, create their own medieval manuscripts and breathe in the fragrance of a monastic herb garden. Complementing the town's Museum and Archaeological Services, a Records and Research Service was opened in a new building in 1995. It has 5½

Fish Street and St Julians Church

miles of material relating to Shropshire past and present, including many original records and extensive microfilm records. Shrewsbury has more than 30 churches and among the finest are St Mary's and St Chad's. **St Mary's**, the town's only complete medieval church, originated in the late Saxon period, but the earliest features of the present building are of the 12th century. The stained glass, monuments and fittings are quite out of the ordinary, and the spire has claims to being the third highest in the land. One of the memorials is to Admiral Benbow, a national hero who died in 1702 and is also remembered in innumerable pub signs. **St Chad's** is the work of Attingham Hall's designer George Steuart, who was commissioned to design a replacement for the original, which fell down in 1788. His church is very unusual in having a circular nave.

The Abbots House

8

Guided tours and suggested walks cover all aspects of this marvellous town, including a **Brother Cadfael Tour** and walks in the beautiful countryside that is all around. One walk takes in the spot to the north of town now known as Battlefield, where in 1403 the armies of Henry IV and the insurgent Harry Percy (Harry Hotspur) met. 50,000 men were deployed in all, and in the brief but bloody battle Hotspur was among the many casualties. A church was built near the mass grave, where 1,600 bodies are buried, a monument to the fallen and also an oasis of wildlife in the town environment.

Shrewsbury Flower Show is Britain's best two-day summer show and each August for more than a century the show has been held in the picturesque setting of **Quarry Park**. Three million blooms fill three giant marquees, and the show includes a musical programme and fireworks displays.

TONG

Tong is an attractive village which once had a castle, founded, according to legend, by the wizard Merlin. Where was he when the castle was blown up in 1954? The Vernons and the Durants were the Lords of the Manor in Tong for many years and they are commemorated in 15th-century **Church of St Bartholomew**. The Vernons were a particularly distinguished lot: one was a Speaker of the House of Commons and another was Lord High Constable to Henry V. In the Golden Chapel, which has a superb gilded, fan-vaulted ceiling, there is a bust of Arthur Vernon, who was a don at Cambridge University. Venetia Stanley, descended from the Vernons and the Earls of Derby, was a famed beauty who was lauded by poets and artists. She counted Ben Jonson, Van Dyck and the Earl of Dorset among her lovers, but in 1625 she made the unfortunate move of marrying Sir Kenelm Digby, whose father had been executed for his part in the Gunpowder Plot. She died tragically young, some say at the hands of her jealous husband.

Charles Dickens is thought to have had Tong in mind when he wrote *The Old Curiosity Shop*: Little Nell's home was right by the church, and some say that she is buried in the churchyard.

A couple of miles east of Tong is **White Ladies Priory**, where the ruins of a 12th-century church may be seen.

WEM

A peaceful enough place now, but Wem has seen its share of strife, being virtually destroyed in the Wars of the Roses and attacked in the Civil War. On the latter occasion, in 1643, Lord Capel at the head of 5,000 Royalist troops got a pretty hostile reception, and his defeat by a much smaller band, including some townswomen, gave rise to this mocking couplet:

"The women of Wem and a few volunteers
Beat the Lord Capel and all his Cavaliers."

It was another woman - actually a 14-year-old girl called Jane Churm - who nearly did what Capel proved incapable of doing. In setting alight the thatch on the roof of her home she started a fire that destroyed 140 properties in one hour. Some notable buildings survived, including **Astley House**, home of the painter John Astley. This and many of the town's most impressive houses are in **Noble Street**. Famous people associated with Wem include Judge Jeffrey's of Bloody Assize fame, who became Baron Wem in 1685, with his official residence at Lowe Hall. Wem is the home of the modern sweet pea, developed by the 19th-century nurseryman Henry Eckford. The **Sweet Pea Show** and the carnival are great occasions in the Wem calendar.

WESTON-UNDER-LIZARD

Just on the border with Staffordshire stands **Weston Park**, a fine restoration mansion that has been the home of the Earls of Bradford for 15 generations. It was recently chosen by the Prime Minister for the Retreat Day of the G8 Summit of World Leaders. Inside, they would have admired a wealth of treasures including paintings by Van Dyck, Gainsborough and Stubbs, fine books, porcelain and Beauvais and Gobelin tapestries. The setting of 1,000 acres of Capability Brown landscape embraces a deer park, pets corner and playground with a miniature railway. Lots of special events take place each year.

WHITCHURCH

First developed by the Romans as *Mediolanum*, Whitchurch is the most important town in the northern part of the county. Its main street is dominated by the tall sandstone tower of **St Alkmund's Church**, in whose chapel lies the body of Sir John Talbot, 1st Earl of Shrewsbury, who was killed at the Battle of Castillon, near

Bordeaux, in 1453. **The Shropshire Way** passes nearby, so too the **Llangollen Canal**, and nature-lovers can explore the local wetland habitats - **Brown Moss** is 2 miles to the south off the A41. Whitchurch is the home of **Joyce Clocks**, the oldest tower clockmakers in the world, and is also, somewhat oddly, where Cheshire cheese was created. Hidden away in the heart of the town are the **Old Town Hall Vaults**, where the composer Edward German (*Merrie England, Tom Jones*) was born in 1862.

ing *For All the Saints*. Dick Whittington may or may not have been born here, but someone who definitely lived at nearby **Halston Hall** for many years was Mad Jack Mytton, a 19th-century hard-living squire and sometime MP for Shrewsbury.

Park Hall Farm Museum houses a splendid display of 19th-century farm implements and is also home to some rare breed animals and some marvellous Shire horses, who work on the land at certain times.

WOLLASTON

The church here has a memorial to Thomas Parr, widely claimed to be the longest-lived Englishman, dying at the ripe old age of 152. He lived through ten reigns, married for the first time at 88, raised a family and married again at 122. He is buried in Westminster Abbey, so someone must have believed his story.

Whitchurch High Street

Whitchurch has a major attraction for anglers at **Dearnford Hall Trout Fishery**, with fishing from bank or boat, tuition and accommodation.

WHITTINGTON

On the eastern edge of Oswestry, Whittington once had a castle, but little now remains. Close by is the parish church where William Walsham How, later Bishop of Wakefield, was the incumbent for almost 30 years. He was a hymnwriter of some standing, one of his finest hymns be-

10   The Admiral Duncan

Newtown, Baschurch,
Shrewsbury,
Shropshire SY4 2AY
Tel: 01939 260397

Directions:

From Shrewsbury take the A5 north towards Oswestry. About 9 miles along this road, turn right on the B4397 to Baschurch (5 miles). As you enter Baschurch, turn right and the Admiral Duncan is on the left.

Dating back to the 1780s, **The Admiral Duncan** is a handsome red brick building which was originally a coaching inn. It takes its name from a popular naval commander of the time, Viscount Duncan, the connection being that the timbers for his flagship were culled from nearby woods. As well as providing hospitality for coach travellers, part of the inn was used as overnight accommodation for convicts on their way to transportation to Australia. One of the windows still has iron bars in place. More congenial reminders of the inn's antiquity are the old beams, the shining brass items and the open fire in the lounge bar.

Ann Ashfield took over here in late 1999 after some 14 years experience in the hospitality business and swiftly established a reputation for serving wholesome traditional food in generous portions as well as "lite bites" and filled jacket potatoes. There are also special dishes for vegetarians and children, and a menu created by students from the local agricultural college. Quench your thirst with one of the 3 real ales on tap, a selection from the wine list, or one of the many popular beverages on display. Meals can be enjoyed in either of the two bars or in the separate, non-smoking dining room which also serves as a function room for parties of up to 20 people. This sociable hostelry lays on live entertainment once a month and in addition to its pool table, darts and dominoes also supports its own football team.

Opening Hours: Mon-Fri: 12.00-15.00; 19.00-23.00 Sat: 11.00-23.00 Sun: 12.00-22.30

Food: Available every lunchtime & evening

Credit Cards: All major cards except Amex & Diners

Facilities: Restaurant/function room; large car park

Entertainment: Pool table; darts; dominoes; live entertainment monthly

Local Places of Interest/Activities: Equestrian Centre, Prescott, 1 mile; Adcote School, Little Ness, 3 miles; Nesscliffe Hill Country Park, 4 miles; Rowley's House, Clive House, St Mary's Church, Brother Cadfael tours, all at Shrewsbury, 7 miles

Internet/Website: annashfield@talk21.com

The Admiral Rodney | 11

Criggion
Nr. Welshpool
Powys SY5 9AU
Tel: 01938 570313

Directions:

At the western end of
the M54 pick up the A5
for Shrewsbury. Follow
the A5 around the
southern side of Shrews-
bury until you reach the
A458. Take this road for
2½ miles and turn right
onto the B4393. Con-
tinue along this road for six miles, passing Alberbury Castle on the right, and the village of
Criggion will be signposted on the left.

Nestling at the foot of Breiddon Hill, not far from the Wales-England border, is the
village of Criggion. Here you will find the long established village hostelry, **The Admiral Rodney**, which dates back to the mid-1700s. The charming black and white inn
takes its name from a naval commander of the 18th century who built his fleet from
oak harvested in the local valleys. In the centre of the village Rodney's Pillar commemorates his victories.

Employing many of the pub's locals is a nearby working quarry - but don't be put
off. Quarry traffic is not allowed to use the road past the pub nor can be quarry be seen
from it. The views that can be enjoyed, from the large beer garden and children's play
area, are of the surrounding green hills and idyllic countryside that many visitors will
enjoy exploring. This is a real locals' pub with all the regulars on first name terms with
both the landlords, Jerry and Mandy Weaver, and each other. Visitors to the area are
also made more than welcome and a friendly, relaxed atmosphere for young and old
exists throughout. The fact that this is a community pub is clearly evidenced by the
number of events that Jerry organises with live entertainment each Saturday night
and the occasional fun day to raise money for charity. The cosy interior comprises two
bar areas and food is served throughout. The menu offers some classic dishes that are
very reasonably priced and served in good sized portions. All meals are freshly cooked
to order and everyone is sure to find something to their taste. To accompany your
meal there is a good selection of wines and tasty, hand-pulled real ales.

Opening Hours: Mon-Fri 12.00-14.00,
17.00-23.00; Sat 12.00-23.00; Sun 12.00-
22.30.

Food: Bar meals and snacks.

Credit Cards: Visa, Access, Delta, Switch.

Facilities: Pool table/games room, Large
Beer garden, Car Park.

Entertainment: Live entertainment every
Saturday.

Local Places of Interest/Activities:
Breiddon Hill, Offa's Dyke 5 miles, Powis
Castle, Welshpool 8 miles, Butterfly World
11 miles, Rowton Castle 10 miles, Shrewsbury 18 miles.

12   The Black Bear

High Street
Whitchurch
Shropshire
SY13 1AZ
Tel: 01948 663624

Directions:

From the M6, take junction 16 and follow the A500 to Nantwich. When you reach the town of Nantwich follow signs for Whitchurch and the A530. After about 6 miles, at the end of the A530, turn right onto the A525. You will reach Whitchurch after about four more miles.

The bustling market town of Whitchurch is popular with visitors to the area, boasting a long and fascinating history dating back to the Roman occupation and beyond. There are a number of fine buildings dating from Medieval, Tudor and Georgian times and the skyline in the centre is dominated by the parish church of St Alkmunds. Next door to the church is the **Black Bear**, one of the many charming black and white timbered buildings that can be found in the town.

Earliest records of the pub go back to 1676 though it is thought that it was actually built in the 1500s, probably originally as a Drover's pub. The interior features a wealth of original features including some exposed beams which are reclaimed ships' timbers. There are two bar areas, the public bar includes the pool table and dart board while the lounge bar has an open fire which is a real draw in winter. There is also a delightful beer garden which is within a courtyard at the back.

Popular with visitors to the town, as well as the town's residents, here you can enjoy some tasty pub food each lunch time and evening. The daily menu is presented on a blackboard with a good selection of light dishes and hearty main meals on offer. Everyone is sure to find something that appeals and all items are reasonably priced. Behind the bar there is a choice of two real ales along with the usual range of lager, cider, wine, spirits and soft drinks.

Opening Hours: Mon-Sat 11.00-23.00; Sun 12.00-22.30.

Food: Bar meals and snacks.

Credit Cards: None.

Facilities: Pool table/games room, Beer garden, Car Park.

Local Places of Interest/Activities: Cholmondeley Castle and Gardens 8 miles, Nantwich 11 miles, Ellesmere 10 miles, Sandstone Trail 8 miles, Dorfold Hall 11 miles, Bridgemere Garden World 13 miles, Stapeley Water Gardens 13 miles.

The Black Horse Inn | 13

Maesbrook
Nr. Oswestry
Shropshire
SY10 8QG
Tel: 01691 682472
Fax: 01691 682472

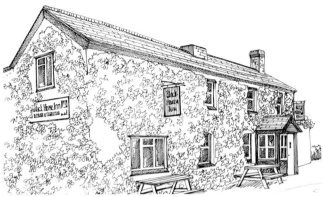

Directions:

From the end of the M54 pick up the A5 and follow it to Shrewsbury. Follow the A5 round Shrewsbury and continue towards Oswestry. About 10 miles from Shrewsbury turn left onto the B4397 where the village of Knockin can be found after about 2 miles. Here turn left onto the B4398. The village of Maesbrook is about 2 miles further on.

The peaceful hamlet of Maesbrook has a long history dating back to the Domesday book, in which it featured as 'Meresbroc'. This is the heart of Oswestry borderland where many of the villages have been both Welsh and English at different stages of history and the landscape is unspoilt and uncrowded.

At the heart of Maesbrook is **The Black Horse Inn**. Dating back to the 17th century this has always been a hostelry, and was probably originally a drovers inn. The large sprawling establishment enjoys a sunny corner and is surrounded by trees, making it look even more like a country inn. The front door can barely be seen for the amount of climbing ivy that covers the front of the building. The interior features an open plan lounge that is divided into three areas, one for dining, one for drinking and the other for a bit of both! The decor is traditional with some exposed stone walls, oak beamed ceilings and a collection of polished brasses scattered throughout. There is food served each lunch time and evening from a wide ranging menu offering a tasty selection of meals and snacks. The offerings are traditional English pub fayre, all freshly prepared and cooked to order. To enjoy with your meal there is a choice of two real ales, a good selection of wines as well as the usual spirits, soft drinks and other beer and lager on draught. Recently under new management there are regular live music nights and quizzes organised.

Opening Hours: Mon 19.00-23.00; Tues-Sat 12.00-15.00, 19.00-23.00; Sun 12.00-15.00, 19.00-22.30.

Food: Bar meals and snacks, Traditional Sunday Lunch.

Credit Cards: Visa, Access, Delta, Switch.

Facilities: Pool table/games room, Car Park.

Entertainment: Live music, monthly quiz.

Local Places of Interest/Activities:
Oswestry 8 miles, Alberbury Castle 9 miles, Adcote House 9 miles, Llangollen 21 miles, Froncysyllte Aquaduct 16 miles, Ellesmere 16 miles, Shrewsbury 16 miles.

14   Bradford Arms

Knockin
Nr. Oswestry
Shropshire
SY10 8HJ
Tel: 01691 682358
Fax: 01691 682358

Directions:

From the end of the M54 take the A5 to Shrewsbury. Follow the A5 round Shrewsbury and continue towards Oswestry. About 10 miles from Shrewsbury turn left onto the B4396. The village of Knockin can be found about 2 miles along this road.

In the turbulent borderland of Shropshire, not far from the Welsh-English border, is the small village of Knockin. The village has a long history dating back to beyond Tudor times, and the church is over 800 years old. **The Bradford Arms** is in the centre of the village and from its car park you can see a telescope which is linked with Jodrell Bank radio telescope in Cheshire. The Bradford Arms was built in the 18th century and was originally a coaching inn. It is able to provide ample car parking and at the rear is a beer garden which is popular in summer. Inside there is a large bar area which is divided into three distinct areas. One is for drinking, one is for eating and the other is for eating and drinking. There is also a separate non-smoking dining room. The emphasis here is most definitely on the food and it is Christine, one half of the husband and wife partnership that owns and runs the Bradford Arms, that supervises the cooking. The menu is wide ranging with a choice of tasty grills, steaks, classic meat dishes, some vegetarian selections and a good range of salads. There is also a children's menu. Everyone is sure to find something to suit and you can rest assured that every dish has been freshly prepared and cooked to order. To accompany your meal the bar offers an extensive wine list, three real ales as well as the usual range of lager, spirits and soft drinks. Occasional live entertainment is organised so ring ahead for details. There is wheelchair access.

Opening Hours: Mon-Sat 12.00-14.30, 18.00-23.00; Sun 12.00-22.30. Midnight Supper License.

Food: Bar meals and snacks, A la Carte.

Credit Cards: Visa, Access, Delta, Switch, Amex.

Facilities: Pool table, Beer garden, Car Park.

Entertainment: Occasional live entertainment.

Local Places of Interest/Activities: Oswestry 8 miles, Alberbury Castle 9 miles, Adcote House 7 miles, Llangollen 21 miles, Froncysyllte Aqueduct 16 miles, Ellesmere 14 miles, Shrewsbury 14 miles.

Internet/Website: e-mail sanks.par@virginnet.com

Bradford Arms

15

Llanymynech,
nr Oswestry,
Shropshire
SY22 6EJ
Tel: 01691 830582

Directions:

Llanymynech is on the A483, about 7 miles south of Oswestry. The Bradford Arms is in the centre of the village

For truly outstanding cuisine and a jaw-dropping choice of fine wines, there are few hostelries in the area to compare with the **Bradford Arms.** Originally built in the 1700s, the inn was substantially altered in 1901 and provided with an attractively ornate late-Victorian frontage. Anne and Michael Murphy, who own and run this appealing old tavern, have maintained the period charm of the interior where the attractive restaurant area is divided into several small areas, giving a cosy, intimate atmosphere. There is also a small conservatory dining area furnished and decorated in similar style. The food served here is quite exceptional, with awards from Routiers, Which Guide to Country Pubs and AA Guide to Good Pubs. Amongst the starters, for example, there's an Oak Roasted Smoked Salmon Cheesecake; main dishes include a tasty Chicken Moglai Curry, a succulent Salmon Bonne Femme, and an appetising Pasta with Walnut Sauce; the dessert list ranges from a memorable Rum & Walnut Gateau to a choice of refreshing sorbets; and to conclude, there's a "Real Cheese List" featuring top quality cheeses from around Britain and Europe. The Bradford Arms wine list is equally impressive - 7 pages of closely printed listings ranging from a choice of 6 wines available by the glass to a connoisseur's treasury of old wines and rare vintages stretching back to the 1920s.

Opening Hours: Tue-Sat 12.00-14.00, 19.00-23.00; Sun 12.00-14.00, 19.00-22.30

Food: Outstanding cuisine available Tuesday-Sunday lunchtime & evening

Credit Cards: All major cards accepted

Facilities: Restaurant; Conservatory dining area; No smoking dining area; Parking

Accommodation: Quality en suite rooms available May/June 2001

Local Places of Interest/Activities: Montgomery Canal, nearby; Cambrian Museum of Transport, St Oswald's Church, both in Oswestry, 7 miles; Rowley's House, Clive House, St Mary's Church, Brother Cadfael tours, all at Shrewsbury, 15 miles

16   Cleveland Arms

High Ercall, Telford,
Shropshire TF6 6AE
Tel/Fax: 01952 770204

Directions:

From the A5, 10 miles west of Telford, take the A49 north towards Whitchurch. About 1.5 miles along this road, turn right on the B5062 to High Ercall (6 miles). At the T-junction with the B5063 you will see the Cleveland Arms facing you.

A spacious Victorian building dating back to at least 1851, the **Cleveland Arms** is well known for its colourful floral displays. Its hanging baskets and tubs have won several awards. For more than 150 years, the inn has provided a traditional village pub atmosphere, serving good food and cask conditioned ales at reasonable prices. Today, landlord Tim Mason also offers his customers a small selection of quality wines. Tim, who is also a British Athletics official, arrived here in 1998 after working in industry for some 30 years. He has made the inn a popular social centre which, incidentally, has raised more than £20,000 for various charities, the elderly and the disabled.

A major reason for the pub's popularity is the excellent food on offer, the regular menu of hearty main courses, lite bites, filled jacket potatoes and vegetarian dishes supplemented by daily blackboard specials. Children are welcome in the restaurant, (a high chair is available if required), and have their very own menu. There's also a special senior citizen's menu for those with smaller appetites. Real ale devotees will be pleased to find a choice of 3 different brews on tap. As in all the best traditional pubs, there's plenty of entertainment available at the Cleveland Arms: a pool table, darts and dominoes inside; a bowling green and adventure playground outside. Incidentally, the pub takes its name from Thomas, 3rd Earl of Cleveland (1591-1667), a prominent supporter of the Royalist cause during the Civil War who commanded a cavalry regiment at the Battle of Worcester in 1651.

Opening Hours: Mon-Sat: 11.00-23.00 Sun: 12.00-22.30

Food: Available every lunchtime & evening; seniors' menu; children's menu

Credit Cards: All major cards except Amex & Diners

Facilities: Restaurant; beer garden; adventure playground; large car park

Entertainment: Pool table; darts; dominoes; bowling green

Local Places of Interest/Activities: Haughmond Abbey, 4.5 miles; Clive House, Rowley's House, Shropshire Regimental Museum, St Mary's Church, Brother Cadfael tours, all at Shrewsbury, 9 miles

Internet/Website: clevelandarms@tesco.net

The Horse and Jockey   17

Church Street
Whitchurch
Shropshire SY13 1LB
Tel: 01948 664902
Fax: 01948 664902

Directions:

From the M6, take junction 16 and follow the A500 to Nantwich. When you reach the town of Nantwich follow signs for Whitchurch and the A530. After about 6 miles, at the end of the A530, turn right onto the A525. You will reach Whitchurch after about four more miles.

In the centre of the attractive market town of Whitchurch, you will find **The Horse and Jockey** lying in the shadow of the parish church. Dating back to the 1600s this was originally built as a travellers rest but did not become licensed until the 1700s. The attractive frontage features the original cobbled yard and an elegant Georgian doorway, while at the back there is a large attractive beer garden. Run by Andy and Marie Thelwell for over four years, they have created a friendly, welcoming establishment. It is Andy who is the chef and his love of cooking is evident from the fabulous menu he puts together. The day's offerings are set out on blackboards from where you can make your selection. The boast is that everyone will find something to suit their taste and appetite, and the meals are very reasonably priced as well. There is a large, mainly non-smoking, restaurant in which to enjoy your meal and there is a small bar, also serving food, with an open log fire to warm the atmosphere throughout in cooler weather. The beamed ceilings are constructed from timbers reclaimed from sailing ships, and some evidence of this can be seen on some! To enjoy on its own, or with a meal, why not have a refreshing drink. Behind the bar there are two real ales on tap as well as the usual other offerings and there is also an extensive wine list.

Opening Hours: Tues-Sat 11.30-14.30, 18.00-23.00; Sun 12.00-22.30.

Food: Bar meals and snacks, extensive A La Carte menu. Restaurant is AA recommended

Credit Cards: Visa, Access, Delta, Switch.

Facilities: Beer garden, Car Park.

Local Places of Interest/Activities:
Cholmondeley Castle and Gardens 8 miles, Nantwich 11 miles, Ellesmere 10 miles, Sandstone Trail 8 miles, Dorfold Hall 11 miles, Bridgemere Garden World 13 miles, Stapeley Water Gardens 13 miles.

Internet/Website:
e-mail andy.thelwell@onmail.co.uk

18   The Horseshoes

Tilstock
Nr. Whitchurch
Shropshire SY13 3NR
Tel: 01948 880396

Directions:

From the M6, take junction 16 and follow the A500 to Nantwich. When you reach the town of Nantwich follow signs for Whitchurch and the A530. After about 6 miles, at the end of the A530, turn right onto the A525. When you reach the outskirts of Whitchurch, follow the A525 ring road round to the south where you can pick up the B5476 heading due south. The village of Tilstock can be found just over a mile along this road.

Located on the quieter of the two roads between Whitchurch and Shrewsbury is **The Horseshoes**. Conveniently positioned it is not surprising perhaps that this establishment is popular with travellers and has been since it first opened - built in the mid-1800s the site was originally used for a coaching inn. The large property conceals ample car parking and to the rear visitors will find a beer garden and children's play area. In summer the beer garden is a lovely spot in which to enjoy a refreshing drink and there are also regular barbecues.

The Horseshoes is popular with locals which is not surprising when you learn that the owner, Christopher Reeves, was sitting in front of the bar himself until fairly recently! Coming from 14 years experience in the trade, he now serves from behind the bar together with his partner Emily and they are bubbly and lively hosts. On draught they can offer four real ales of which one is rotated regularly and there is a reasonable wine selection. You will also find the usual selection of lager, cider, spirits and soft drinks. There is just the one, large bar area and the games room, which boasts a pool table and darts board, is attached. There is satellite TV which enables customers to enjoy live sporting events regularly and parties can be catered for by prior arrangement. Food is served each lunch time and evening with a selection of classic pub fayre on offer.

Opening Hours: Mon-Fri 17.00-23.00; Sat 12.00-23.00; Sun 12.00-22.30.

Food: Bar meals and snacks.

Credit Cards: None.

Facilities: Pool table/games room, Beer garden, Children's Play Area, Car Park.

Entertainment: Satellite TV, Barbecues.

Local Places of Interest/Activities: Cholmondeley Castle and Gardens 10 miles, Nantwich 13 miles, Ellesmere 12 miles, Sandstone Trail 10 miles, Dorfold Hall 13 miles, Bridgemere Garden World 15 miles, Stapeley Water Gardens 15 miles.

The Narrowboat Inn 19

Ellesmere Road,
Whittington,
Shropshire
SY11 4DJ
Tel: 01691 661051
Fax: 01691 662424

Directions:

From Oswestry take the A495 towards Whitchurch.

Whittington is about 3 miles along this road. Continue through the village towards Ellesmere and after about 2 miles you will see The Narrowboat Inn on your left

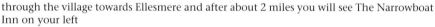

The Narrowboat Inn takes it name from the fact that it stands beside a feeder water-way of the Shropshire Union Canal. From here, given time, you could travel by water as far south as Bristol and Bath in the southwest, or northwards to Ripon in North Yorkshire. Although built in the late 1800s, the inn was originally just a canalside cottage and it was only in the early 1980s that Martin Hill and his family converted it into a welcoming hostelry.

Inside, there's is one large bar and a separate non-smoking dining room which also doubles as a function room capable of accommodating up to 28 guests. Food is served every lunchtime and evening and the menu offers a good choice of starters, a "light bite" menu, main courses ranging from Steak & Kidney Pie to Grilled Trout with Almonds, and a selection of desserts. Vegetarian options are available as well as daily specials complementing the regular menu.

Real ale devotees will find a choice of 3 brews which are rotated on a regular basis and for wine lovers there's a comprehensive wine list. If the weather is kind, enjoy your refreshments in the pleasant beer garden overlooking the canal.

Opening Hours: Mon-Sat: 11.00-15.00; 18.00-23.00 Sun: 12.00-15.00; 18.00-22.30

Food: Main meals and bar snacks available every lunchtime & evening

Credit Cards: All major cards except Amex & Diners

Facilities: Beer garden; dining room/ function room for 28; large car park

Local Places of Interest/Activities: Whittington Castle, 2 miles; Park Hall Farm Museum, 2.5 miles; Chirk Castle, 5 miles; Offa's Dyke, 5 miles; Plas Newydd (NT), 10 miles

Internet/Website: website: www.the narrowboat.co.uk

20   The Penrhos Arms

Station Road,
Whittington,
Oswestry
SY11 4DA
Tel: 01691 679977

Directions:
From Oswestry take the A495 towards Whitchurch.
  Whittington is about 3 miles along this road. As you enter the village, you will see The Penrhos Arms on your left

Owned at one time by Lord Harlech, **The Penrhos Arms** began life in the 1600s as a coaching inn and in those days of stagecoach travel had stabling for 6 horses. Although no longer in use, the stables are still intact. The inn gained its licence some time prior to 1841 and today it's an inviting-looking hostelry with its cream coloured walls and the name picked out in gilt letters. The pub sign shows a pleasant rural scene - a reference to the inn's name which derives from the Welsh pen, meaning head, and rhos, the term for a common meadow. Inside, there are two bars, each with its ancient beams, polished brass and open fire.

Amanda and Roger Woof took over here in November 1999 although they have lived in the next village for many years. Customers are promised "Good Ale, Good Food and Good Company" and all three pledges are fully honoured. There are 3 real ales on tap, including one guest ale, as well as a good selection of wines. The bar snack menu is available every lunchtime and evening, except Mondays, and offers a wide choice of wholesome light meals, jacket potatoes, hot baguettes, ploughmans, sandwiches and snacks-in-a-basket. The evening menu ranges from fish dishes ("The Water"), through "The Field" (steaks), to The Sty - dishes such as Shropshire Ham or Penrhos Scrumpy Pork. Vegetarian options, daily specials and the famous Penrhos Curries are also available.

Opening Hours: Mon: 17.00-23.00 Tue: 12.00-15.00; 17.00-23.00 Wed-Sat: 12.00-23.00 Sun: 12.00-22.30

Food: Bar snacks every lunchtime & evening except Mon lunchtime; evening meals, daily

Credit Cards: All major cards except Amex & Diners

Facilities: Beer garden; children's play area; pets' corner; large car park

Entertainment: Pool table; darts

Local Places of Interest/Activities: Whittington Castle, nearby; Park Hall Farm Museum, 1 mile; Chirk Castle, 5 miles; Offa's Dyke, 5 miles; Plas Newydd (NT), 10 miles

2 Bridgnorth and South Shropshire

PLACES OF INTEREST:

Acton Scott 23
Aston-under-Clun 23
Atcham 23
Billingsley 24
Bishop's Castle 24
Bridgnorth 24
Bromfield 25
Broseley 25
Church Stretton 25
Cleobury Mortimer 26
Clun 26
Craven Arms 27
Ironbridge 27

Little Stretton 28
Ludlow 28
Morville 29
Much Wenlock 29
Onibury 30
Quatt 30
Shifnal 30
Stokesay 30
Telford 31
Wellington 31
Wenlock Edge 31
Wroxeter 32

PUBS AND INNS:

The Acton Arms, Morville 33

The Baron of Beef , Bucknell 34

The Church Inn, Ludlow 35

The Crown Inn, Clunton 36

The Crown Inn, Wentnor 37

The Green Dragon, Little Stretton 38

The Kynnersley Arms, Leighton 39

The Rose & Crown, Ludlow 40

The Seven Stars, Beckbury 41

The Stable Tavern, Cleobury Mortimer 42

The Stokesay Castle Inn, Craven Arms 43

The Swan, Dorrington 44

The Talbot Inn, Much Wenlock 45

The Three Horseshoes, Alveley 46

The Hidden Inns of the Welsh Borders

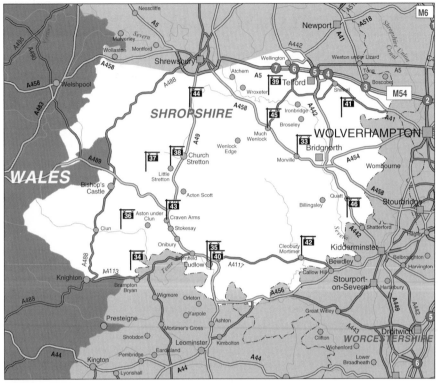

© MAPS IN MINUTES ™ (2000)

33 The Acton Arms, Morville		**40** The Rose & Crown, Ludlow
34 The Baron of Beef , Bucknell		**41** The Seven Stars, Beckbury
35 The Church Inn, Ludlow		**42** The Stable Tavern, Cleobury Mortimer
36 The Crown Inn, Clunton		**43** The Stokesay Castle Inn, Craven Arms
37 The Crown Inn, Wentnor		**44** The Swan, Dorrington
38 The Green Dragon, Little Stretton		**45** The Talbot Inn, Much Wenlock
39 The Kynnersley Arms, Leighton		**46** The Three Horseshoes, Alveley

Please note all cross references refer to page numbers

Bridgnorth and South Shropshire   23

This part of the county boasts some of Britain's most important Roman sites, notably at Wroxeter, which at one time was the fourth largest Roman town in the land. The southern part of the county beckons with a landscape of great variety: amazing parallel hill ranges, Clun Forest, and Ironbridge Gorge, called "the birthplace of the Industrial Revolution". Add to this the churches and the stately homes and the glorious gardens and you have a part of the world just waiting to be explored, whether by car, on a bike or on foot. South Shropshire affords a trip through romance and history, including the wonderful and historic town of Ludlow and the spectacular scenery of Wenlock Ridge and Long Mynd.

PLACES OF INTEREST

ACTON SCOTT

Signposted off the A49 just south of Church Stretton, **Acton Scott Historic Working Farm** offers a fascinating insight into farming and rural life as practised in the South Shropshire hills at the close of the 19th century. Owned by Shropshire County Council, it is a living museum with a commitment to preserving both traditional farming techniques and rural craft skills. Every day, visitors can see milking by hand and butter-making in the dairy. There are weekly visits from the wheelwright, farrier and blacksmith, while in the fields the farming year unfolds with ploughing, sowing and harvesting; special attractions include lambing, shearing, cider-making and threshing with steam and flail. Shropshire County Council also run Ludlow Museum and Much Wenlock Museum.

ASTON-UNDER-CLUN

Aston-under-Clun's **Arbor Tree Dressing** ceremony has been held every year since 1786. Following the Battle of Worcester in 1651, King Charles spent some time up a tree; to commemorate his escape he proclaimed Arbor Day, a day in May, as a national holiday when tree-dressing took place. The custom generally died out, but was revived here in 1786 when a local landowner married. As Aston was part of his estate, he revived the tradition of dressing the Black Poplar in the middle of the village, a custom which still survives.

ATCHAM

This village stands at the point where the Severn is crossed by the Roman road. The splendid old seven-arched bridge is now redundant, having been replaced by a new neighbour some time ago, but is still in situ. The old bridge was designed by John Gwynne, who was a founder member of the Royal Academy and the designer of Magdalen Bridge in Oxford.

Attingham Park, run by the National Trust, is perhaps the finest house in Shropshire, a splendid neo-classical mansion set in 250 delightful acres. Designed by George Steuart for the 1st Lord Berwick, it has the grandest of Regency interiors, ambassadorial silver, Italian furniture and Grand Tour paintings hanging in the John Nash gallery. The tea room is lined with paintings of the 5th Lord Berwick's Herefordshire cattle. Humphrey Repton landscaped the park, where visitors can enjoy woodland and riverside walks and see the deer.

Attingham Home Farm, the original home farm of the grand house, comprises buildings dating mainly from about 1800, and the yard retains the atmosphere of a traditional Shropshire farm. Many breeds of farm animals are represented: pigs - Oxford, Sandy, Iron Age, Vietnamese pot-bellied; sheep - Jacob, Shetland and Ryeland; cattle - Jerseys, Longhair, Dexter, Red Poll, British White. The rabbit house is particularly popular with youngsters, and there are usually some orphaned lambs for children to bottle-feed.

24

BILLINGSLEY

In a beautiful wooded valley near the village, Rays Farm Country Matters is home to many farm animals including Highland cattle, deer, donkeys, goats and pigs, plus more than 50 owls. The longest bridleway in Shropshire, and one of the longest in the country, starts at the farm. This is the Jack Mytton Way, named after a 19th-century hard-living squire and sometime MP for Shrewsbury. It runs all the way to Llanfair Waterdine in the Teme Valley, a distance of some 70 miles.

BISHOP'S CASTLE

This small and ancient town lies in an area of great natural beauty in solitary border country. Little remains of the castle, built in the 12th century for the Bishops of Hereford, which gave the place its name, but there is no shortage of fine old buildings for the visitor to see. The **House on Crutches Museum**, sited in one of the oldest and most picturesque of these buildings, recounts the town's history. Its gable end is supported on wooden posts - hence the name. North of Bishop's Castle lie the **Stiperstones**, a rock-strewn quartzite outcrop rising to a height of 1,700 feet at the Devil's Chair. A bleak place of brooding solitude, the ridge is part of a 1,000-acre National Nature Reserve and on the lower slopes gaunt chimneys, derelict buildings and neglected roads and paths are silent reminders of the lead-mining industry that flourished here from Roman times until the 19th century. To the west, on the other side of the A49 near **Chirbury** is **Mitchell's Fold** stone circle, a Bronze Age circle of 15 stones. This is Shropshire's oldest monument, its origins and purpose unknown.

BRIDGNORTH

The ancient market town of Bridgnorth, straddling the River Severn, comprises **Low Town**, and, 100 feet up sandstone cliffs, **High Town**. 1101 is a key date in its history, when the Norman Castle was built by Robert de Belesme from Quatt. All that remains of the castle is part of the keep tower, which leans at an angle of about 15 degrees as a result of an attempt to demolish it after the Civil War. The castle grounds offer splendid views of the river, and when King Charles l stayed here in 1642 he declared the view from the **Castle Walk** to be the finest in

Northgate Museum

his dominion. The **Bridgnorth Museum** is a good place to start a tour of this interesting town. It occupies rooms over the arches of the **North Gate**, which is the only one of the town's original fortifications to survive - though most of it was rebuilt in the 18th century. The **Costume and Childhood Museum** incorporates a costume gallery, a complete Victorian nursery and a collection of rare minerals. It's a really charming place that appeals to all ages. The Civil War caused great damage in Bridgnorth and the lovely **Town Hall** is one of many timber-framed buildings put up just after the war. The sandstone arched base was completed in 1652 and later covered in brick; Charles ll took a great interest in it and when improvements were needed he made funds available from his own purse and from a collection he ordered be made in every parish in England.

St Mary's Street is one of the three streets off High Street which formed the planned new town of the 12th century. Many of the houses, brick faced over timber frames, have side passages leading to gardens which contained workshops and cottages. **Bishop Percy's House** is the oldest house standing in the town, a handsome building dating from 1580 and one of the very few timber-framed houses to survive the fire of 1646. It is named after the Reverend Dr Percy, who was born in the house in 1729 and became Bishop of Dromore.

For many visitors the most irresistible attraction in Bridgnorth is the **Castle Hill Cliff Railway**, funicular railway built in 1892 to link the two parts of the town. The track is 200 feet long and rises over 100 feet up the cliff. Originally it operated on a water balance system, but it was converted in 1943 to electrically driven colliery-type winding gear. John Betjeman likened a ride on this lovely little railway to a journey up to heaven. For all but the very energetic it might

Bridgnorth and South Shropshire

A mile or so north of Bromfield, near the River Corve, is the village of **Stanton Lacy** and the Church of St Peter with some Saxon features and Victorian stained glass.

BROSELEY

Broseley, which stands on the south side of the River Severn opposite Ironbridge, was the head-quarters of John Wilkinson, the great ironmaster and head of a giant empire. It was while he was living at **The Lawns** in Broseley that he commissioned the Shrewsbury architect Thomas Pritchard to design the world's first iron bridge. He also launched the first iron boat, *The Trial*, on the Severn in 1787 and even designed his own iron coffin. Broseley was the centre of an ancient local industry in clay products and tobacco pipes, and the **Pipe Museum**, untouched for more than 40 years, is a time-capsule factory where the famous Broseley Churchwarden pipes were made until 1957.

Just north of Broseley off the B4375, on a

Bishop Percy's House

Benthall Hall

feel like heaven compared to the alternative ways of getting from Low to High Town - seven sets of steps or **Cartway**, a meandering street that's steeped in history.

The bridge across the Severn, rebuilt in 1823 to a Thomas Telford design, has a clock tower with an inscription commemorating the building, in 1808, of the first steam locomotive at John Hazeldine's foundry a short distance upstream.

Talking of steam locomotives, Bridgnorth is the northern terminus of the wonderful **Severn Valley Railway**.

Eardington is a southern suburb of Bridgnorth, where, a mile out of town on the B4555, stands **Daniel's Mill**, a picturesque working watermill powered by an enormous (38') wheel. Family-owned for 200 years, the mill still produces flour.

BROMFIELD

St Mary's Church is noted for its exotic interior, particularly its famous painted ceiling and a Victorian triptych. Also at Bromfield is **Ludlow Racecourse**, where Bronze Age barrows have been brought to light.

plateau above a gorge, stands **Benthall Hall**, a 16th-century building in the care of the National Trust, with mullioned windows and a magnificent interior with a carved oak staircase, elaborate plaster ceilings and the Benthall family's collection of furniture, ceramics and paintings. There's a carefully restored plantsman's garden and, in the grounds, an interesting Restoration church.

CHURCH STRETTON

The town has a long history - King John granted a charter in 1214 - and traces of the medieval

26

town are to be seen among the 18th and 19th-century buildings in the High Street.

Many of the town's black-and-white timbered buildings are not so old as they look, having been built at the turn of the century when the town had ideas of becoming a health resort. Just behind the High Street stands the **Church of St Laurence**, with Saxon foundations, a Norman nave and a tower dating from about 1200. Over the aisle is a memorial to a tragic event that happened in 1968 when three boys were killed in a fire. The memorial is in the form of a gridiron, with flakes of copper simulating flames. The gridiron is the symbol of St Laurence, who was burnt to death on one in AD258. The Victorian novelist Sarah Smith, who wrote under the name of Hesba Stretton, was a frequent visitor to nearby All Stretton, and there is a small memorial window to her in the south transept.

Carding Mill Valley

A mile from the town centre are **Carding Mill Valley** and the **Long Mynd**. The valley and the moorland into which it runs are National Trust property and very popular for walking and picnicking. This wild area of heath affords marvellous views across Shropshire to the Cheshire Plains and the Black Mountains. Tea room, shop, information centre.

A short drive north of Church Stretton, on minor roads off the A49, is Acton Burnell, where Parliament met in the reign of King Edward I. It has a small but interesting castle, which, like Stokesay, was a fortified residence rather than a fortress.

CLEOBURY MORTIMER

A famous landmark at Cleobury Mortimer is the crooked spire of **St Mary's Church**, whose east window commemorates William Langland. His best known work is *Piers Ploughman*. It was in this village that Maisie Bloomer, a witch, gained notoriety in the 18th century. Curses and love potions were her speciality, and the villagers were in no doubt that she was in league with the Devil.

Two miles east of Cleobury stands **Mawley Hall**, an 18th-century stone house with some very fine internal features.

Five miles west of Cleobury, at Clee Hill on the A4117, the **Clee Hills** to the north of the village include the highest peaks in the county. The summit of **Brown Clee** is 1,750 feet above sea level.

CLUN

This is a quiet, picturesque little town in the valley of the River Clun, overlooked by the ruins of its **castle**, which was once the stronghold of the Fitzalan family. The shell of the keep and the earthworks are the main surviving features. The **Church of St George** has a fortress-

Clun Castle

like tower with small windows and a lovely 17th-century tiered pyramidal top. There are also some splendid Norman arcades with circular pillars and scalloped capitals. The 14th-century north aisle roof and restored nave roof are an impressive sight that will keep necks craning for some time. Some wonderful Jacobean woodwork and a marvellous medieval studded canopy are other sights worth lingering over at this beautiful church, which is a great tribute to G E Street, who was responsible for its restoration in 1876. Geological finds are the main attractions in the little **Local History Museum** in the Town Hall. The real things are to be found on site at **Bury Ditches**, north of Clun on the way to **Bishop's Castle**. The Ditches are an Iron Age fort on a 7-acre tree-covered site.

Down the valley are other Cluns: **Clunton**, **Clunbury** and **Clungunford**. This quartet was idyllically described by A E Housman in *A Shropshire Lad*:

> *In valleys of springs and rivers,*
> *By Onny and Teme and Clun,*
> *The country for easy livers,*
> *The quietest under the sun.*

CRAVEN ARMS

The village takes its name from the hotel and pub built by the Earl of Craven. The coming of the railways caused the community to be developed, and it was also at the centre of several roads that were once used by sheep-drovers moving their flocks from Wales to the English markets. In its heyday Craven Arms held one of the largest sheep auctions in Britain, with as many as 20,000 sheep being sold in a single day.

IRONBRIDGE

This is it, the town at the centre of Ironbridge Gorge, an area which has been designated a World Heritage Centre by UNESCO, ranking it alongside the likes of the Pyramids, the Grand Canyon and the Taj Mahal. It was the first British site on the list. The **bridge** itself is a pedestrian right of way with a tollgate at one end, and the series of museums that spread along the banks of the Severn in **Ironbridge**, **Coalbrookdale**, **Coalport** and **Jackfield** pay tribute to the momentous events that took place here 250 years ago. The first iron wheels were made here, and also the first iron rails and the first steam railway locomotive.

The **Ironbridge Visitor Centre** offers the ideal introduction to the attractions, and plenty of time should be devoted to the individual museums. The **Museum of Iron** in Coalbrookdale in the most historic part of the valley shows the whole story of ironmaking. Next to it is the original furnace used by Abraham Darby when he first smelted iron with coke; a little way north are **Rosehill House**, one of the homes of the Darby family, and **Dale House**, where Abraham Darby's grandson made his plans for the iron bridge.

Also at Coalbrookdale is the **Ironbridge Open Air Museum of Steel Sculpture**, a collection of 60 modern steel sculptures of all shapes and sizes set in 10 acres of beautiful countryside.

The **Jackfield Tile Museum**, on the south bank, stands on the site of a world centre of the tile-making industry. The museum houses a fine collection of wall and floor tiles from Victorian times to the 1950s. Demonstrations of traditional tile-making take place regularly. Back across a footbridge to the **Coalport China Museum**, with its marvellous displays of two centuries of porcelain. Coalport was once one of the country's largest manufacturers of porcelain, starting life here but moving its factory to Stoke in the 1920s. Nearby is the extraordinary **Tar Tunnel** with its gushing spring of natural bitumen. It was a popular attraction for tourists in the 18th century, and it remains one of the most interesting geological phenomena in Britain. The tunnel was started in 1786, under the direction of ironmaster William Reynolds, who intended that it should be used for a canal to reach the shafts to the coal seams 3/4 of a mile away on Blists Hill. After they had driven the tunnel about 300 yards the miners struck a spring of natural bitumen. Reynolds immediately recognised the scientific interest of the discovery and sent samples of the bitumen to eminent scientists, who declared that the properties of the bitumen were superior to those of tar made of coal. The tunnel was almost forgotten over the years, but in 1965 the Shropshire Mining Club persuaded the owner of the village shop in **Coalport** to let them explore the darkness which lay beyond a door opening from his cellar. They rediscovered the Tar Tunnel, but it was another 18 years before visitors were allowed access to a brief stretch.

At **Blists Hill Victorian Town** visitors can experience the atmosphere and way of life of a working Victorian community; there's a shop, domestic animals, a squatter's cottage, a schoolhouse and a bank which distributes its own legal tender.

Passport tickets are available to admit holders to all the Ironbridge Gorge Museums.

Two miles west of Ironbridge, on a minor road off the B4378, stands **Buildwas Abbey**, one of the finest ruined abbeys in England. After 850 years the church is virtually complete except for the roof, and the setting, in a meadow by the Severn against a backdrop of wooded grounds, is both peaceful and evocative. The place is full of things of interest, like the lead-glazed tiles depicting animals and birds in the Chapter House.

27

28   LITTLE STRETTON

The village of Little Stretton nestles in the **Stretton Gap**, with the wooded slopes of Ragleth to the east and **Long Mynd** to the west. It is a peaceful spot, bypassed by the A49, and is a delightful place to stroll for a stroll. The most photographed building is **All Saints Church**, with a

Castle Lodge

All Saints Church

black and white timbered frame, a thatched roof and the general look of a cottage rather than a church. When built in 1903 it had an iron roof, but this was soon found to be too noisy and was soon replaced with thatch (heather initially, then the straw that tops it today). Among many other interesting buildings are **Manor House**, a cruck hall dating from 1500, and Bircher Cottage, of a similar vintage.

LUDLOW

Often called "the perfect historic town", Ludlow has more than 500 listed buildings, and the medieval street pattern has been kept virtually intact. **Ludlow Castle** was built by the Normans

Ludlow Castle

in the 11th century, one of a line of castles along the Marches to keep out the Welsh. Under its protection a large town was planned and built - and prospered, due to the collection and sale of wool and the manufacture of cloth. The Castle has been home to many distinguished families and to Royalty: Edward V, Prince Arthur and other Royal children were brought up in Ludlow, and the Castle became the headquarters of the Council of the Marches, which governed Wales and the border counties until 1689. Nowadays the past combines dramatically with the future in the **Holodeck**, where hologram images create ultra-realistic 3D illusions. The Giant Kaleidoscope gives the viewer the sensation of standing before a globe of light and an ever-changing surface of colours, and the **Well of Infinity** is an apparently bottomless hole in the ground - on the first floor.

The parish church of St Laurence is one of the largest in the county, reflecting the town's affluence at the time of its rebuilding in the 15th century. There are fine misericords and stained glass, and the poet A E Housman, author of *A Shropshire Lad*, is commemorated in the churchyard. Other places which should be seen include **Castle Lodge**, once a prison and later home of the officials of the Council of the Marches, and the fascinating houses that line Broad Street.

The historic Corve district of Ludlow is liberally scattered with buildings going back to the 17th century. **Ludlow Museum**, in Castle Street, has exhibitions of local history centred on, among other things, the Castle, the town's trade and special features on local geology and archaeology.

The **Ludlow Festival**, held annually since 1960 and lasting a fortnight in June/July, has become one of the major arts festivals in the country. The centrepiece of the festival, an open-air performance of a Shakespeare play in the Castle's inner bailey, is supported by a number of events that have included orchestral concerts, musical recitals, literary and historical lectures, exhibitions, readings and workshops.

Broad Street

At one time in the last century glove-making was one of the chief occupations in the town. Nine master glovers employed some 700 women and children, each required to produce ten pairs of gloves a week, mainly for the American market.

MORVILLE

Morville Hall, 16th-century with 18th-century additions, stands at the junction of the A458 and B4368. Within its grounds, the **Dower House Garden** is a 1½-acre site designed by Dr Katherine Swift and begun in 1989. Its aim is to tell the history of English gardens in a sequence of separate gardens designed in the style of different historical periods. Particular attention is given to the use of authentic plants and construction techniques. Old roses are a speciality of the garden. Parking is available in the churchyard of the fine Norman Church of St Gregory, which is also well worth a visit.

Another fine Norman church is located in nearby **Aston Eyre**. A tympanum over the door-

way represents Christ's entry into Jerusalem and shows him sitting not astride his mount but sideways. He is flanked by two men, one with a young ass, the other spreading palm leaves.

MUCH WENLOCK

The narrow streets of Much Wenlock are a delight to explore, and among the mellow buildings are some absolute gems. The **Guildhall** is one of them, dating from 1540 and added to in 1577 with a chamber over the stone medieval prison. The Guildhall was until recently used as a courtroom, and the Town Council still meets here once a month. The **Museum** is housed in the former market hall, which was built in 1878. There are interesting displays on the geology, flora and fauna of **Wenlock Edge**, as well as local history items including Dr

Wenlock Priory

William Penny Brookes's Olympian Games. A forerunner of, and inspiration for the Olympic Games, they are an annual event in the town every year, having started in 1850. The good doctor lived in what is now Lloyds Bank.

Holy Trinity Church, "mother" to ten churches in villages around Much Wenlock, is a dominant presence in the town, though less conspicuous than it was until 1931, when its spire was removed. Its nave and chancel are

The Hidden Inns of the Welsh Borders

Norman, the porch 13th-century. The Parish Registers date from 1558.

The sight that simply must not be missed on a visit here is the ruins of the **Priory of St Milburga**. The Priory was originally a nunnery, founded in the 7th century by a Mercian princess and destroyed some 200 years later. Leofric, Earl of Mercia and husband of Lady Godiva, re-established it as a priory in 1050 and the current spectacular ruins belong to the Cluniac Priory rebuilt in the 12th and 13th centuries. The best remaining features are the wall carvings in the cloisters and the Norman interlacing of arches and doorways in the Chapter House. The Prior's Lodge,

Much Wenlock

dating from about 1500, is particularly impressive with its steeply pitched roof of sandstone tiles above the rows of mullioned windows. Away from the main site is **St Milburga's Well**, whose waters are reputed to cure eye diseases.

ONIBURY

A fascinating day out for all the family is guaranteed at **The Wernlas Collection**, a living museum of rare poultry. The setting of this 20-acre smallholding is a joy in itself, and the collection is an internationally acclaimed conservation centre where over 10,000 chicks are hatched each year. Besides the chickens there are rare breeds of goats, sheep and pigs, and some donkeys. The gift shop is themed on chickens - a chickaholic's paradise, in fact.

QUATT

Quatt is the location of the National Trust's **Dudmaston Hall**, a late 17th-century house with fine furniture, Dutch flower paintings, modern pictures and sculptures (Hepworth, Moore), botanical art, watercolours, family and natural history and colourful gardens with lakeside walks, a rockery and a wooded valley. The church at Quatt contains some splendid monuments and memorials to the Wolryche family.

Nearby, in the grounds of Stanmore Hall on the Stourbridge road, is the **Midland Motor Museum**, with an outstanding collection of more than 100 vehicles, mostly sports and racing cars. The grounds also include a touring caravan site.

SHIFNAL

Once a staging post on the Holyhead Road, Shifnal has an unexpectedly large church with a Norman chancel arch, a carved Italian pulpit and an Italian reredos. On the A41, at Cosford near Shifnal, the **RAF Museum** is home to an important collection of aircraft, aero engines and missiles from all over the world. Classic British airliners like the Comet, Britannia, Viscount and VC10 share space with warplanes such as the Spitfire, Mosquito, Lincoln and Liberator. The missile collection, numbering over 40, charts the development of these weapons of war from the 1920s to the present time.

STOKESAY

The de Say family of nearby Clun started **Stokesay Castle** in about 1240, and a Ludlow wool merchant, Lawrence de Ludlow, made

Great Hall, Stokesay Castle

considerable additions, including the Great Hall and fortified south tower. It is the oldest fortified manor house in England and is substantially complete, making it easy to see how a rich medieval merchant would have lived. Entrance to this magnificent building is through a splendid timber-framed gatehouse and the cottage-style gardens are an extra delight. An audio tour guides visitors round the site.

The adjacent parish church of St John the Baptist is unusual in having been restored during Cromwell's rule after sustaining severe damage in the Civil War. A remarkable feature in the nave is a series of biblical texts written in giant script on the walls.

Telford

Telford is a sprawling modern development that took several existing towns in the region of the Shropshire coalfield. **Wellington, Hadley, Ketley, Oakengates, Madeley** and **Dawley** were among the towns to be incorporated, and the name chosen in the 1960s commemorates Thomas Telford, whose influence can be seen all over the county. Thomas Telford was a Scot, born in Eskdale in 1757, who came to Shrewsbury in 1786. Appointed County Surveyor, he quickly got to work on such enterprises as Shrewsbury jail, Bridgnorth, a host of bridges, an Aqueduct, canals and the Holyhead Road. He designed distinctive milestones for the road, one of which is now at the Blists Hill Museum. Telford's many ambitious developments include the huge (450-acre) Town Park, with nature trails, sports fields, lakes, gardens and play areas. Wonderland is an enchanting and enchanted woodland whose fairytale attractions include Snow White's Cottage, the Three Little Pigs and the Wrekin Giant. On the northern outskirts, at Preston-on-the-Weald Moor, is **Hoo Farm Animal Kingdom**, which numbers among its inhabitants ostriches, chipmunks, deer and llamas. Events include lamb feeding, milking and the famous sheep steeplechase. Christmas brings Santa and his animals to the magic grotto.

Telford Steam Railway Trust keeps a number of old locomotives, some of them ex-GWR, in working condition at the old shed and yard at Horsehay.

Oakengates, on the eastern edge of Telford, is the birthplace of Sir Gordon Richards, perhaps the greatest jockey this country has ever produced. His father was a miner and the young

Gordon first learned to ride on pit ponies. When he retired from the saddle, he had ridden 4,872 winners and was champion jockey for 20 years. Frankie and Kieren have a long way to go!

The celebrated Oakengates Theatre is on Market Street.

Wellington

Wellington is part of the new town of Telford, but still retains much of its Victorian look. The Church of All Saints is the work of George Steuart, better known for St Chad's in Shrewsbury. One of the town's attractions is the National Trust's **Sunnycroft**, a late-Victorian gentleman's suburban villa typical of the kind that were built for wealthy business and professional men. The house and its contents are largely unaltered, and in the grounds are pig sties, a kitchen garden, orchards, a conservatory and a Wellingtonia avenue.

A couple of miles north of Wellington, at **Longdon-on-Tern**, stands the **aqueduct** built by Thomas Telford as a pilot for other, better-known constructions.

South of here, on the other side of the M54/A5, is one of the best-known landmarks in the whole country. **The Wrekin**, which reaches up over 1,300 feet, is the site of a prehistoric hill fort, visible for many miles around and accessible by a network of public footpaths. The reward for reaching the top is beautiful panoramic views across to the neighbouring counties. In Roman times it was used as a base by the Cornovii tribe before they were moved to Viroconium. Shropshire folklore tells us that it was "put" there by a malicious giant who was carrying a huge load of earth to dam the Severn and flood Shrewsbury, simply because he didn't like the people. The giant met a cobbler, who persuaded him against this evil act, whereupon the giant dropped the load he was carrying - and that's The Wrekin.

Wenlock Edge

Wenlock Edge is one of the most spectacular and impressive landmarks in the whole county, a limestone escarpment dating back 400 million years and a paradise for naturalists and lovers of the outdoors. It runs for 15 miles all the way down to Craven Arms. For centuries its quarries have produced the stone used in

32 many of the local buildings; it was also a source of lime for agricultural fertiliser and much went into the blast furnaces that fired the Industrial Revolution.

WROXETER

In the village of Wroxeter, beside the B4380, is one of the most important Roman sites ever brought to light. *Viroconium* was the first town to be established by the Romans in this part of the country and developed from being a military settlement to a sizeable civilian town where the Cornovii tribe were settled. It's an absolutely fascinating place, where the highlights include extensive remains of a 2nd-century bathhouse complex. Some of the major excavated items are on display here, many more at **Rowley's House Museum** in Shrewsbury. Also in the village is Wroxeter Roman Vineyard, where there is not only a vineyard producing both red and white wines but additional delights in the shape of rare-breed animals and a lavender field.

The Acton Arms   33

Morville
Nr. Bridgnorth
Shropshire WV16 4RJ
Tel: 01746 714209

Directions:

From junction 4 of the M54 take the A442 south to Bridgnorth. From Bridgnorth take the A458 towards Shrewsbury. About three miles from Bridgnorth you will come to the village of Morville.

The Acton Arms can be found on the A458 Shrewsbury to Bridgnorth road in the village of Morville. It is thought that there has been a building on this site since the reign of Henry VIII and the dissolution of the monasteries, when this was probably a priory. The present building is from the 18th century, when it would have been a coaching inn serving travellers along the busy road, as well as the local community. Nothing much has changed in 250 years with the clientele being much the same mix. The large interior comprises a village bar and a large lounge bar, which is divided into a restaurant and a drinking area, with some parts being designated as non smoking. The menu served in the restaurant offers a good choice of starters and main dishes with a delicious selection of desserts to round things off and the offerings are regularly updated to make the most of seasonal produce. To enjoy with a meal, or simply on its own, there is an equally tasty selection of drinks on offer behind the bar. There is a choice of wines and three real ales of which one is a guest and regularly changed.

The Acton Arms has recently been taken over by father and son team, Jack and Aaron Lynn, although between them they have many years experience in the trade. In addition to running a fine inn and restaurant they can also offer bed and breakfast accommodation with two double rooms available.

Opening Hours: Mon-Fri 11.00-15.00, 17.30-23.00; Sat 11.00-23.00; Sun 12.00-22.30.

Food: Bar meals and snacks, A la Carte.

Credit Cards: Visa, Access, Delta, Switch.

Accommodation: 2 double rooms.

Facilities: Pool/Games Room, Beer garden, Children's Play Area, Car Park.

Entertainment: Monthly live music acts.

Local Places of Interest/Activities:
Bridgnorth 4 miles, Acton Round Hall 3 miles, Ironbridge 10 miles, Wenlock Priory 5 miles, Benthall Hall 9 miles, Shipton Hall 7 miles, Coalport 8 miles.

Internet/Website:
e-mail acton_arms@madasafish.com

34 Baron of Beef

Chapel Lawn Road,
Bucknell,
Shropshire SY7 0AH
Tel: 01547 530549
Fax: 01547 530445

Directions:

From the A4113, Ludlow to Knighton road, turn right on the B4367 to Bucknell (1 mile). The Baron of Beef is signposted from the A4113 and from the outskirts of Bucknell village.

Originally built as a barn, the **Baron of Beef** is a delightful old stone building located on the fringes of Bucknell village and surrounded by unspoilt countryside. A Grade II listed building, the inn has a wealth of olde worlde features, - exposed beams, stone walls and perhaps most striking of all, the original cider press, dating from 1777, and mill wheel which form the focal point in the Cider Bar. On Saturday evenings during the summer the Cider Bar provides an ideal setting for live music. There are 2 other bars, the Lounge Bar and Stable Bar, where you'll find an extraordinarily wide choice of bar meals, snacks and sandwiches on offer. There's something for every palate, with special listings for vegetarians and children. The 80-seater restaurant on the first floor offers a choice of table d'hôte or à la carte menus, complemented by an extensive wine list.

The inn is very much a family business, run by Jon and Joan Martin together with daughter Isla and son-in-law Matt. Jon and Joan have more than 25 years experience in the hospitality profession and are ready to rise to any challenge. The inn's level lawn is perfect for special occasions such as wedding receptions, and the Martins can supply one of their superbly fitted out marquees. They are also happy to organise your own corporate function or private dinner dance. By the time you read this, their programme of themed dinners should also be under way, - just call for details.

Opening Hours: Mon-Fri: 12.00-14.30; 18.30-23.00. Sat: 12.00-23.00. Sun: 12.00-22.30

Food: Mon-Fri: Extensive choice of bar meals available every lunchtime & evening; Sat-Sun: available all day; Carvery, Sat 19.00-22.00; Sun 13.00-16.00

Credit Cards: All major cards except Amex & Diners

Facilities: Restaurant; beer garden; children's play area; function room for 80 guests; large car park

Entertainment: Pool table; darts; entertainment most Saturday nights in summer

Local Places of Interest/Activities: Offa's Dyke Path, 5 miles; Discovery Centre, Craven Arms, 8 miles; Stokesay Castle, 9 miles; The Judge's Lodging, Presteigne, 10 miles

The Church Inn

35

The Buttercross, Ludlow,
Shropshire SY8 1AW
Tel: 01584 872174 Fax: 01584 877146
Directions:
Ludlow is on the A49, 28 miles south of
Shrewsbury; and on the A4117, 23 miles
west of Kidderminster. The Church Inn is
right in the centre of the town, directly be-
hind the Buttercross

During the course of some seven centuries of history, the premises now known
as **The Church Inn** have appeared in a
multiplicity of roles. Recorded in 1446 as
belonging to Ludlow's notable Palmers
Guild, the venerable building has served
as a blacksmith's, saddler's, druggist's and
barber-surgeon's. The inn's name has
been equally volatile: known mostly as
The Cross Keys, but also answering to The
Wine Tavern near the Cross (1792),
Wollaston's Wine Vaults (1876), Ex-
change Vaults (1895) and The Gaiety
(1974) before finally settling down in
1979 as The Church Inn, - so-named be-
cause of its proximity to Ludlow's magnificent St Laurence's Church.

Today, this historic old hostelry provides its patrons with a choice of appetising,
freshly cooked meals, served in the restaurant, (where booking is strongly recommended
at weekends), and a selection of snacks, sandwiches and meals in the spacious bar
with its open fire. Devotees of real ales will be delighted to find a choice of no fewer
than 6 brews on tap, and wine lovers are well-catered for with a wine lists that includes 6 house wines, available by the glass or bottle. If you are planning to stay in
this enchanting old town, The Church Inn has 9 guest bedrooms to let, (a mix of
family, double, twin and single rooms), all of which are en suite and available all year
round.

Opening Hours: Mon-Sat: 11.00-23.00
Sun: 12.00-22.30

Food: Available every lunchtime &
evening

Credit Cards: All major cards accepted

Facilities: Restaurant; public car park
nearby

Accommodation: 9 rooms, all en suite

Local Places of Interest/Activities:
Ludlow Castle, St Laurence's Church,
Ludlow Museum, Shropshire Way foot-
path, all nearby; Ludlow Racecourse, 3
miles; Clee Hill viewpoint, 5 miles;
Berrington Hall (NT), 7 miles

Internet/Website:
e-mail: reception@thechurchinn.com
web site: www.thechurchinnludlow.co.uk

36   The Crown Inn

Clunton, Nr. Craven Arms
Shropshire SY7 0HU
Tel: 01588 660265
Fax: 01588 660147

Directions:

From the end of the M54 pick up the A5 and follow it to Shrewsbury. Follow the A5 round Shrewsbury and pick up the A488 for about 25 miles to the junction with the B4368 at the village of Clun. Turn left onto the B4368 where Clunton can be found about 2 miles further on.

The River Clun gives its name to a number of villages of varying sizes in this western corner of Shropshire. Clun is perhaps the most notable as it was the centre of the centuries-long tug of war between England and Wales. A Medieval bridge leads over the river to the ruins of the imposing 13th-century castle where only the keep remains standing.

The hamlet of Clunton is just a couple of miles along the B4368 from Clun and right on the cross-roads in the centre is the **Crown Inn**. Built in the 1600s there is a car park across the road and a small beer garden. Popular with locals, tourists and walkers there are two cosy bar areas with the lounge bar featuring an open fire. There is also a separate non-smoking dining room. Most customers sample the food on offer, with a bar menu in addition to the a la carte selection in the restaurant. The dishes are selected to make the most of seasonally available produce and are freshly prepared to order. Run by Lee and Bev Martin, it is Lee who is a qualified chef and supervises the running of the kitchen. To accompany your meal, the couple offer a small select wine list, featuring new world wines, and there is always a choice of real ales. Small local breweries are supported so you could find a real treat in store. To add to the atmosphere there are occasional live entertainers so ring ahead for details. This is fine walking country and Shropshire County Council has produced two leaflets suggesting a number of walks around Clunton. Varying in length and designed to suit a variety of abilities, copies of the leaflets are available in the pub, and all walks start from the car park opposite.

Opening Hours: Mon-Fri 14.00-23.00; Sat 12.00-23.00; Sun 12.00-22.30.

Food: Bar meals and snacks, A la Carte.

Credit Cards: None.

Facilities: Pool table/games room, Beer garden, Car Park.

Entertainment: Occasional live entertainment.

Local Places of Interest/Activities: Clun Castle 2 miles, Stokesay Castle 8 miles, Craven Arms 7 miles, Ludlow 15 miles, Offa's Dyke 6 miles, Church Stretton 14 miles, Acton Scott Working Farm Museum 12 miles.

Internet/Website:
e-mail crownclunton@barbox.net

The Crown Inn 37

Wentnor, Bishops Castle
Shropshire SY9 5EE
Tel: 01588 650613
Fax: 01588 650436

Directions:

From the end of the M54 take the A5 into Shrewsbury. Follow the A5 and pick up the A49 heading south towards Ludlow. At Marshbrook, about 15 miles, turn right onto the B4370. At the end of the road, about 3 miles, turn right onto the A489. After 3 miles the village of Wentnor will be signposted to the right.

Long Mynd and Stipperstones are prominent features of this corner of Shropshire, although they are somewhat bleak hill ranges. There are hardly any trees to be found and the open moorland is scenic. The area is redeemed by several lovely valleys, such as Ashes Hollow and Carding Mill, where there is an abundance of hawthorn and whymberry bushes and some pleasant walks along the streams can be enjoyed.

The village of Wentnor lies beyond the western edge of Long Mynd on the River East Onny. Here visitors will find **The Crown Inn** which is a real gem, run in fine style by Simon and Joanna Beadman. The inn, which in summer is a riot of colour with the many flowers and plants that are grown at the front, dates back to the 16th century. Its historic character has been preserved inside with the bar featuring exposed wooden beams and polished brasses. There is a separate restaurant area where waitress service serves Joanna's excellent cooking to the tables. The daily menu is presented on a blackboard and there is always a good choice of snacks, starters and main dishes catering to all appetites. Vegetarians are also well provided for with at least three choices of main dish. As the restaurant can get busy at weekend, advance reservations are recommended. Behind the bar there is equally friendly service, and there are four real ales, an extensive wine list and the usual selection of lager, spirits and soft drinks on offer. The Crown can also boast three outstanding letting bedrooms with en-suite bath or separate shower room, making it an ideal base for touring this lovely part of the country and its many places of interest.

Opening Hours: Mon-Sat 12.00-15.00, 19.00-23.00; Sun 12.00-15.00, 19.00-22.30.

Food: Bar meals and snacks, A la Carte.

Credit Cards: Visa, Access, Delta, Switch,

Accommodation: 3 rooms.

Facilities: Car Park.

Local Places of Interest/Activities: Long Mynd 2 miles, Acton Scott Working Farm Museum 11 miles, Stokesay Castle 12 miles, Ludlow 18 miles, Shipton Hall 22 miles.

Internet/Website:
e-mail crowninn@wentnor.com
www: wentnor.com

38 The Green Dragon

Ludlow Road,
Little Stretton,
Church Stretton,
Shropshire
SY6 6RE
Tel/Fax: 01694 722925

Directions:

From the A49, about 2 miles south of Church Stretton, turn right on the B4371 to Little Stretton (0.5 miles). The Green Dragon is on the right as you enter the village

The Green Dragon stands on the edge of this attractive village which nestles on the lower slopes of Long Mynd. It's inviting-looking black and white frontage is set off with lots of colourful hanging baskets, creepers and plants. Inside the inn, which is believed to have been built in the 1600s as an alehouse, there's an L-shaped bar with a separate, non-smoking dining room attached. Mine hosts, Angela and Gary Medlicott, offer a good selection of wholesome, home-cooked meals and snacks which includes a children's menu and daily specials.

Real ale lovers will be pleased to find a choice of 3 genuine brews and there's also an extensive wine list for those who favour the grape. If you are lucky with the weather, the beer garden at the rear provides a pleasant setting in which to enjoy your refreshments. Angela is always happy to accommodate special functions in the dining room which can seat up to 45 guests and the inn has ample parking. Only a short distance from the Green Dragon, walkers can join one of several paths that cross the Long Mynd, a glorious tract of more than 5000 acres of ancient hills and moorlands which is now in the care of the National Trust.

Opening Hours: Mon-Sat: 12.00-15.00; 18.00-23.00 Sun: 12.00-15.00; 19.00-22.30

Food: Available every lunchtime & evening

Credit Cards: Not accepted

Facilities: Dining room; beer garden; large car park

Entertainment: occasional entertainment

Local Places of Interest/Activities: All Saints Church, walking on Long Mynd (NT), both nearby; Historic Working Farm, Acton Scott, 2.5 miles; Jack Mytton Way, 2.5 miles; Stokesay Castle, 7 miles

The Kynnersley Arms 39

Leighton
Shrewsbury
Shropshire SY5 6RN
Tel: 01952 510258
Fax: 01952 510258

Directions:

From the M54 leave the motorway at junction 6 near to Telford. Follow the A442 south towards Coalbrookdale. After just over 2 miles turn right onto the

A4169. After another 1½ miles, turn right onto the B4380 signposted for Buildwas. The village of Leighton can be found about 2 miles along this road.

Within the valley of the River Severn, not far from the industrial region of Ironbridge, is the village of Leighton. Situated on the main through road, **The Kynnersley Arms** doesn't look much like your typical country pub. Not surprising when you learn that the building possibly dates back to the 12th/14th century when it originally housed a furnace later used for making cannon balls for the Civil War. It pre-dates Abraham Darby's factory in nearby Coalbrookdale by several hundred years. When the demand for cannon balls declined, in the early 1800s, the building was turned into a corn mill, and the workings for this are still intact. It wasn't until the 20th century that it became a pub. The Kynnersley Arms has now developed a solid reputation for providing a warm and friendly welcome to both the locals and the many tourists that find themselves walking through the doors. Inside there is one of the longest copper-topped bars in the area and it really is a magnificent feature. The large bar area has a small circular greenhouse at one end in which the floor has been removed to reveal the corn mill workings below. There is also a separate, small, non-smoking dining room seating just 20 people. The menu offers a range of quality, fresh food which uses organic produce from a local supplier wherever possible. The menu is limited, due to the lack of space available in the kitchen, and every meal is cooked to order. The French chef specialises in crêpes, both sweet and savoury, and these come highly recommended. As the restaurant is quite small, and is very popular, advance booking is advisable.

Opening Hours: Mon 17.00-23.00; Tues-Thur 12.00-14.00, 17.00-23.00; Fri-Sat 12.00-23.00; Sun 12.00-22.30.

Food: Bar meals and snacks, A la Carte.

Credit Cards: None.

Accommodation: 1 family room.

Facilities: Pool table/games room, Car Park.

Entertainment: Occasional quiz night.

Local Places of Interest/Activities: Buildwas Abbey 2 miles, Wroxeter Roman City 3 miles, Wenlock Priory 6 miles, Museum of Iron 4 miles, Ironbridge Gorge 5 miles, Blists Hill Open Air Museum 4 miles, Coalport Museum 6 miles, Attingham Park 6 miles

40 Rose & Crown

8 Church Street,
Ludlow,
Shropshire SY8 1AP
Tel: 01584 872098

Directions:

Ludlow is on the A49, 28 miles south of Shrewsbury; and the A4117, 23 miles west of Kidderminster. The Rose & Crown is in the centre of the town, just off the Market Square

Tucked away in the heart of this captivating town, the **Rose & Crown** looks absolutely delightful with its whitewashed and half-timbered walls decked with hanging baskets. The inn stands on the site of a medieval monastery and was gradually extended over the years, finally becoming an inn some time in the 1500s. Inside the L-shaped bar, ancient beams and vintage pictures recall the Ludlow of yesteryear and create an olde worlde atmosphere which is enhanced by the open fire.

Mine host, Pamela Childs, took over here in the summer of 2000 and quickly made the old hostelry popular with those who appreciate wholesome, appetising food, carefully prepared and attractively presented. There's a very extensive menu which caters for just about every culinary preference, - traditional roasts of the day served between noon and 3pm, a main menu that ranges from a 12oz T-bone steak to faggots, a good choice of vegetarian dishes and an excellent selection of jacket potatoes, salads, ploughmans, baguettes, sweets and puddings. To complement your meal, there is an extensive range of all the popular beverages, and a small selection of quality wines. On fairweather days, enjoy your refreshments either in the small courtyard at the front, or on the patio to the rear.

Opening Hours: Mon-Sat: 12.00-23.00; Sun: 12.00-22.30

Food: Available all day

Credit Cards: Not accepted

Facilities: Patio; courtyard; public car park nearby

Accommodation: Expected to be available in Summer 2001

Local Places of Interest/Activities: Ludlow Castle, St Laurence's Church, Ludlow Museum, Shropshire Way footpath, all nearby; Ludlow Racecourse, 3 miles; Clee Hill viewpoint, 5 miles; Berrington Hall (NT), 7 miles

Seven Stars

41

Madeley Road,
Beckbury,
nr Shifnal, Telford,
Shropshire
TF11 9DN
Tel: 01952 750229

Directions:

From Telford, take the
A442 south towards
Bridgnorth. At Sutton
Madock, turn left on
the B4176 towards
Dudley, then first left
on minor road to Beckbury (2 miles). The Seven Stars is on the left.

Built in the 1700s as a private residence, the **Seven Stars** didn't become a pub until 1867. This spacious old hostelry has two bars and a separate, non-smoking dining room attached to the lounge. Old beams, polished brass and the unique wooden bars all add to the character and atmosphere of this welcoming, family-run inn. Steve and Sheila Tattershall take care of the kitchen, their daughter Liz presides over the bar.

The food at the Seven Stars enjoys a very good reputation, - always freshly prepared and served with seasonal vegetables the extensive choice ranges from a mighty 20oz T-bone steak, through a "Stars Special" of two pork steaks topped with bacon, onions, mushrooms and melted cheddar cheese, to fish dishes and vegetarian options. Bar snacks are also available, on Sundays there's a Carvery, (booking essential), and from time to time Steve and Sheila arrange themed evenings. Amongst the drinks on offer are 3 permanent real ales, plus a guest ale, and a fairly extensive wine list which also includes fruit wines. Weather permitting, customers can enjoy their refreshments on the patio and there's also a children's play area. Sheila is a keen walker and can direct you to the best paths, and for anyone interested in England's industrial heritage a visit to Ironbridge and the world's first iron bridge, just a few miles distant, should definitely not be missed.

Opening Hours: Mon-Wed: 19.00-23.00; Thu-Sat: 12.00-15.00; 19.00-23.00; Sun: 12.00-15.00; 19.00-22.30

Food: Available lunchtimes Thu-Sun; evenings, daily

Credit Cards: All major cards except Amex & Diners

Facilities: Restaurant/function room; patio; barbecue area; children's play area;
large car park

Entertainment: Pool table; darts; dominoes

Local Places of Interest/Activities: Blists Hill Victorian Town, Coalport, 5 miles; Pipe Museum, Benthall Hall (NT), both at Broseley, 5 miles; Ironbridge Visitor Centre, Iron Museum, 6 miles

42   The Stable Tavern

Talbot Square,
Cleobury
Mortimer,
Shropshire
DY14 8BQ
Tel: 01299 270382

Directions:

Cleobury Mortimer is on the A4117, about 12 miles west of Kidderminster. The Stable Tavern is located in the town centre, behind the Talbot Hotel

Dating back to 1561, **The Stable Tavern** was originally built as stables for the nearby Talbot Hotel but when that hostelry was destroyed by fire the stables were converted into a pub, - hence the name. It's an attractive building, long, low and whitewashed with its sign, rather unusually, mounted on the wall rather than hanging from a bracket. The interior is just as inviting, with lots of low ceilings, old beams and cosy, welcoming atmosphere, - a genuine country pub in fact which has not been spoiled by modernisation. Mine hosts at this Free House are Ursula Downs and Gary Willis and the fact that The Stable is popular with local people provides testimony to the quality of the food and drink on offer here. Main meals, bar snacks and sandwiches are available all day and the menu ranges from a 10oz rump steak to Sizzling Prawn Cantonese, from home-made Chicken & Broccoli Bake or Chicken & Mushroom Pie to fish dishes, curry and lasagne. Vegetarian options are always available as well as a Children's Menu which includes a 5oz rump steak & chips. To complement your meal, there's a wide selection of beers, lagers, cider and a tasty real ale, Tetley's Bitter. The Stable also has a spacious function room which accommodate up to 50 people for a seated meal, 70 for a buffet.

Opening Hours: Mon-Sat: 12.00-23.00; Sunday: 12.00-22.30

Food: Home-cooked food served all day; children's menu

Credit Cards: All major cards except Amex

Facilities: Function room; parking

Entertainment: Pool table; darts; quoits; cards

Local Places of Interest/Activities: St Mary's Church, nearby; Clee Hills, 5 miles; Ludlow Castle, 12 miles

Stokesay Castle Inn · 43

School Road,
Craven Arms,
Shropshire SY7 9PE
Tel: 01588 672304
Fax: 01588 673877

Directions:

From Shrewsbury take the A49 towards Ludlow. Craven Arms is 21 miles along this road. As you leave Craven Arms, take the last turning on the left into School Road

Only a short walk from Stokesay Castle, the most perfectly preserved 13th century manor house in the country, the **Stokesay Castle Inn** is an impressive old coaching inn located in the heart of unspoilt Shropshire countryside at the nub of four delightful valleys. Inside, there's a very traditional atmosphere with lots of old beams in the lounge and also in the cosy tavern bar with its roaring log fire in winter. The bar also has a selection of time-honoured pub games, including dominoes, pool and darts. In the lounge, mine hosts Chris Borowik and Mary Lewis offer a wide range of traditional ales, wines and spirits, and an appetising choice of home cooked dishes.

The regular menu, which includes a "fresh fish of the day" course as well as meat and poultry dishes, is supplemented by a regular vegetarian Dish of the Day. Excellent food, based on the finest and freshest ingredients, mostly sourced from Shropshire farms and estates, is also served in the intimate and atmospheric wood-panelled Portcullis Restaurant. Or, in good weather, customers can enjoy their refreshments in the pleasant beer garden where there's also a children's play area. Located close to many of the county's top attractions, the inn is an ideal place to stay. There are 12 guest bedrooms, all attractively furnished and decorated with a country theme, with pine furniture, colour TV, direct dial telephone, hospitality tray and, of course, en suite facilities. The inn has AA 4 crowns grading.

Opening Hours: Mon-Sun: 07.00-24.00

Food: Home-cooked food available every lunchtime & evening; OAP menu

Credit Cards: All major cards accepted

Facilities: Restaurant; beer garden; children's play area; function room; large car park

Entertainment: Pool table; darts; dominoes

Accommodation: 12 rooms, all en suite

Local Places of Interest/Activities: Stokesay Castle, nearby; Shropshire Way, 1 mile; walking, riding, hang-gliding on Long Mynd, 4 miles; Ludlow Castle, Ludlow Racecourse, Ludlow Museum, all 7 miles

Internet/Website:
e-mail: stokesaycastleinn@talk21.com
website: www.go2.co.uk/stokesaycastleinn

44

The Swan

Dorrington, Shrewsbury,
Shropshire SY5 7HA
Tel: 01694 731208

Directions:

Travel south from Shrewsbury along the A49 and through the village of Dorrington. After a further 1 mile, take the left turn signposted for Longnor and Frodesley. Having passed through Longnor, at the next crossroads turn left for Frodesley. The Swan is 1.5 miles on your right with the car park to the rear

Built in 1829, **The Swan** was refurbished in November 2000 and redecorated to a rustic decor more in keeping with the beautiful South Shropshire valley and countryside in which it is located. Long Mynd lies a short 15-minute drive to the west, and Wenlock Edge a similar distance to the east, with other National Trust properties in the vicinity.

Described by regular patrons as "a restaurant that serves beer", The Swan's menu is comprised totally of home prepared meals boasting a wealth of unique dishes created by the well-travelled chef. Mediterranean and European flavours complement the wide selection of food available on the lunch and evening menus. Choices can be made from poultry, game, beef, pork and fish, whilst the vegetarian has also been considered and is catered for to a high degree. The Swan does not compete in any of the traditional pub food markets but has retained a modest pricing structure whilst providing excellent cuisine. With advance notice, dishes for people with special dietary needs can also be catered for. A varied selection of New World wines is detailed in the comprehensive wine list.

Cask ales from the local Salopian Brewery in Shrewsbury are on tap and also from the Hereford-based Wye Valley Brewing Company. Carling, Guinness and Worthington complete the selection from the keg offerings.

Opening Hours: Varies according to the time of year - Phone for details

Food: Varies according to the time of year - Phone for details

Credit Cards: Credit cards are not accepted but cheques, cash and debit cards are welcome

Facilities: Covers for 55; large patio and lawn; parking for 40+

Local Places of Interest/Activities: Golf, 2 miles; Burnell Castle, 2 miles; Rowley's House, Clive House, St Mary's Church, Brother Cadfael tours, all at Shrewsbury, 6 miles; Attingham Park (NT), 7 miles

The Talbot Inn   45

High Street,
Much Wenlock,
Shropshire TF13 6AA
Tel: 01952 727077
Fax: 01952 728436

Directions:
From the A5 near Shrewsbury, take the A458 towards Bridgnorth. Much Wenlock is about 11 miles along this road. The Talbot Inn is in the centre of the town

The Welsh Borders are richly supplied with ancient hostelries but few can match the long history of **The Talbot Inn**. Back in 1361, the inn was already accommodating visitors to the Priory and during the following century it became part of Wenlock Abbey, serving as the Almoner's house where travellers were provided with food and shelter, and the poor received alms. Of the many guests who have crossed its threshold, the most distinguished was perhaps James II who stayed at The Talbot in 1687. This delightful old tavern is approached by an archway which leads into a charming courtyard.

Overlooking the Courtyard, the former Malthouse of 1762 has been converted into 6 spacious en suite bedrooms, all attractively appointed and equipped with television, hair dryer and hospitality tray. (Please note that all rooms are non-smoking, including the residents' lounge). The inn itself, with its old beams and open log fire, is full of character and atmosphere, and the much-praised food truly lives up to its reputation. All the dishes are based on prime quality ingredients, carefully prepared, attractively presented and served by courteous and efficient staff. A vegetarian menu is available and the regular menu is supplemented by daily specials. The home made puddings and speciality ice creams provide a really satisfying conclusion to a meal here. The Talbot's wine list offers an excellent choice of wines from around the world; there are 2 real ales on tap, and a selection of 10 single malts is also available.

Opening Hours: Mon-Sat: 10.30-14.30; 18.00-23.00 Sun: 12.00-15.00; 19.00-22.30

Food: Main meals & bar snacks available every lunchtime & evening

Credit Cards: All major cards accepted

Facilities: Restaurant/function room; small car park (large public park nearby)

Accommodation: 6 rooms, all en suite

Local Places of Interest/Activities: Priory of St Milburga, Guildhall, Museum, all nearby; walking on Wenlock Edge, 1 mile: Benthall Hall (NT), 3 miles; Ironbridge Gorge & Bridge, 5 miles; Rowley's House, Clive House, St Mary's Church, Brother Cadfael tours, all at Shrewsbury, 11 miles

46 The Three Horseshoes

Alveley, Bridgnorth,
Shropshire
WV15 6NB
Tel: 01746 780642

Directions:

From Kidderminster take the A442 northwest towards Bridgnorth. About 7 miles along this road, turn left on minor road to Alveley (1.5 miles). Go through the village to the T-junction at the top of the hill and you will see The Three Horseshoes facing you

Dating back to 1406 **The Three Horseshoes** is believed to be the oldest pub in Shropshire. It has been much extended since those days and is now an impressive whitewashed building, made colourful during the summer with window tubs and hanging baskets. Picnic tables and benches at the front provide a perfect vantage point for watching village life pass by. Inside, there are two bars, a public bar with an open fire which is much favoured by local people, and a lounge bar split into two areas, one of them the non-smoking elevated dining area. Old beams, gleaming brass and an inglenook fireplace all add to the character and charm.

Mine hosts at The Three Horseshoes are Jeff Wright and Matthew and Jacqui Small who, in addition to the welcoming atmosphere they create, have made this ancient hostelry well known for its outstanding food. Jeff is a very experienced chef with more than 20 years experience in the catering business and his menu offers an interesting choice of traditional country dishes with specialities of the house including pheasant, wild boar, salmon and hare. To accompany your meal, there are 2 real ales on tap or you can choose from an extensive wine list. In good weather, enjoy your food and drink in the pleasant beer garden where there's also a children's play area.

Opening Hours: Mon-Fri: 12.00-15.00; 18.00-23.00; Sat 12.00-23.00 and Sun: 12.00-22.30

Food: Traditional country fare available every lunchtime & evening

Credit Cards: All major cards except Amex & Diners

Facilities: Beer garden; children's play area; function room for 45; large car park

Entertainment: Darts

Local Places of Interest/Activities: Severn Valley Country Park, riverside walks, 0.5 miles; golf, Severn Valley Railway, 1.5 miles; Dudmaston Hall (NT), 3 miles; Shatterford Wildlife Sanctuary, 3 miles; Kidderminster Railway Museum, 7 miles; Midland Motor Museum, 8 miles

3 Leominster and North Herefordshire

PLACES OF INTEREST:

Almeley 49
Ashton 49
Brampton Bryan 49
Bromyard 49
Dilwyn 50
Eardisland 50
Eardisley 50
Hope under Dinmore 50
Kimbolton 51
Kington 51
Kinnersley 52

Leominster 52
Lyonshall 52
Moreton Jeffries 52
Mortimer's Cross 52
Orleton 52
Pembridge 53
Shobdon 53
Sutton St Nicholas 53
Weobley 53
Wigmore 54
Yarpole 54

PUBS AND INNS:

The Chase Inn, Bishop's Frome   55

The Cliffe Arms, Mathon   56

England's Gate Inn, Bodenham   57

The Hop Pole Inn, Leominster   58

The Lamb Inn, Stoke Prior   59

The Maidenhead Inn, Orleton   60

The Malvern Hills Hotel, Malvern   61

The Marshpools Country Inn,
    Ledgemoor   62

The Nags Head Inn, Canon Pyon   63

The Red Lion Inn, Pembridge   64

Roebuck Inn, Brimfield   65

The Wheatsheaf Inn, Fromes Hill   66

The Hidden Inns of the Welsh Borders

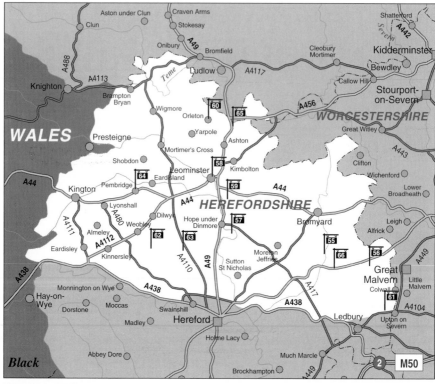

© MAPS IN MINUTES ™ (2000)

55 The Chase Inn, Bishop's Frome

56 The Cliffe Arms, Mathon

57 England's Gate Inn, Bodenham

58 The Hop Pole Inn, Leominster

59 The Lamb Inn, Stoke Prior

60 The Maidenhead Inn, Orleton

61 The Malvern Hills Hotel, Malvern

62 The Marshpools Country Inn, Ledgemoor

63 The Nags Head Inn, Canon Pyon

64 The Red Lion Inn, Pembridge

65 Roebuck Inn, Brimfield

66 The Wheatsheaf Inn, Fromes Hill

Please note all cross references refer to page numbers

"Wherever one goes, there will not be a mile that is visually unrewarding." Sir Nikolaus Pevsner was clearly impressed, and today's visitors will also find delights at every turn in the rolling landscape, the pretty villages and the charming market towns of Herefordshire.

Just north of Hereford is the start of this journey through the northern part of the county, including the towns of Bromyard, Leominster and Kington, and the wonderful Black and White villages that are among the most picturesque in the whole of England. **The Black and White Trail** was devised in 1987 by David Gorvett, who wanted to encourage visitors to take a leisurely look at some of the most beautiful countryside and the most picturesque villages in England. The trail can be used by motorists and cyclists, but best of all is to walk from village to village, each of them a treasury of cottages, inns and shops and each with a fascinating parish church. Skirmishes with the Welsh were a common occurrence for many centuries, and one of the county's best-known landmarks, **Offa's Dyke**, was built in the 8th century as a defence against the marauders.

PLACES OF INTEREST

ALMELEY

A small village with many fine old timbered buildings, a handsome 15th-century manor house, a massive cruck-beamed barn (at Castle Froome Farm) and the 14th-century Church of St Mary with a sturdy tower and unusual painted roof. **Almeley Castle** was once the home of Sir John Oldcastle, a follower of Wycliffe and, it is thought, the model for Shakespeare's Falstaff.

ASHTON

Three miles north of Leominster on the road to Ludlow stands the National Trust's **Berrington Hall**, an elegant 18th-century mansion designed by Henry Holland (later architect to the Prince Regent) in parkland laid out by his father-in-law Capability Brown. Features of the interior include a spectacular staircase hall, gilt tracery, fine furniture and paintings, a nursery, Victorian laundry and tiled Georgian dairy. Most notable of all are perhaps the beautifully decorated ceilings: in the drawing room, the central medallion of Jupiter, Cupid and Venus is a composite scene taken from The Council and The Banquet of the Gods by Penni and del Colle in the Villa Farnesina in Rome. In the grounds are a walled garden with a collection of old-fashioned local apple trees, a woodland walk and a living willow tunnel in the children's play area.

BRAMPTON BRYAN

Many of the thatched cottages in the village as well as its castle, had to be rebuilt after a siege during the Civil War in 1643. The chief relic of the castle is the gatehouse, which now stands in the gardens of a charming 18th-century house near the Church of St Barnabus. Sir Robert Harley, a relation of Thomas Harley of Berrington Hall, owned the castle, and it was due to his allegiance to Cromwell that it was besieged not once but twice by the Royalist army. Following the eventual destruction of the castle by the Royalists, Harley fell out with Cromwell. They remained at loggerheads until the day that Cromwell died, and on that day in September 1658 it is said that a violent storm swept through Brampton Bryan Park, destroying a great number of trees. Harley was convinced that the storm was the Devil dragging Cromwell down to Hell.

BROMYARD

A super little market town on the River Frome, with hills and good walking all around. In the town itself the **Teddy Bear Museum**, housed in an old bakery, is a magical little world of bears, dolls and Disney-related toys. It also has a bear hospital.

Bromyard Heritage Centre tells the stories of the local hop-growing industry, the railway age and life in Bromyard through the centuries. Find time to look at the 12th-century St Peter's Church with its historic Walker organ. Late June and early July see Bromyard's **Great Hereford Show and Steam Rally**, an event which has been built up to major proportions over the years. Later on, in early September, Bromyard's **Folk Festival** brings in the crowds.

Great walking is to be enjoyed on rugged **Bringsty Common**, in Stanford Bishop, two miles east of Bromyard off the B4220. For the energetic the walk can take in the National Trust property of **Lower Brockhampton**, a 14th-century half-timbered moated farmhouse with a very unusual, tiny detached gatehouse. Springtime sees it at its best, when the daffodils provide a mass of colour. South of Bringsty Common, the church at Stanford Bishop has the very chair occupied by St Augustine at a 7th-century bishops' conference. The yew tree in the churchyard is the largest in the area.

Four miles north of Bromyard off the B4203, in the village of Edvin Loach, can be found the remains of one of Britain's rare Saxon churches. The church at nearby Edwyn Ralph is noted for its unusual monument and medieval effigies under the tower.

DILWYN

The village lies in a hollow, so its Old English name of "Secret Place" is an appropriate one. The main body of the parish church was built around 1200, with additions in the following century and a spire put up in the 18th. The workmen who built the church were also associated with nearby **Wormsley Priory**, and one of the figures in Dilwyn's church is thought to be a member of the Talbot family, founders of the priory. The church registers go back over 400 years, providing a valuable trail of local history.

EARDISLAND

"An uncommonly pretty village", said Pevsner of this renowned spot on the banks of the River Arrow. Certainly glorious Eardisland is one of the most beuatiful villages in the county (and

Eardisland

the competition is very strong), and with its inns, bowling green, river and charming buildings spanning the centuries, this is essential England. Dominating the scene is the 12th-century **Church of St Mary the Virgin**, where each year, from Easter until late autumn, an exhibition of village and parish life is staged. A mile outside the village is **Burton Court**, whose centrepiece is the sumptuous 14th-century Great Hall. Many additions have been made to the building down the years, and the present entrance, dating from 1912, is the work of Sir Clough Williams-Ellis of Portmeirion fame. Highlight of the various attractions is a collection of European and Oriental costumes, but of interest too are a model ship collection, a wide range of natural history specimens and a working model fairground. Also pick-your-own fruit.

EARDISLEY

The greatest treasure of Eardisley's **Church of St Mary Magdalene** is its font, dating from the early 12th century. The figures depicted round the font represent not only familiar religious themes but also two men in armed struggle. It is thought that these are a 12th-century lord of the manor, Ralph de Baskerville, and his father-in-law, whom he killed in a dispute over land. Outside the village, the most notable feature, standing majestically by an old chapel, is the **Great Oak**, which is probably 800 years old.

HOPE UNDER DINMORE

Queen's Wood Country Park is a popular place for walking and enjoying the panoramic views, and the most visited spot of all is the arboretum with its wonderful variety of specimen trees.

Adjoining the park is **Dinmore Manor and Gardens**, where the Knights Hospitallers had their local headquarters. The gardens are sheltered, but as they rise some 550 feet above sea level, they afford marvellous views across to the Malvern Hills. The gardens are a sheer delight, and among the many attractions are a 12th-century chapel near the rock garden and pools, a cloister with a roof walk, wonderful stained glass, a yew tree believed to be 1,200 years old, medieval sundials and a grotto. Many varieties of plants, shrubs, alpines and herbs are available for sale in the Plant Centre.

KIMBOLTON

There are two delightful gardens to visit near Kimbolton. At **Stockton Bury** (turn right off the A49 on to the A4112) the sheltered four-acre garden has an extensive variety of plants set among medieval buildings, a kitchen garden, pigeon house, tithe barn, cider press and ruined chapel. At **Grantsfield** (turn right off the A49) are the gardens of an old farmhouse with a wide range of unusual plants and shrubs, old roses, climbers, orchard, kitchen garden - and superb views. Private visits welcome.

KINGTON

The road up to Kington passes many places of interest, and for two in particular a short pause will be well worth while. The National Trust's **Cwmmau Farmhouse**, which lies 4 miles south of Kington between the A4111 and A438 at **Brilley**, is an imposing timber-framed and stone-tiled farmhouse dating from the early 17th century. Viewing is by guided tour only.

Half a mile off the A44 on the Welsh side of Kington are **Hergest Croft Gardens**, four distinct gardens that include rhododendrons up to 30 feet tall, spectacular azaleas, an old-fashioned kitched garden and a marvellous collection of trees and shrubs.

Nearby is the impressive **Hergest Ridge**, rising to around 1,400 feet, and, on its southern edge, **Hergest Court**, once owned by the Vaughan family, whom we met at Kinnersley. Two members of the family who gained particular notoriety were Thomas 'Black' Vaughan and his wife, who was known as 'Gethen the Terrible'. She is said to have taken revenge on a man who killed her brother by taking part in an archery competition disguised as a man. When her turn came to compete, she shot him dead at point blank range and escaped in the ensuing melee. Thomas died at the Battle of Banbury in 1469, but, being a true Vaughan,

that was not ther last of him. He is said to have haunted the church in the guise of a bull, and even managed to turn himself into a horsefly to annoy the local horses. He was back in taurine form when he was finally overcome by a band of clerics. One of the band managed to shrink him and cram him into a snuff box, which was quickly consigned to the waters of Hergest Pool. Later owners of the estate found and unwittingly opened the box, letting Black Vaughan loose once more. The next band of intrepid clerics confined the spirit under an oak tree, but he is currently at large again - though not sighted for many years. These feisty Vaughans are buried in the Vaughan Chapel in Kington parish church.

Kington itself lies on the England/Wales border and, like other towns in the area known as the Marches, had for many years to look closely to the west, whence the wild Welsh would attack. Kington's castle was destroyed many centuries ago, but outside the town, on **Wapley Hill**, are earthworks of an ancient hill fort which could be the site of King Caractacus' last stand.

Most notable by far of all the defences in the region is **Offa's Dyke**, the imposing ditch that extends for almost 180 miles along the border, from the Severn Estuary at Sedbury Cliffs near Chepstow, across the Black Mountain ridge, through the Wye Valley and north to Prestatyn on the North Wales coast. Offa was a Mercian king of great influence, with strong diplomatic links with the Popes and Charlemagne, who ruled the land south of the Humber from 757 to 796. Remnants of wooden stakes unearthed down the years suggest that the Dyke had a definite defensive role, rather than acting merely as a psychological barrier. It was a truly massive construction, in places almost 60' wide, and although nowadays it disappears in places, much of it can still be walked, particularly in the Wye Valley. A stretch north of Kington is especially well preserved and provides excellent, invigorating walking for the energetic. The walk crosses, at **Bradnor Hill**, the highest golf course, over 1,200 feet above sea level. Other major traces of the Dyke remain, notably between Chepstow and Monmouth and by Oswestry, and at many points Offa's Dyke Path, opened by the Countryside Commission in 1971, diverts from the actual Dyke into magnificent scenery.

KINNERSLEY

On the main road lie the village and **Kinnersley Castle**, which has the look of a fortified manor house. Famous occupants down the years include the Morgans (Sir Henry Morgan was one of them) and the Vaughans. Black Vaughan's huge dog is believed to have been the inspiration for Conan Doyle's *Hound of the Baskervilles*. The eight acres of grounds contain many fine specimen trees.

LEOMINSTER

The hub of the farming community and the largest town in this part of the county, made wealthy in the Middle Ages through wool, and still prospering today. Leominster (pronounced Lemster) is well known as one of the most important antiques centres in the region. Some have linked the unusual name with Richard the Lionheart, but there was in fact an earlier king who earned the title. In the 7th century, Merewald, King of Mercia, was renowned for his bravery and ferocity and earned the nickname of "the Lion". He is said to have a dream concerning a message from a Christian missionary, while at the same time a religious hermit had a vision of a lion coming to him and eating from his hand. They later met up at what was to be Leominster almost by accident, and when the King heard of the hermit's strangely coincidental dream, he was persuaded to convert to Christianity. Later, the King requested that a convent and church be built in the town; a stone lintel on the west door of the church depicts the chance meeting of King and hermit. Other, more likely explanations of the name revolve around Welsh and medieval Latin words for "stream" and "marsh".

The Priory Church of **St Peter and St Paul**, originally King Merewald's convent, became a monastery in the 11th century, and the three naves, built in the 12th, 13th and 14th centuries, attest to its importance. A curio here is a ducking stool which, in 1809, was the last to be used in England.

A short walk away, in Priory Park, is **Grange Court**, a fine timbered building which for many years stood in the market place. Built in 1633, it is the work of John Abel, and shows typical Abel flamboyance in its elaborate carvings.

Other buildings to be visited in Leominster are the **Leominster Folk Museum**, the Lion Gallery, featuring the best of local arts and crafts, and the Forbury, a 13th-century chapel dedicated to Thomas à Becket.

LYONSHALL

Church and castle remains are at some distance from the main body of the village, a fact which is often attributed to the plague causing older settlements to be abandoned. The Church of St Michael and All Angels dates mainly from the 13th century and was restored in 1870 when close to collapse. The ruins of the castle include some walls and part of the moat, making this the most "complete" of all the castle ruins in the area. Among the fine old buildings in the village itself are the Royal George Inn, Ivy House, The Wharf and The Woodlands. There are two 12th-century watercorn mills in the parish, one of them, **Bullock's Mill**, being documented continuously from 1580 to 1928.

MORETON JEFFRIES

Worth a visit here is a long, low church with a little slatted bell tower. Note the elaborately carved Jacobean puplit, complete with sounding board and reading desk - a sophisticated touch in generally simple surroundings.

MORTIMER'S CROSS

The site of one of England's greatest and bloodiest battles. Here, on 3 February 1461, was enacted the final episode in the War of the Roses, with the Yorkists defeating the Lancastrians. Hundreds died that day, but Edward Mortimer, the Duke of York's eldest son, survived and was crowned King Edward IV in the following month. Visit the Battle Centre at Watermill.

ORLETON

The churchyard at Orleton is thought by some to be the likely setting for the Resurrection at the Day of Judgemnt, and for that reason people from all over the country used to ask to be buried here in the hope that they would be among the first in the queue when life began again. The road north from Orleton leads to **Richard's Castle** on the Shropshire border. This Norman castle, which lies in ruins on the hillside above the church, was, like so many others, built as a defence against the marauding Welsh. The church played a similar role, and in the 14th century it was refurbished for use as a chapel by the Knights Hospitallers.

Pembridge

The influential Mortimer family were responsible for the medieval prosperity of historic Pembridge, and many handsome buildings bear witness to their patronage and its legacy. The most famous building is the 14th-century church, a three-storey structure in stone and timber with a marvellous timber **belfry**. The bell and the clock mechanism can be viewed from inside the church. Two other buildings which the visitor should not miss are the delightful 16th-century market hall standing on its eight oak pillars and the Old Chapel Gallery in a converted Victorian chapel.

A little way south of Pembridge is **Dunkerton's Cider Mill**, where cider and perry are produced from organically grown local fruit.

Shobdon

The **Church of St John the Evangelist**, which stands on the site of a 12th-century priory, is one of the most remarkable in the county. Behind a fairly unremarkable facade, the interior is stunning. The overall effect is of being in a giant wedding cake, with white and pale blue icing everywhere, and lovely stained glass adding to the dazzling scene.

Just north of here are the "**Shobdon Arches**", a collection of Norman sculptures which have sadly been greatly damaged by centuries of exposure to the elements, but which still demonstrate the high skills of the sculptors of the 12th century.

Country roads signposted from the B4362 lead west from Shobdon to **Lingen**, where the **Nursery and Garden** are a horticultural haven for visitors to this remote area of the Marches. The gardens are home to National Collections of Iris Sibirica and Herbaceous Campanula.

Even nearer the Welsh border, between **Kinsham** and **Stapleton** (signs from the B4362 at Combe) is **Bryan's Ground**, a three-acre Edwardian garden with topiary, parterres, formal herb garden, shrubbery and apple orchard, plus a specialist collection of old roses.

Sutton St Nicholas

Just outside the village is a group of stones known collectively as the **Wergin Stone**. In the hollow base of one of the stones, rents or tithes were laid, to be collected later by the local squire. There is a story that in 1652 the Devil picked up the stone and removed it to a spot a little distance away. It took a team of nine oxen to return the stone to its original place, though why the villagers bothered is not related. South of the village is the Iron Age hill fort of **Sutton Walls**, where King Offa once had a palace. One day in 794, Offa, the King of Mercia, promised the hand of his daughter Alfreda to Ethelbert, King of East Anglia. Ethelbert journeyed to Sutton Walls, but the trip was full of bad omens: the earth shook, there was an eclipse of the sun, and he had a vision that his mother was weeping bloody tears. In spite of all this he pressed on, but after he had reached the palace, and before the wedding ceremony, Offa had him beheaded. There is little now to see at the camp, as a lot of the land has been worked on. Many skeletons have been unearthed, some showing signs of very violent ends.

Just outside Sutton, **Overcourt Garden Nursery** is situated in the grounds of a Grade II listed 16th-century house with connections to the Crusader Knights of St John. A wide range of unusual plants is for sale. Private visits welcome.

Weobley

The steeple of the parish church of St Peter and St Paul is the second highest in the county, a reminder that this prettiest of places (call it Webbly) was once a thriving market town. One of its more unusual sources of wealth was a successful glove-making industry which flourished in the early 19th century when the Napoleonic

Weobley

54

Wars cut off the traditional French source of gloves. At certain times in its history Weobley returned two Members of Parliament, but there have been none since 1832. One of the effigies in the church is of Colonel John Birch, who was rewarded for his successes with Cromwell's army with the Governorship of Hereford and who later became a keen Royalist and Weobley's MP. Little but the earthworks remain of Weobley Castle, which was built before the Norman Conquest and was captured by King Stephen in 1138. One of Weobley's many interesting buildings is called **The Throne**, but it was called The Unicorn when King Charles I took refuge after the Battle of Naseby in 1645.

care of the National Trust. Behind a defensive exterior that tells of the troubled times of Marcher territory, the state rooms are elegant and comfortable, with rare furniture, fine plasterwork and portraits of the Croft family, who have occupied the place with only one break since it was built in the 14th century. In the park are ancient oaks and an avenue of 350-year-old Spanish chestnut trees. Also looked after by the National Trust, and just a short walk away, is **Croft Ambrey**, an Iron Age fort which affords stunning views.

WIGMORE

A few miles on from Mortimer's Cross, Wigmore is noted for its ruined **castle** and abbey. With its impressive vantage point, the hillside at Wigmore was a natural site for building a castle, which is what William FitzOsbern did in the 11th century. This was one of a chain of fortifications built along the Welsh border. By the time of his death in 1071, FitzOsbern had also built Chepstow, Berkeley, Monmouth, Guenta (perhaps Winchester?) and Clifford, and had rebuilt Ewyas Harold. Wigmore passed into the hands of the Clifford family, then the ambitious Mortimers, and it was no doubt here that the future Edward IV prepared himself for the battle at Mortimer's Cross. Enough of the ruins remain to show that Wigmore was once a very serious castle, and one which protected the village and its environs for many centuries, until the Civil War. Two miles north of the village are signs to the 12th-century **Wigmore Abbey**, now in use as a private residence.

YARPOLE

In this delightful village with its jumble of cottages and their colourful gardens stands the Church of St Leonard, which has a detached bell tower, a wooden structure with a stone outer wall. At neighbouring **Eye** are **Eye Manor** and the **Church of St Peter and St Paul**, where Thomas Harley, a Lord Mayor of London, is buried. An unusual feature of this church is the pulpit with carvings of Red Indians.

Near Yarpole, reached from the B4362 between Bircher and Mortimer's Cross, stands **Croft Castle**, an atmospheric property in the

The Chase Inn

55

Bishop's Frome
Herefordshire
WR6 5BP
Tel: 01885 490234
Fax: 01885 490547

Directions:

From the M5 take junction 7 and follow the A44 into Worcester. Continue out on the A44, bearing left onto the A4103. After 14 miles turn right onto the B4214 which will bring you to Bishop's Frome. The Chase Inn is on the left.

The valley of the River Frome has become famous as a hop growing region, and the town of Bishop's Frome is the largest of the villages that take their name from the river. Here you will find **The Chase Inn** where a warm welcome awaits all. The inn was built in 1874 to cater for the hop pickers who flooded the area at that time, and takes its name from a cider chase (an old fashioned method of crushing cider apples). Inside, the inn is beamed in places, has a warming log fire and lots of antique memorabilia. One of the bars serves as a games room with a pool table and dart board. Recently taken over by husband and wife team, Sarah and Mark Low, this has the feel of being a well loved, family business. Sarah is a London trained chef and has brought her expertise to bear in the kitchen with the food being of a very high standard. There are no printed menus, just a blackboard which is updated weekly. All the dishes are freshly cooked and the specialities are the steaks. In addition to the bars there is a separate restaurant area and children are welcome to join their parents there for a meal. Bishop's Frome would be an ideal base for a short stay or longer visit to the region, and The Chase Inn can provide comfortable bed and breakfast accommodation. There are seven rooms, all en-suite. In 2001 a large barn adjoining the pub will be converted to provide a swimming and solarium and further, luxury accommodation. Ring for further details.

Opening Hours: Mon-Thur 12.00-15.00, 18.00-23.00; Fri-Sat 12.00-23.00; Sun 12.00-22.30.

Food: Bar meals and restaurant.

Credit Cards: Visa, Access, Delta, Switch.

Accommodation: 7 en-suite rooms.

Facilities: Pool table/games room, Function room, Car Park.

Entertainment: Theme nights.

Local Places of Interest/Activities: Worcester 15 miles, Great Malvern 10 miles, Three Counties Showground 11 miles, Ledbury 8 miles, Eastnor Castle 9 miles.

Internet/Website: www.chaseinn.co.uk

56 Cliffe Arms

Mathon,
nr Malvern,
Herefordshire WR13 5PW
Tel/Fax: 01886 880782

Directions:
From Worcester take the A4103 towards Hereford. 3½ miles past the village of Leigh Sinton, turn left signposted "Cradley". Continue to Mathon and the Cliffe Arms is on the left, 350 yards beyond the church

The Cliffe Arms, parts of which date from the 14th Century, nestles at the foot of the Malvern Hills alongside the River Rundle in the tiny hamlet of Mathon, an area once noted for cider orchards and hop fields. All that remains of the hops is a China Design called the "Mathon Hop". The timbered and whitewashed walls of the Cliffe Arms, with creeper covered porch, invite you inside where you will find old crook beams, brass, some stone floors and seasonally welcoming fires.

Philip and Cara Jenkins have been running the Cliffe Arms since 1987 with Philip in charge of the kitchen. The menu offers a choice of traditional fare adjusted to the seasons including vegetarian dishes, sandwiches and filled baguettes. A children's menu is also available. Three real ales are on tap, a sensible wine list plus most of the usual popular beverages. You may enjoy your refreshment in the attractive bars and, weather permitting, outside in the garden.

The Cliffe Arms also has an interesting galleried function room, which can accommodate 60 guests seated and up to 80 for a buffet.

Opening Hours: Mon: 19.00-23.00. Tues-Sat: 12.00-15.00; 18.30-23.00. Sun: 12.00-15.00; 19.00-22.30

Food: Available every lunchtime & evening, except Sun & Mon evening (unless it's a Bank Holiday)

Credit Cards: All major cards accepted

Facilities: Beer garden; function room; large car park

Entertainment: Very occasionally

Local Places of Interest/Activities: Good walks all around; Malvern Hills, 3 miles; Worcestershire Beacon viewpoint, 3.5 miles; golf, 4 miles; Three Counties Showground, 5 miles; Priory Church, Abbey Gatehouse, Malvern Museum, all at Great Malvern, 5 miles

England's Gate Inn 57

Bodenham
Herefordshire
HR1 3HU
Tel: 01568 797286

Directions:

8 miles north of Hereford, between the A49 and A417.

The **England's Gate Inn** enjoys a delightful setting in the village of Bodenham, between Hereford and Leominster. This characterful establishment has a history going back to the 1600s when the first property on the site was probably built as a farmhouse. Over the centuries there have been many changes resulting in the sizeable establishment we see today. The interior has retained many original features including a flagstone floor and low beamed ceilings and the furnishings are also in keeping with the age and character of the building.

There is a separate dining room and the quality of the food makes this a popular night out for residents from the surrounding area. The menu ranges from bar snacks and sandwiches at lunchtime, to a more sophisticated a la carte selection in the evenings. There is also a daily specials board and a traditional Sunday lunch menu. In the summer months meals and drinks can be enjoyed in the attractive gardens which surround the inn, and this is also an ideal play area for children.

Adding to the community spirit that can be found here, is the programme of entertainment that is arranged on a regular basis. Events range from live singers and bands, to karaoke, quiz and race nights.

Opening Hours: Mon-Sat 11.00-23.00; Sun 12.00-22.30.

Food: Bar meals and snacks, A la carte menu, Traditional Sunday Lunch.

Credit Cards: Visa, Access, Delta, Switch, Diners Club.

Entertainment: Local Bands, Quiz Night, Karaoke, Race Nights.

Local Places of Interest/Activities:

Queenswood Country Park 2 miles, Leominster 5 miles, Hereford 8 miles.

58 · The Hop Pole Inn

Bridge Street
Leominster
Herefordshire
HR6 8DX
Tel: 01568 612779

Directions:
In the centre of the town of Leominster.

In the centre of the town of Leominster you will find the delightful **Hop Pole Inn**. A typical Herefordshire building the well presented exterior is white painted brick with black painted woodwork, decorated with colourful hanging wall baskets. Dating back to the 1600s this was originally a cider house and was later used for brewing of beer - hence its unusual name. This is a popular cider brewing region though Leominster itself grew up around the wool trade. It is however still a country market town and a popular meeting place for the local farming communities.

The Hop Pole is a quiet, cosy establishment, much like a remote country pub, popular with locals and other visitors to the town. The spacious interior comprises comfortable bar areas in addition to a separate dining room. The quality of the food adds to the popularity with a fine menu offering a good choice of meals and snacks, all home cooked and very reasonably priced. Children can choose from a special menu and their meals come complete with a free soft drink and dessert. Sunday Lunches are very popular here so booking ahead is strongly recommended. To accompany your meal, or simply to enjoy on its own, there is a very good selection of real ales, beer and cider on tap.

The size of The Hop Pole lends itself very well to medium sized functions and the management offer catering services for receptions, working breakfasts and dinners. A full information pack is available, just ring for further details or to receive a copy.

Opening Hours: Mon-Sat 11.00-23.00; Sun 12.00-16.00, 1900-22.30.

Food: Bar meals and snacks, Traditional Sunday Lunch.

Credit Cards: Visa, Access, Delta, Switch.

Facilities: Beer garden, Conference Facilities, Car Park.

Local Places of Interest/Activities: Grange Court, Leominster, Burton Court 5 miles, Queenswood Country Park 5 miles, Hampton Court 6 miles, Berrington Hall 3 miles.

The Lamb Inn

59

Stoke Prior
Leominster
Herefordshire
HR6 0NB
Tel: 01568 760308

Directions:

From the centre of Leominster follow the A49 south before turning left onto the A44 signposted to Worcester. Almost immediately there will be a turning on the right for Stoke Prior. The centre of the village will be found about 2 miles along the road.

The Lamb Inn, in the centre of the village of Stoke Prior, is a traditional country hostelry that has been serving the local community since the 16th century. The deceptively large interior retains some hint of its historic character with beamed ceilings throughout. The atmosphere is cosy and welcoming and the bar area is comfortably furnished with wooden tables and easy chairs.

Food is available from a select menu offering a choice of home made hearty main dishes or lighter snacks to suit all tastes. The food is freshly prepared to order and is served throughout the bar areas while there is also a separate dining area. A traditional roast lunch is served on Sundays and advance booking is recommended. Children are more than welcome in the restaurant and high chairs can be supplied on request. Behind the bar they stock a good range of lager, spirits and soft drinks and there are two real ales on tap.

Opening Hours: Mon-Fri 12.00-15.00, 18.00-23.00; Sat 12.00-23.00; Sun 12.00-15.00, 18.00-22.30.

Food: Bar meals and snacks, Traditional Sunday Lunch.

Credit Cards: None.

Facilities: Pool table, Darts, Beer garden, Car Park.

Local Places of Interest/Activities: Leominster 3 miles, Folk Museum in Leominster, 9 hole golf course 1 mile, Queenswood Country Park 5 miles, Hampton Court 3 miles.

60   The Maidenhead Inn

Orleton,
nr Ludlow,
Herefordshire
SY8 4JB
Tel: 01584 831686

Directions:

From Ludlow, take the A49 towards Leominster. After 4 miles, at Woofferton, turn right on the B4362. Stay on this road for about 2 miles to the junction with the B4361. Turn left and after about 0.3 miles you will see the Maidenhead Inn on your right.

It's believed that **The Maidenhead Inn** was built in the 16th century as a coaching inn and the flagstone floors, ancient beams and open fire certainly suggest it has enjoyed a long history. From the outside, it looks very enticing with its creepered walls and a patio with colourful parasols and flower-boxes. The inn is very much a family business where Nicky Turner, who has been in the trade since 1986 and here since 1999, is ably assisted by her four daughters.

Perhaps not surprisingly, the Maidenhead is a child-friendly hostelry. Children are welcome in the restaurant, where they can choose from their own menu, and in good weather they can take advantage of the play area outside. The inn's wholesome menu is available every lunchtime and evening with a choice of snacks and sandwiches in the bar, or more substantial meals in the dining area of the lounge bar. In addition to the regular menu, there's also a choice of daily specials. To complement your meal, make a selection from the extensive wine list, sample one of the 2 real ales on tap, or choose from the wide range of other popular beverages.

Opening Hours: Mon-Sat: 12.00-14.30; 18.00-23.00 Sun: 12.00-14.30; 19.00-22.30

Food: Available every lunchtime & evening

Credit Cards: All major cards except Amex & Diners

Facilities: Restaurant; beer garden; patio at front; children's play area; large car park

Entertainment: Darts; pool table; crib; dominoes

Local Places of Interest/Activities: Richard's Castle, 2.5 miles; Berrington Hall (NT), 3.5 miles; Croft Hall (NT), 3.5 miles; Ludlow Castle, Ludlow Museum, both 6 miles

The Malvern Hills Hotel | 61

Wynds Point, Malvern,
Herefordshire WR13 6DW
Tel: 01684 540690
Fax: 01684 540327

Directions:
From Exit 2 of the M50, take the A417 towards Ledbury. At the first roundabout (4.5 miles) take the A449 towards Great Malvern. The Malvern Hills Hotel is on this road, at the junction with the B4232, on the left.

Perched 800ft above sea level in an area of outstanding natural beauty, **The Malvern Hills Hotel** offers walks with breathtaking views in all directions. The hotel dates back to the early 1800s but there has been a hostelry on this picturesque site for some 500 years. Oswald and Karen Dockery, who bought the hotel in 1997, continue that great tradition of hospitality. Arriving guests will find a very warm and friendly atmosphere along with outstanding food, drink and accommodation. The hotel has two bars, one decorated in contemporary style, the other oak-panelled and named after Jenny Lind, "The Swedish Nightingale", who was born in Stockholm in 1820 and died in the house next door to the hotel in 1887.

Appetising bar meals are served here, or guests can choose from the extensive fixed price menu served in the elegant surroundings of Nightingales Restaurant. Chef Paul Carney offers his own rustic English style of cooking with influences from around the world, - Thai Spiced Marrow & Ham soup, for example, or a pan fried fillet of John Dory on a butternut squash purée. The hotel is a great base for walkers and an ideal centre for touring the Malverns. Overnight accommodation comprises 14 well-equipped bedrooms, all en suite and many enjoying views over either the tranquil Herefordshire countryside or British Camp, one of the best-preserved Iron Age hill forts in the land.

Opening Hours: Mon-Sat: 11.00-23.00 Sun: 12.00-22.30

Food: Bar or restaurant meals available every lunchtime & evening

Credit Cards: All major cards accepted

Facilities: Restaurant; garden; function room for 50; large car park

Entertainment: Pool table; live entertainment every Tue & Fri

Accommodation: 14 rooms, all en suite. Children & pets welcome

Local Places of Interest/Activities:
Walking on the Malvern Hills, nearby; Herefordshire Beacon viewpoint, 0.5 miles; Three Counties Showground, 2 miles; golf, 2.5 miles; St Anne's Well, Abbey Gateway, Church of St Mary & St Michael, Victorian Winter Gardens, all at Great Malvern, 3.5 miles; Eastnor Castle, 4 miles

Internet/Website:
e-mail: malhilhotl@aol.com
www.malvernhillshotel.com

62 The Marshpools Country Inn

Ledgemoor, Weobley
Herefordshire HR4 8RN
Tel: 01544 318215
Fax: 01544 318847
Directions:

From Leominster follow the A44 southwest towards Brecon. After 5 miles carry straight on to the A4112. After 4 miles turn left on to the B4230 to Weobley. Turn left off the B4230 onto a smaller country road following signs to Tillington. Follow this road for a mile before turning left which will bring you into Ledgemoor.

Tucked away in the country lanes to the south west of Leominster, in the small village of Ledgemoor, is **The Marshpools Country Inn**. This modern built establishment is worth seeking out if you are travelling through the area and in need of some refreshment, or are simply wanting a leisurely drive to enjoy a meal out. The roomy interior is furnished in a traditional style to create a comfortable ambience. Drawing a loyal following from the surrounding area it is the quality and variety of food on offer that is so popular. The extensive menu offers an excellent choice ranging from omelettes, pizzas, jacket potatoes and filled Yorkshire puddings to ploughmans, sandwiches and salads - and that's only the range of snacks and light dishes. There is an equally impressive selection of starters and main courses for those that would like a heartier meal. The dishes are a good mixture of classic English cuisine and pub fayre with a few Continental-style selections as well. Everyone is sure to find something to suit, all meals are freshly prepared to order and are very reasonably priced.

If you are need of a comfortable place to stay in this part of the Welsh Borders, then there are three en-suite rooms available for bed and breakfast. This is certainly a delightfully quiet location with the grounds of the pub extending to two acres and provided with a safe children's play area. Overnight guests can also make use of the coarse fishing which is within the grounds.

Opening Hours: Mon-Sun 12.00-15.00; 19.00-23.00.

Food: Bar meals and snacks.

Credit Cards: Visa, Access, Delta, Switch, Diners.

Accommodation: 3 en-suite rooms - ETC 3 diamonds.

Facilities: Darts, Petanque Court, Coarse Fishing, Children's Play Area, Car Park.

Local Places of Interest/Activities: Herefordshire Golf Club 1½ miles, Go-Karting 2 miles, Dunkerton's Cider 5 miles, Burton Court 5 miles, Offa's Dyke 7 miles, Hereford 12 miles, Leominster 11 miles, Hay on Wye 14 miles

Nags Head   63

Canon Pyon
Herefordshire
HR4 8NY
Tel: 01432 830252

Directions:
On the A4110, 6 miles north-west of Hereford.

The Nags Head Inn can be found on the main A4110 road in the centre of the village of Canon Pyon.

This listed building can trace its history back 430 years when it was originally built as a farmhouse and retains many original features including flagstone flooring, open fires and exposed wooded beams. Outside there is a large car park which can also accommodate coach parties when required and there is a large garden with a well-equipped children's adventure playground.

Food is served at every session and there is a great choice on offer from a varied and interesting menu. The dishes are freshly prepared, home cooked and served in good sized portions to suit even the heartiest of appetites. In addition to the a la carte menus there is also a good choice of sandwiches and snacks. There is a large dining area which is tastefully furnished and features an illuminated well around which there is a table seating eight people - a highly unusual and popular feature! The restaurant can get busy so advance booking is recommended at all times, especially for Sunday lunch. To complement your meal there is an equally good choice of beer, real ale and lager served behind the bar.

If you need somewhere to stay then you need look no further - there is a total of six en-suite bedrooms on offer here with a single room, four double rooms and a family room. All the rooms are comfortably furnished and are provided with tea/coffee making facilities and a TV.

Opening Hours: Mon-Sat 11.00-14.30;18.00-23.00; Sun 12.00-22.30. Closed Monday lunchtime except bank holidays

Food: Bar meals and snacks, A la carte, Traditional Sunday lunch.

Credit Cards: Visa, Access, Delta, Switch.

Accommodation: 4 double rooms en-suite, 1 single room en-suite, 1 family room en-suite.

Facilities: Large Beer Garden, Children's Play Area, Large Car Park.

Local Places of Interest/Activities: Hereford 6 miles, 18 hole golf course 2 miles, Queenswood Country Park 4 miles.

64

Red Lion

Pembridge
Herefordshire
Tel: 01544 388188

Directions:

From Leominster follow the A44 west towards Kington. The village of Pembridge will be found about 6 miles from Leominster on this road.

Half-timbered cottages, inns and almshouses all lend an air of old English charm to the village of Pembridge which is very popular with tourists. There are some beautiful examples of the traditional 'black and white' building style and they are well worth a look. The jewel is undoubtedly the delightful market hall which lies in the tiny market square and dates from the early 16th century. The Church of St Mary is also worth a visit, dating from 1320 it is one of the best examples of a detached bell tower, a feature of churches that is common in this part of England. The church has a slightly oriental feel, looking a little like a pagoda, and slits in the walls indicate that the church doubled up as a stronghold during the time of the border skirmishes.

In the centre of the village stands the **Red Lion inn**. This 200 year old inn is a comfortable, locals' pub that is also popular with visitors to the area because of its prominent location. The Red Lion boasts a cosy, welcoming atmosphere, enhanced by the open log fire which is lit when the weather turns cool. The bar is complemented by a small restaurant area and here you will find a small, select menu offering some traditional fayre. To enjoy with your meal there is the usual selection of beer, ale and lager.

Opening Hours: Mon-Sat 11.00-15.00, 18.00-23.00; Sun 11.00-15.00, 18.00-22.30.

Food: Bar meals and snacks.

Credit Cards: None.

Local Places of Interest/Activities: Leominster 8 miles, Burton Court 2 miles, Dunkertons Cider 2 miles.

The Roebuck Inn 65

Brimfield, Ludlow
Herefordshire SY8 4NE
Tel: 01584 711230
Fax: 01584 711654

Directions:

Leave the M5 at junction 3 and take the A456 round Kidderminster and on to Tenbury Wells. Continue until you reach the A49, about 5 miles. Turn left onto the A49 and almost immediately left again into the village of Brimfield. The Roebuck Inn is about 200 metres on the left.

The elegant **Roebuck Inn** can be easily found just off the main A49 Ludlow to Leominster road. Dating back to the 15th century this has always been an inn, catering to the locals from the surrounding area and travellers passing through, and there is ample parking for those who arrive by car. A warm and friendly welcome is extended to all who pass through the door by hosts David and Susan. They have been here for over four years and have brought many years' experience in the trade to the Roebuck, resulting in the popular and successful establishment you find today. There is no doubt that one of the main reasons for their success is the high quality of the food available. All dishes are freshly prepared by the resident chefs using the best local produce available and everything that is served in the restaurant, including the bread, is made on the premises. The exciting selection is sure to stimulate every palate and everyone can be sure of finding something that appeals to their taste and appetite. The al fresco dining area is an ideal setting for a romantic night out or to celebrate a special occasion. More casual dining can be enjoyed in the lounge bar, or visitors can simply enjoy a refreshing drink. The bar stocks three real ales, one of which is a guest beer. There is an extensive wine list together with a good selection of exclusive malts, armangnac, cognac and vintage port. The Roebuck Inn can also offer comfortable bed and breakfast accommodation with three en-suite guest rooms available. Ring for details of rates and availability.

Opening Hours: Mon-Sat 11.30-1400, 18.30-23.00; Sun 12.00-15.00, 19.00-22.30.

Food: A la carte.

Credit Cards: Visa, Access, Delta, Switch.

Accommodation: Three rooms.

Facilities: Car Park.

Local Places of Interest/Activities:
Berrington Hall 3 miles, Eye Manor 3 miles, Croft Castle 6 miles, Leominster 7 miles, Burford House Gardens 5 miles, Ludlow Castle 4 miles, Ludlow Racecourse 6 miles.

Internet/website:
e-mail dave@roebuckinn.demon.co.uk
website www.roebuckinn.demon.co.uk

66 The Wheatsheaf Inn

Fromes Hill
Ledbury
Herefordshire
HR8 1HT
Tel: 01531 640888

Directions:

The village of Fromes Hill lies on the A4103 between Worcester and Hereford. Located just to the east of the B4214, it is about 13 miles from Worcester.

The Wheatsheaf Inn enjoys a prime location on the busy A44 between Worcester and Hereford. It is known to have been an inn since 1702 though the main building was probably built even earlier than this. This is an area well-known for hop growing, an industry which was well-established by the 19th century, and this probably contributed to the growth of this popular hostelry.

Set slightly back from the road, The Wheatsheaf Inn is positioned at the top of a steep hill, surrounded by a large car park, making this a convenient and popular stopping place for travellers along the road. In addition to the car park the surrounding grounds, which extend to 9 acres, include a football pitch and beer garden. Inside the inn there are two bar areas, one with a non-smoking restaurant attached seating 50. Food is served each lunchtime and evening with a range of bar snacks available throughout and a table d'hote menu available in the restaurant. The menus feature fresh local produce as much as possible and all meals are freshly prepared to order. If you would like to enjoy a drink of wine with your meal there is an extensive wine list, while behind the bar they serve four real ales of which two are regularly changed.

This is a new venture for the present owners and they have made this a friendly family-run business. They help to keep the atmosphere lively for regular customers by arranging live music each week. Bed and breakfast accommodation is also available with six en-suite rooms and the location of The Wheatsheaf Inn makes this a convenient overnight stop when travelling through or touring the area.

Opening Hours: Mon-Sat 11.00-23.00; Sun 12.00-22.30.

Food: Bar meals and snacks, Table d'hote.

Credit Cards: Visa, Access, Delta, Switch, Amex, Diners.

Accommodation: 6 en-suite rooms.

Facilities: Function room, Car Park, Football pitch, Beer Garden.

Entertainment: Live music each week.

Local Places of Interest/Activities: Worcester 13 miles, Great Malvern 8 miles, Three Counties Showground 9 miles, Ledbury 8 miles, Eastnor Castle 9 miles.

4 Hereford and South Herefordshire

PLACES OF INTEREST:

Abbey Dore 70
Brockhampton 70
Dorstone 70
Garway 71
Goodrich 71
Grosmont 71
Hay-on-Wye 71
Hereford 71
Hoarwithy 73
Holme Lacy 73
How Caple 73
Kilpeck 73
Ledbury 73
Madley 74

Moccas 75
Monnington-on-Wye 75
Much Marcle 75
Peterstow 75
Ross-on-Wye 75
Sellack 76
Skenfrith 76
Swainshill 76
Symonds Yat 76
Welsh Newton 77
Weston-under-Penyard 77
Whitchurch 77
Wilton 77

PUBS AND INNS:

Alma Inn, Linton   78
The Black Lion, Hereford   79
The Boat Inn , Whitney on Wye   80
The Crown Inn , Longtown   81
The Red Lion Inn , Kilpeck   82
The Red Lion Inn, Madley   83
The Temple Bar , Ewyas Harold   84
The Travellers Rest , Stretton Sugwas   85
Ye Olde Ferrie Inne, Symonds Yat West   86

The Hidden Inns of the Welsh Borders

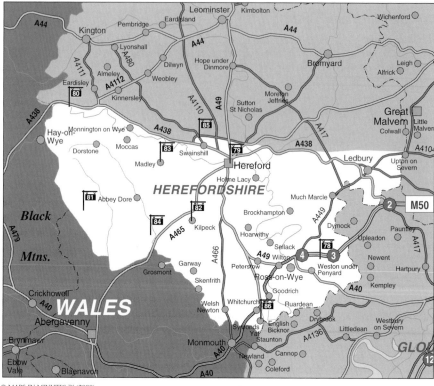

© MAPS IN MINUTES ™ (2000)

78 Alma Inn, Linton

79 The Black Lion, Hereford

80 The Boat Inn , Whitney on Wye

81 The Crown Inn , Longtown

82 The Red Lion Inn , Kilpeck

83 The Red Lion Inn, Madley

84 The Temple Bar , Ewyas Harold

85 The Travellers Rest , Stretton Sugwas

86 Ye Olde Ferrie Inne, Symonds Yat West

Please note all cross references refer to page numbers

This chapter takes the reader from the very south of the county and along the Wye Valley, taking in the county town of Hereford. The River Wye rises in the Plynlimon mountains east of Aberystwyth, near the spot where the Severn also has its source. The Wye enters England by Hay-on-Wye and winds its way through some of the most delightful scenery in the whole land, changing mood and direction from time to time and finally joining its original neighbour at the Severn Estuary. The whole of its length offers great touring and walking country, and the **Wye Valley Walk**, waymarked with the logo of the leaping salmon, follows the river closely for 112 miles, almost half of which are in Herefordshire. The valley was designated an Area of Outstanding Natural Beauty (AONB) in 1971, and the river itself was the first to be recognised as a Site of Special Scientific Interest (SSSI). The salmon logo is, of course, wholly appropriate, as the Wye is a mecca for anglers, with salmon the king of a realm that also includes perch, pike, tench, roach and eels. In the 18th century, artists, poets and the leisured classes enjoyed the Wye Tour, a highly agreeable alternative to the European Grand Tour, and two centuries later the car, train and bicycle have brought the charm of the valley within the reach of all.

A trip up from Monmouth along the the River Monmow, on and around the A466, will reward the motorist with not just beautiful scenery but a real glimpse into the often turbulent history of this Border country.

Herefordshire has only ever had few natural resources, so the industrial scars that spoil many counties are mercifully absent; the beauty remains relatively intact, so too the peace, and motorists will generally find jam-free roads. Apples and hops are the traditional crops of Herefordshire, and the cider industry is still a thriving one. The days when almost every farm produced its own cider are long gone, but many of the old mills are preserved on the farms or in museums. 9,500 acres of the county are given over to cider orchards, and 63 million gallons of cider are produced here each year - well over half the UK total. In western Herefordshire perry is something of a speciality, the drink being made on similar lines to cider but with pears instead of apples. Hops have been cultivated in the county since the 16th century and once provided late summer work for thousands of pickers, mainly from the Black Country and South Wales. The industry is considerably smaller than before, and mechanisation has greatly reduced the need for human effort. The poles and wires are a less common sight than previously, but they can still be seen, along with the occasional kiln for drying the hops - the Herefordshire equivalent of Kent's oast houses. Among the animals, sheep and cattle are a familiar sight; Hereford cattle still abound, and their stock are now to be found in many parts of the world, particularly the Americas. Industry was never developed to any great extent, partly through the remoteness of the location and the poverty of communications, and the visible traces of the county's heritage are confined largely to castles (this is Border territory) and churches. The castles were mainly of the straightforward motte and bailey variety, the motte being a tower-topped earthen mound surrounded by a small court, the bailey a larger yard with the stables and workshops and accommodation.

70 PLACES OF INTEREST

ABBEY DORE

A Cistercian **abbey** was founded here in the 12th century and the building, which was substantially restored by John Abel in the 17th century, is still in use as a parish church.

The garden at **Abbey Dore Court**, where the River Dore flows through the grounds, is home to many unusual shrubs and perennials, with specialist collections of euphorbias, hellebores and peonies. There's also a small nursery, a gift shop and a restaurant.

At nearby **Bacton**, a mile along the same B4347, is **Pentwyn Cottage Garden**, where visitors can walk round the peaceful garden before enjoying a cream tea. From the remote, lonely roads that lead west towards Offa's Dyke and the boundary with Wales, motorists should leave their cars, stretch their legs and drink in the wonderful scenery. The villages of **Longtown** and **Clodock** lie at the foot of the **Olchon Valley**, while further north are the **Olchon Waterfall**, **Black Hill**, the rocky ridge of the **Cat's Back** and the ruins of **Craswall Priory**, which was founded in the 13th century by the rare Grandmontine order and abandoned 200 years later.

Back in the Golden Valley are the twin towns of **Turnastone** and **Vowchurch**, linked by a stone bridge over the river. These neighbours each have their own parish church.

BROCKHAMPTON

The **Church of All Saints** is one of only two thatched churches in the country and dates from 1902, designed by William Lethaby, who had close ties with Westminster Abbey, and built by Alice Foster as a memorial to her parents. The Norfolk thatch is not the only unusual aspect here, as the church also boasts stained glass made in the Christopher Whall studios and tapestries from the William Morris workshop from Burne-Jones designs. Continuing up the B4224 in the direction of Hereford, the visitor will come upon the village of **Fownhope**, where every year on Oak Apple Day in May or June the Green Man Inn celebrates the restoration of Charles ll with the Heart of Oak Club Walk. The inn's most famous landlord was Tom Spring, a champion bare-knuckle

prize fighter who died in 1851. Fownhope church, 'The Little Cathedral', has a special treasure in the form of a tympanum of the Virgin and Child.

Minor roads lead eastward to another village not to be missed. **Woolhope** is named after Wuliva, Lady Godiva's sister, who owned the manor in the 11th century. In the 13th-century sandstone Church of St George is a modern stained-glass window depicting the siblings.

This is, like so much of the county, great walking country, with the **Marcle Ridge**, the 500 foot **Woolhope Dome** and the Forestry Commission's **Haugh Wood** among the attractions and challenges. The last is best approached from **Mordiford**, once a centre of the mining industry and now free from the baleful man-eating Mordiford Dragon. The story goes that the dragon was found by a local girl while it was still small. She nurtured it lovingly, and although it was at first content to feed on milk, and later chickens and the odd duck, it eventually developed a taste for cows and finally people. The beast terrorised the locals, and indeed one of the paths leading from the woods is still known as Serpents Lane. It was here that he would slink along the river to drink, and it is said that no grass ever grows there. No one was brave enough to face the beast until a man called Garson, who happened to be awaiting execution, decided that he had nothing to lose. He hid in a barrel by the river, and when the creature appeared he shot it through the heart. That was the end of the dragon, and also of poor Garson, who was killed in the fiery breath of the dragon's death throes. Mordiford stands on the River Lugg, just above the point where it joins the Wye, and the River Frome joins the Lugg a little way above the village. **Mordiford Bridge**, with its elegant span of nine arches, was once the source of regular revenue for the kings of this land: apparently every time the king crossed the bridge the locals lords had to provide him with a pair of silver spurs as a levy on the manor.

DORSTONE

A very attractive village with neat sandstone cottages set around the green. St Faith's Church has a connection with Canterbury, as Richard de Brito, one of the knights who murdered Thomas à Becket, established a church here after serving 15 years' penance in the Holy Land for his crime. He returned to build the church and is buried in the churchyard.

South of Dorstone lie the ruins of **Snodhill Castle**, from which the views are spectacular even for this part of the world. To the north, on wild, exposed Merbach Hill, is the much-visited landmark of **Arthur's Stone**, a megalithic tomb of great antiquity which was used for the burial of tribal chieftains. Some say (but few believe it!) that the body of King Arthur himself was buried here.

GARWAY

Marvellous views from the wild and remote **Garway Hill** take in the river valley, the Forest of Dean beyond Symonds Yat to the east, and the Black Mountains. The church at Garway was built by the Knights Templar and the influences from the Holy Sepulchre in Jerusalem can clearly be seen. During the purges of Henry VIII's reign, the Abbot of Monmouth was one of many who sought refuge in the church tower. The most unusual building in Garway is undoubtedly the famous **dovecote**, the first of several to be mentioned in this book. A contemporary construction (also probably the work of the good knights) in a farmyard next to the church, the dovecote has precisely 666 pigeon-holes.

GOODRICH

Goodrich village is notable for the landmark 14th-century broach spire of its parish church. The vicar at a critical point in the Civil War was one Thomas Swift, grandfather of Jonathan Swift, author of *Gulliver's Travels*. This staunch Royalist hid some of the church's treasures, including a superb silver chalice, from the marauders, and, it is said, sewed 300 pieces of gold into his waistcoat to take to the King.

In a village of predominantly yellow sandstone houses, there are some notable Gothic exceptions; the most dramatic of these is Ye Hostelrie Hotel, whose pinnacles and tall lattice windows are a dramatic feature on the small village street. The core of the building dates from the 16th century and the present facade was added in 1850 - the work of Edward Blore, who had a hand in the design of Buckingham Palace.

GROSMONT

71

In the village of Grosmont lies a castle with impressive remains, and another interesting church, this one dedicated to St Nicolas of Myra.

A little way beyond Grosmont is **Kentchurch Court**, a one-time border castle rebuilt by John Nash around 1800 and featuring some splendid wood carvings by Grinling Gibbons. The Court has for many centuries been the home of the Scudamore family, one of whose number married Owen Glendower.

HAY-ON-WYE

Bookworms will wriggle with delight as they browse through Hay-on-Wye's 38 secondhand bookshops. Richard Booth, known as the King of Wye, opened the first bookshop here 40 years ago, and is a leading player in the annual **Hay Book Festival**. The famous diarist Francis Kilvert was a local man, and his *Diary* is just one of millions of books on for sale. But books are not the only attraction: Hay also has a large number of antique shops, and the River Wye in never far away, with its shifting moods and ever-changing scenery.

HEREFORD

The county town-to-be was founded as a settlement near the unstable Welsh Marches after the Saxons had crossed the Severn in the 7th century. A royal demesne in the 11th century, it

Hereford Cathedral

had a provincial mint, and was an important centre of the wool trade in the Middle Ages. Fragments of Saxon and medieval walls can still be seen, but the city's crowning glory is the magnificent 'Cathedral of the Marches'. Largely Norman, it also has examples of Gothic, Early English, Decorated, Perpendicular and Modern architecture. The Cathedral demands an extended visit, as it contains, in the impressive New Library building, two of the country's most important historical treasures. *Mappa Mundi* is the renowned medieval world map, the work of Richard of

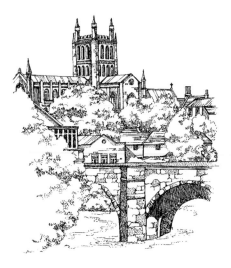

Hereford Cathedral

Haldingham. Drawn on vellum, it has Jerusalem as its centre and East at the top, indicating that direction as the source of all things good and religiously significant. Richard was Treasurer of Lincoln Cathedral, which might explain why Lincoln appears rather more prominently on the map than Hereford. The **Chained Library**, the finest in the land, houses 1,500 rare books, including over 200 medieval manuscripts, all chained to their original 17th-century book presses. The Cathedral has many other treasures, including the shrine of St Thomas of Hereford in stone and marble, the Norman font, the Bishop's Throne and the John Piper tapestries. There's also a brass-rubbing centre.

Hereford is full of fascinating buildings and museums which visitors should try to include in their tour. **Hereford Museum and Art Gallery** has a changing art gallery programme and hands-on exhibitions. The **Old Hall Museum**, right in the centre of High Town, brings alive the 17th century in a three-storey black-and-white house filled with fascinating exhibits. **Churchill House Museum**, whose grounds include a fragrant garden, displays furniture, costumes and paintings from the 18th and 19th centuries; among its rooms are a costume exhibition gallery and Victorian nursery, parlour, kitchen and butler's pantry. The **Hatton Gallery** shows the work of local artist Brian Hatton. **St John Medieval Museum** at Coningsby is a 13th-century building in an ancient quadrangle of almshouses. Displays include costume models of Nell Gwynne, a famous daughter of Hereford, and the history of the Ancient Order of St John and its wars during the Crusades. Hereford's restored pumping station is home to the **Waterworks Museum**, where Victorian technology is alive and well in the shape of a collection of pumps (some of which can be operated by visitors), a Lancashire Boiler and Britain's largest triple expansion engine. The **Regimental Museum** houses an important collection of uniforms, colours, medals, equipment, documents and photographs - and the flag and pennant of Admiral Doenitz.

Hereford and cider are old friends, and the **Cider Museum** tells the intersting story of cider production down the years. One of the galleries houses the King Offa distillery, the first cider brandy distillery to be granted a licence for over 200 years. Also on the outskirts of the city are the Cider Mills of HP Bulmer, the world's leading cider producer. Look, learn and taste on one of the organised tours.

The original Saxon part of the city includes historic Church Street, full of 17th-century listed buildings (mostly modernised in the 19th century). Church Street and Capuchin Yard - the name derives from the hood worn by the Franciscan friars who built a chapel nearby - are renowned for their small specialist shops and craft workshops.

Hereford stages important musical events throughout the year, and every third year hosts the **Three Choirs Festival**, Europe's oldest music festival.

The A465 out of Hereford soon reaches **Belmont Abbey**, whose architect, the renowned

Pugin, was responsible for part of the House of Commons. One of the stained-glass windows in the church at **Clehonger** is probably also his work. The church at **Eaton Bishop**, just north of the B4352, is famous for its east window, with 14th-century stained glass depicting the Crucifixion, Madonna and Child, and the Archangel Gabriel.

HOARWITHY

By far the most extraordinary of the three walk-linked churches lies in the unspoilt village of Hoarwithy on the willow-lined banks of the Wye. **St Catherine's Church** is a splendid piece of architecture which owes its origin to the Reverend William Poole, who arrived in1854, didn't like what he saw and spent the next 30 years supervising the building of a new church round the chapel. The result is an Italianate building complete with a campanile, arcades, beautiful tiled floors and a white marble altar with lapis lazuli inlay. Further on up or near the A49 are the villages of **Much Birch** and **Little Birch**, both with interesting churches. Also worth a look in Little Birch is Higgin's Well, named after a local farmer and restored at the time of Queen Victoria's Diamond Jubilee in 1897.

HOLME LACY

Holme Lacy was originally the estate of the de Lacy family in the 14th century, but later passed into the hands of the illustrious Scudamore family. The first Viscount Scudamore was the first person to classify the varieties of cider apple, and actually introduced the well-known Red Streak Pippin strain. The fine Palladian mansion dates from 1672 and once sported woodwork by Grinling Gibbons. St Cuthbert's Church, standing away from the village on a bend of the Wye, has a remarkable collection of 16th and 17th-century monuments of the Scudamores, and also some fine furnishings and medieval stalls with misericords.

Near the village of Holme Lacy is **Dinedor Court**, a splendid 16th-century listed farmhouse with an impressive oak-panelled dining hall. English Heritage is responsible for **Rotherwas Chapel** in Dinedor. This is a Roman Catholic chapel dating from the 14th and 16th centuries and featuring an interesting mid-Victorian side chapel and high altar.

HOW CAPLE   **73**

The Edwardian gardens at **How Caple Court**, set high above the Wye in park and woodland, are magnificent indeed, with formal terraces, yew hedges, statues, pools, a sunken Florentine water garden and woodland walks. How Caple's medieval **Church of St Andrew and St Mary** contains a priceless 16th-century German diptych depicting, among pther subjects, the martyrdom of St Clare and St Francis, and Mary Magdalene washing the feet of Christ.

KILPECK

The parish church of **St Mary and St David** is one of the most fascinating in the whole county. Built by Hugh de Kilpeck (son of William Fitznorman, who built Kilpeck Castle) round an earlier Saxon church, it has changed little since the 12th century. Much of the church is unique in its rich decoration, but the gem is the portal over the south doorway, with all manner of elaborate carvings. Most of the carvings throughout the church have no apparent religioius significance, with some bordering on the bizarre, if not downright bawdy! Very little remains of the castle, it having been largely demolished by Cromwell's men, but on a clear day the castle mound affords very fine views.

LEDBURY

A classic market town filled with timber-framed black-and-white buildings, mentioned in the Domesday Book as Ledeberge and accorded its market status in the 12th century. The centre of the town is dominated by the **Barrett Browning Institute** of 1892, erected in memory of

Ledbury Market Hall

74

Elizabeth Barrett Browning, whose family lived at nearby Colwall. Alongside it are the almshouses of St Katherine's Hospital, founded in 1232 for wayfarers and the poor. **Church Lane**, much in demand for calendars and film location scenes, is a cobbled medieval street where some of the buildings seem almost to meet across the street. Here are the **Heritage Centre** in a timber-framed former grammar school, **Butcher's Row Museum** and, upstairs in the old council offices, the **Painted Room**, graced with a series of remarkable 16th-century frescoes.

The town's symbol is the **Market House**, dating from about 1650 and attributed to John Abel, the royal carpenter; another notable landmark is the Norman parish church of St Michael and All Angels, with a soaring spire set on a separate tower, some magnificent medieval brasses and bullet holes in the door - the scars of the Battle of Ledbury. The town's history has in general been fairly placid, but its peace was broken with a vengeance in April 1645, when Royalist troops under Prince Rupert surprised a

Roundhead advance from Gloucester. In the fierce fighting that followed there were many deaths, and 400 men were taken prisoner.

Annual events at Ledbury include a poetry festival in July, a street carnival in August and a hop fair in the autumn. Among the famous sons of the town is one of our most distinguished Poets Laureate, John Masefield. William Langland, who wrote *Piers Ploughman*, was from nearby Colwall. The town is a great place for walking, and on the fringes nature-lovers will find plenty to delight in **Dog Hill Wood**, **Frith Wood** and **Conigree Wood**, as well as on **Wellington Heath** and along the **Old Railway Line**.

2½ miles outside Ledbury on the A438 towards Tewkesbury stands **Eastnor Castle**, overlooking the Malvern Hills. This fairytale castle, surrounded by a deer park, arboretum and lake, has the look of a medieval fortress but was actually built between 1812 and 1824 and is a major example of the great Norman and Gothic architectural revival of the time. The first Earl Somers wanted a magnificent baronial castle, and, with the young and inspired architect Robert Smirke in charge, that's exactly what he got; the combination of inherited wealth and a judicious marriage enabled the Earl to build a family home to impress all his contemporaries. The interior is excitingly beautiful on a massive scale: a vast 60-feet high hall leads into a series of state rooms including a library in Italian Renaissance style containing a treasure house of paintings and tapestries, and a spectacular Gothic drawing room designed by Pugin. The grounds, part of which are a Site of Special Scientific Interest, are home to a wonderful variety of flora and fauna, and throughout the year the castle is the scene of special events.

MADLEY

There's fine stained glass in the church at Madley, where the immense stone font also takes the eye. St Dyfrig, the man who some say crowned King Arthur, was born here.

In the ancient village, just down the road from the famous church, **Marston Exotics** is home to one of the most exciting groups of plants in the world - the Insectivorous plants. This working nursery is the biggest in the country for its speciality. It is also home to the Natural Council for the Conservation of Plants & Gardens National Collection of Sarracenia, with

Church Lane, Ledbury

more than 65 varieties and species. There's a café with a picnic area and home-made produce and crafts.

MOCCAS

Moccas Court, designed by Adam and built by Keck, stands in seven acres of Capability Brown parkland on the south bank of the Wye. In the village itself stands the beautiful Church of St Michael, built of the local stone known as tufa.

MONNINGTON-ON-WYE

The grounds of **Monnington Court**, part of the Bulmer Estate, cover 20 acres and include a lake, river, sculpture garden, a famous mile-long avenue of firs and yews, and the foundation farm of the British Morgan horse. There's also a cider mill. Private visits by appointment.

MUCH MARCLE

This is Big Apple Country, with major cider attractions in the shape of **Westons Cider Mill** (see below) and **Lyne Down Farm**, where traditional methods of making cider and perry are still employed. In the church at Much Marcle is a rare painted wooden effigy, carved from solid oak and thought to be the likeness of a 14th-cenruty landowner called Walter de Helyon. Up until the 1970s he was painted a rather sombre stone colour, but was then loaned for an exhibition of Chaucer's London and was repainted in his original colours. The **Great Marcle Yew** is a talking point among all visitors to the village, its massive trunk hollowed out allowing up to eight people to enjoy cosy comfort on the bench inside.

A short distance north of Much Marcle, **Hellens** is an untouched Tudor/Stuart house set in 15 acres of grounds with coppices, lawns and fishponds.

Closer to Ledbury, on the A4172 at **Little Marcle**, is **Newbridge Farm Park**, where families can enjoy a day out on the farm in the company of a large assortment of friendly farm animals.

PETERSTOW

At **Broome Farm**, half a mile off the A49, traditional farmhouse cider has been brewed since the early 1980s, winning many prizes throughout the 90s and featuring apples with evocative names like Fox Whelp or Yarlington Mill. Also at Peterstow is **Kyrle House**, whose coun-

try garden contains herbaceous borders, a small grotto, sunken garden and secret garden. Private visits welcome.

ROSS-ON-WYE

The lovely old market town of Ross-on-Wye is signalled from some way out by the towering spire of St Mary's Church, surrounded up on its sandstone cliffs by a cluster of attractive houses. Opposite the church is a row of Tudor almshouses which have an ancient yet ageless look and which show off the beauty of the rosy-red sandstone to great effect. The town was visited by the Black Death in 1637, and over 300 victims are buried in the churchyard. A simple stone cross commemorates these hapless souls, who were interred in the dead of night in an effort to avoid panicking the populace. Notable features in the church include 15th-century stained-glass figures and a tomb chest with effigies of William Rudhall, Attorney General to Henry VIII and founder of the almshouses, and his wife. Pride of place in the market square goes to the 17th-century **Market House**, with an open ground floor and pillars supporting the upper floor, which is a Heritage Centre. Spot the relief of Charles II on the east wall. The **Lost**

Market Hall, Ross-on-Wye

Street Museum is a time capsule of shops and a pub dating from 1885 to 1935, while the **Button Museum** in Kyrle Street is unique in being the first museum devoted entirely to the humble - and sometimes not so humble - button, of which there are more than 8,000 examples on show spanning working clothes and uniforms, leisure pursuits and high fashion. A fascinating little place and a guaranteed hit with visitors - right on the button, in fact.

Ross is full of interesting buildings, and besides those already noted is **Thrushes Nest**, once the home of Sir Frederick Burrows, a railway porter who rose above his station to become the last Governor of Bengal. Opposite Market House stands the half-timbered house (now shops) of the town's greatest benefactor, John Kyrle. A wealthy barrister who had studied law at the Middle Temple, Kyrle settled in Ross around 1660 and dedicated the rest of his life to philanthropic works: he donated the town's main public garden, **The Prospect**; he repaired St Mary's spire; he provided a constant supply of fresh water; and he paid for food and education for the poor. Alexander Pope was as impressed as anyone by this benefactor, penning these lines some time after the great man died in 1724 at the age of 87:

"Rise, honest Muse, and sing the Man of Ross,

Health to the sick and solace to the swain,

Whose causeway parts the vale in shady rows,

Whose seats the weary traveller repose,

Who taught that heav'n directed spire to rise?

'The Man of Ross', each lisping babe replies."

The **Ross International Festival** of music, opera, theatre, comedy and film takes place each August and grows in stature year by year. In and around Ross are several examples of modern public art, including leaping salmon metal sculptures (Edde Cross Street) and a mural celebrating the life of locally-born playwright Dennis Potter. At Ross-on-Wye Candlemakers in Gloucester Road are a shop and workshop showing the manufacture of all types of candles, with evening demonstrations and group visits by appointment.

SELLACK

A popular waymarked walk takes in three marvellous churches in three delightful villages. The church in Sellack is uniquely dedicated to St Tysilio, son of a king of Powys, and is Norman in origin.

A short drive north of Sellack, in the churchyard at **King's Caple**, is a plague cross remembering victims of the Black Death of 1348. The church dates mainly from the 13th century and a fascinating little detail is to be found on the benefactors' board on the west wall. The local charities listed include Cake Money, a gift in

perpetuity from a former vicar of King's Caple and Sellack. Pax cakes, signifying peace, are still distributed to the congregations on Palm Sunday.

SKENFRITH

A drive or an energetic walk takes in the remains of **Skenfrith Castle** (the round tower is an impressive sight), an ancient mill and the Church of St Bridget, dating, like the castle, from the 12th and 13th centuries. And that's just in Skenfrith!

SWAINSHILL

The Weir in Swainshill is a charming riverside garden, spectacular in early spring, with 'drifts of flowering bulbs'. Views of the Wye and the Welsh Hills. National Trust.

At Credenhill, a little way north of Swainshill on the A480, the **National Snail Farming Centre** is a unique attraction showing snail farming and a display of wild British snails both static and alive.

Further along the same road, seven miles from Hereford, is the village of **Yazor**, whose church, dating from the mid-19th century, features good stained glass and monuments, as well as a very colourful sanctuary.

SYMONDS YAT

The beauty spot of Symonds Yat is an inland resort to which visitors flock to enjoy the views, the walks, the river cruises, the wildlife (peregrine falcons nest at Coldwell Rocks), the history and the adventure. Into the last category fall canoeing - rushing down the Wye gorge south of the village - and rock climbing. Symonds Yat (yat means pass) is divided into east and west by the Wye, with no vehicular bridge at that point. Pedestrians can make use of the punt ferry, pulled across the river by chain, but the journey by car is 4½ miles. Walking in the area is an endless delight, and at **The Biblins** a swaying suspension bridge provides vertiginous thrills across the river. Notable landmarks include the **Seven Sisters Rocks**, a collection of oolitic limestone crags; **Merlin's Cave**; King Arthur's Cave, where the bones of mammoths and other prehistoric creatures have been found; **Coldwell Rocks** and **Yat Rock** itself, rising to 500 feet above sea level at a point where the river performs a long and majestic loop. Also on the Symonds Yat walkabout is a

Symonds Yat Ferry

Wye and the Forest of Dean, and certainly one of the loveliest and most fertile valleys in the region. It is an area of wooded hills and spectacular views, of farms and small settlements, with the tiny village of Hope Mansell itself at the far end. The **Forest of Dean**, over the border in Gloucestershire, is a vast and ancient woodland full of beauty and mystery, with signs of Iron Age settlement. Later a royal hunting ground, and the home of charcoal-burners and shepherds, it became the first National Forest Park.

77

massive boulder measuring 60 by 40 feet, one of the largest in the country.

Other entertainment in the area is provided by the **Jubilee Maze**, an amazing hedge puzzle devised by brothers Lindsay and Edward Heyes to celebrate Queen Elizabeth's 1977 Jubilee. On the same site is a museum of mazes and a puzzle shop. In the **Jubilee Park**, at Symonds Yat West, is **The Splendour of the Orient**, with Oriental water gardens, Chinese furniture, gifts from the Orient and a tea room and restaurant. Another major attraction in the Park is a garden centre with an extensive range of plants plus garden furniture and a gift shop. The church in Symonds Yat, built in the 14th century, is dedicated to St Dubricius, a local who converted the area to Christianity and who, according to legend, crowned King Arthur.

WELSH NEWTON

The village lies right on the A466, and just off it stands **Pembridge Castle**, now in use as a private house. In the village churchyard of St Mary the Virgin lies the body of John Kemble, a Roman Catholic who was executed in 1679 for daring to hold a mass in the castle. A plain slab commemorates this martyr, who was 80 years of age when he met his violent end.

Several more castles along the River Monmow are further reminders that this pretty part of the world was once very turbulent.

WESTON-UNDER-PENYARD

Leave the A40 at Weston Cross to Bollitree Castle (a folly), then turn left to Rudhall and you'll come upon Kingstone Cottages, whose delightful informal gardens contain the National Collection of old pinks and carnations. Private visits welcome. South of Weston lies **Hope Mansell Valley**, tucked away between the River

WHITCHURCH

Just north of Symonds Yat, in the shadow of the Rock, lies the village of Whitchurch, where at the **World of Butterflies** visitors can experience the warmth of a tropical hothouse with butterflies flitting freely about their heads. A little further up, and off, the A40, is **Kerne Bridge**, a settlement which grew around a bridge built in 1828, where coracles are still made, and from where the energetic walker can hike into history at the majestic **Goodrich Castle** in a commanding position above the Wye. Built of red sandstone in the 11th century by Godric Mapplestone, the castle is now ruined but still magnificent. It was the last bastion to fall in the Civil War, attacked by 'Roaring Meg', a siege gun cast in Whitchurch which could hurl a 200lb ball and which can now be seen in Hereford. The siege lasted four and a half months and marked the end of the castle's 'working life'. English Heritage maintain the ruins in excellent condition, and the 12th-century keep and elements from the next two centuries are well worth a visit, to walk the ramparts or just to imagine the glorious sight it once presented.

WILTON

Wilton, just a short walk from Ross, stands at a crossing point of the River Wye. The bridge was built in 1599, some years after a river disaster which claimed 40 lives. Over the bridge are the ruins of **Wilton Castle**, of which some walls and towers still stand. An 18th-century sundial on the bridge bears this numinous inscription:

"Esteem thy precious time,
which pass so swiftly away:
Prepare them for eternity
and do not make delay."

78

Alma Inn

Linton, Ross-on-Wye
Herefordshire HR9 7RY
Tel: 01989 720355

Directions:

From the junction at the end of the M50 motorway, take the B4221 east towards Newent. About 3 miles along this road, a minor road leads to Linton. Alternatively, leave Junction 3 of the M50 and take the B4221 Upton Bishop road. Linton is signposted (1 mile)

In the centre of the village of Linton stands the quiet **Alma Inn**. Dating back to the early 19th century, the establishment was named after the Crimean Battle of the 1854 campaign. This cosy and welcoming inn is run by Graham and Linda. The interior has a Victorian feel though the main structure of the building is much older, with traditional decor. Food is available at lunchtimes, Wednesday to Sunday, and in the evenings from Thursday to Saturday. The varied menu provides a choice of good food, with vegetarians catered for, and with additional specials at the weekend. Traditional Sunday Lunches, which are very reasonably priced, are served each week. Advance booking is recommended as they prove to be very popular with customers from the surrounding area. Meals are served in the non-smoking dining bar - small parties and private functions can be catered for.

Behind the bar they serve a good range of beers, lager and cider with local real ales and a guest beer. In warm weather, the beer garden overlooking open countryside is an ideal spot for a refreshing drink, while inside there's a pool table and dart board. Accommodation is available in the form of 2 double/family bedrooms both of which have en suite facilities. The main stairs leading to the accommodation have the facility of a chair lift. It is hoped that a self-catering cottage, sleeping 4 - 6 people, will be available from summer 2001.

Opening Hours: Mon-Tue 18.30-23.00; Wed-Thu 12.00-14.30, 18.30-23.00; Fri-Sat 12.00-14.30, 18.00-23.00; Sun 12.00-14.30, 19.00-23.00

Food: Bar snacks, Traditional Sunday Lunch.

Credit Cards: None.

Accommodation: 2 double/family bedrooms (both en suite); self-catering cottage available from summer 2001

Facilities: Pool table, Darts, Beer garden, Car Park.

Local Places of Interest/Activities: Ross-on-Wye 5 miles; Shambles Museum of Victorian Life, National Birds of Prey Centre, both at Newent, 5 miles; Forest of Dean 6 miles; Three Choirs Vineyard, Botloe's Green; Goodrich Castle 10 miles, Symonds Yat 15 miles.

Black Lion

79

31 Bridge Street
Hereford
Herefordshire
HR4 9DG
Tel: 01432 354016

Directions:

In the centre of Hereford near to the Old Wye Bridge and the Cathedral.

The Black Lion can be found in the real heart of the charming city of Hereford, enjoying a central location close to the Cathedral and the old Wye Bridge. This is thought to be the oldest pub in the city and has a reputation for being haunted, with a number of ghosts making occasional appearances to staff and customers! The frontage is in keeping with the many other historic buildings, being of the black and white timbered variety, and the interior also features some exposed beams.

Catering to local and tourist trade, the Black Lion is popular for its food, and is open for lunch and in the evening. There is a regular menu with a wide choice of dishes, together with daily specials, with all meals being home prepared and using locally sourced ingredients where possible. Behind the bar there is an equally wide choice of beers, lagers and cider.

Opening Hours: Mon-Sat 11.00-23.00; Sun 12.00-22.30.

Food: Bar meals and snacks, Traditional Sunday lunch.

Credit Cards: Visa, Access, Delta, Switch.

Facilities: Function room.

Local Places of Interest/Activities:
Hereford Cathedral, Hereford racecourse 2 miles, Belmont Abbey 2 miles.

80   The Boat Inn

Whitney on Wye
Herefordshire
HR3 6EH
Tel: 01497 831223

Directions:

On the A438 Hereford to Hay-on-Wye road, 4 miles northwest of Hay-on-Wye

One of very few pubs situated alongside the River Wye, **The Boat Inn** is an imposing, solid building set back from the main road in the village of Whitney on Wye. The property was built by a local landowner in a solid style and it has recently been taken over by new owners, Carol and Robert Taylor. They have owned many pubs throughout Wales and at the Boat Inn they have continued their policy of providing quality and value for money.

The food here is excellent and the restaurant attracts diners from far and wide, including a number of celebrities. Carol is the chef and has received many awards for her cuisine, the most recent being a Dawn of the Millennium award. Her menu offers a superb choice of dishes ranging from locally-reared duck to steaks of prime Hereford beef, from hearty roasts to fish dishes based on the day's catch which Robert will have collected directly from the Swansea docks. Seasonal vegetables are obtained locally and are organically grown. To accompany your meal, there's an equally fine selection of real ales, beer and lager, along with two regularly changing guest ales. The comfortable lounge bar looks out over the River Wye and to the open countryside beyond. Boat trips can be arranged with advance notice. This fine inn also offers a beer garden which is a popular drinking spot on warm summer days, and there is a large car park. Adjoining the pub is a field which is made available to campers and caravans - ring for full details.

Opening Hours: Mon-Sat: 11.00-23.00 Sat: 12.00-22.30

Food: Bar meals and snacks; supper licence to 24.30, Mon-Sat

Credit Cards: Access, Delta, Visa, Switch

Facilities: Beer garden; caravan & camping site

Accommodation: Available during 2001

Local Places of Interest/Activities: Hay-on-Wye, 4 miles; canoeing, 4 miles, Offa's Dyke, 10 miles; Hereford, 16 miles

Crown Inn 81

Longtown
Herefordshire
HR2 0LT
Tel: 01873 860217

Directions:

From Hereford take the A465 towards Abergavenny. About 18 miles south west of Hereford, at the village of Pandy, turn right onto a small country road. About five miles along the road is the village of Longtown.

The village of Longtown is where the Escley, Ochlon and Monmow rivers converge. To the west the Black mountains rise and the village seems to straggle up the hillside to the ruins of Longtown Castle. Dating back to the 12th century, the Castle was built on the site of a much earlier Roman Fort and must have been a spectacular vantage point from which to keep an eye on the surrounding mountain ranges.

Lying in the shadow of the castle stands **The Crown**. This country inn is reputedly 300 years old, with some later additions, and is constructed of stone with a slate tiled roof. The most recent alterations were made in the 1950s and these now house a pool room. Very much a locals' pub catering to the local farming community you could be mistaken for thinking you had stepped back in time when you step through the door! There is no pretence at modernisation, no juke box or karaoke machine here, just good beer and fresh food served with a friendly smile. If you want to while away a quiet evening entertainment is provided in the form of pool, darts or quoits.

The menu offers a choice of classic dishes with an additional children's menu and a vegetarian selection. Bar snacks are available and Sunday lunch is served if booked in advance. If you are on the move, or have no time to stop for something to eat, then there is also the option of take away meals. Behind the bar there is a selection of beer, traditional real ales and cider.

Opening Hours: Summer - Mon 18.00-23.00; Tues-Sun 12.00-15.00, 18.00-23.00; Winter - Tues 12.00-15.00, 18.00-23.00; Thur-Sun 12.00-15.00, 18.00-23.00

Food: Bar meals and snacks, Take-away, Traditional Sunday Lunch.

Credit Cards: None.

Facilities: Pool table/games room, Car Park.

Local Places of Interest/Activities: Longtown Castle, Llanfihangel Court 7 miles, Grosmont Castle 14 miles.

82   The Red Lion Inn

Kilpeck
Herefordshire
HR2 9DN
Tel: 01981 570464

Directions:
In the centre of the village of Kilpeck, just off the A465 Hereford to Abergavenny road, 9 miles south-west of Hereford.

The Red Lion Inn is a comfortable and popular village pub in the centre of the small village of Kilpeck. The delightful rural setting means there are some lovely views from the beer garden and in summer this is a very popular stopping place for visitors to the area. Inside, the country style furniture adds to the warm and friendly atmosphere where everyone is made very welcome. The bar serves a varied selection of real ales, cider and lager. There is a small but carefully chosen menu of bar meals and snacks with all dishes being home cooked and freshly prepared to order. The charming country village of Kilpeck is home to a fine Norman church which is well worth a look around. First time visitors should keep an eye out for the rather naughty corbels!

Opening Hours: Summer: Mon-Fri 12.00-14.30, 18.00-23.00; Sat 12.00-15.00, 18.00-23.00; Sun 12.00-15.00, 19.00-22.30. Winter: Mon-Thur 12.00-14.30, 18.00-23.00; Fri 18.00-23.00; Sat 12.00-15.00, 18.00-23.00; Sun 12.00-15.00.

Food: Bar meals and snacks.

Credit Cards: None.

Entertainment: Occasional Folk Music, Morris Men.

Facilities: Pool, Darts, Table skittles.

Local Places of Interest/Activities: Kilpeck Norman Church, Hereford 9 miles, Black Mountains 10 miles.

The Red Lion Inn 83

Shaw Lane
Madley
Herefordshire
HR2 9PH
Tel: 01981 250292

Directions:

On the B4325 Hereford to Hay-on-Wye road, 7 miles west of Hereford.

Enjoying a prime location in the village of Madley, situated between Hereford and Hay-on-Wye, is **The Red Lion Inn**. This former coaching inn retains much of its historic character with a charming interior featuring a Victorian fireplace and beamed ceilings. The main bar is cosy and welcoming and while being a convenient meeting place for locals is equally appealing to visitors to the area. Occasional live entertainment is arranged with a variety of tastes being catered for.

Open each lunch time and evening, and all day at weekends, the quality of the food is evident from its popularity with customers. There are a variety of menus for the bar, dining area and non smoking restaurant with an excellent range of dishes on offer. All meals and snacks are freshly prepared and cooked to order and everyone is sure to find something to suit their taste and appetite. Considering the quality the prices are very reasonable too. The dining area and restaurant can get busy so booking is recommended at all times. To accompany your meal there is a good choice of traditional ales, beer, lager and wines available.

If you were hoping to linger in the area then en-suite accommodation is available in the recently converted granary. Rooms of varying sizes are comfortably furnished and provided with colour TV and hot drinks tray. Ring for further details.

Opening Hours: Mon-Fri 12.00-15.00, 19.00-23.00; Sat 11.00-23.00; Sun 11.00-20.30.

Food: Bar meals and snacks, A La Carte, Traditional Sunday Lunch.

Credit Cards: Visa, Access, Delta, Switch.

Accommodation: En suite accommodation - call for details

Entertainment: Occasional Live Music.

Facilities: Games Room.

Local Places of Interest/Activities: Hay on Wye 15 miles, Hereford 7 miles.

84 Temple Bar Inn & Restaurant

Ewyas Harold
Herefordshire
HR2 0EU
Tel: 01981 240423

Directions:

In the centre of the village of Ewyas Harold on the B4347, just off the A465 Hereford to Abergavenny road, 12 miles southwest of Hereford.

The Temple Bar Inn is a fine Georgian country pub located in the centre of the charming village of Ewyas Harold. The atmosphere is friendly and welcoming and there is an air of this establishment being well loved and cared for. The interior is comfortably furnished and customers are well provided with pub games in the form of pool, darts and quoits. Attracting a loyal local following this is also a popular stop for visitors to the area.

The bar serves an excellent selection of traditional beers and these are complemented by the usual selection of lagers, local ciders, spirits and soft drinks with a comprehensive wine list. Food is served each lunchtime and evening from a large menu including home-cooked classic dishes, continental and vegetarian food, á la carte and traditional Sunday lunches. Meals are served in a choice of the lounge bar, public bar or the non-smoking dining room.

Although there is no accommodation available here the proprietors are happy to make arrangements for visitors to the area and there is a wide selection available nearby. There is a function room available for private hire and the pub also offers an outside catering service ranging from simply provision of food to a licensed bar.

Opening Hours: Mon-Fri 11.00-15.00; Sat 11.00-23.00; Sun 12.00-16.00, 19.00-22.30.

Food: Bar meals and snacks.

Credit Cards: Visa, Access, Delta, Switch.

Entertainment: Live Entertainment.

Facilities: Beer Garden, Non-smoking Dining Room, Pool, Darts, Quoits, Skittles, Children's Play Area, Function Room, Outside catering.

Local Places of Interest/Activities: Dore Abbey 1½ miles, Abbydore Gardens 2 miles, Grosmont Castle 3 miles, Hereford 12 miles.

The Travellers Rest | 85

Stretton Sugwas
Herefordshire
HR4 7AL
Tel: 01432 760268

Directions:
In the centre of the village of Stretton Sugwas, 3 miles north-west of Hereford.

The Travellers Rest is a charming red-brick country inn located at the centre of the village of Stretton Sugwas. Set slightly back from the road, with a large car park to the front, the Victorian building is softened by the ivy climbing over the walls. It is thought that the building was originally a farmhouse which has been much extended over the years, resulting in the spacious establishment that you find today. The interior is cosy and welcoming with exposed beams adding to the character.

A quiet inn, the Travellers Rest opens each lunch time and evening catering to a loyal local trade as well as to visitors to the area. Food is offered from a menu which gives a choice of tasty dishes and this can be enjoyed in the separate restaurant or in the main bar. Traditional Sunday lunches are served and Senior Citizens can enjoy reduced rates on Thursdays (must be pre-booked). To accompany your meal, or to enjoy on its own, are a selection of beers and lagers with at least one real ale also on tap. There are a variety of pub games to while away a quiet evening and there is an outdoor children's play area.

Opening Hours: Mon-Thurs 11.00-15.00, 18.00-23.00; Fri-Sat 11.00-23.00; Sun 12.00-15.30, 19.00-22.30.

Food: Bar meals and snacks, Traditional Sunday Lunch.

Credit Cards: None.

Facilities: Beer Garden, Pool, Darts, Quoits, Skittles, Children's Play Area.

Local Places of Interest/Activities: Hereford 3 miles, Hereford racecourse 2 miles.

86 Ye Olde Ferrie Inne

Symonds Yat West
Nr. Ross-on-Wye
Herefordshire
HR9 6BL
Tel: 01600 890232

Directions:

From Ross-on-Wye, take the A40 south west towards Monmouth. After about seven miles Symonds Yat will be clearly signposted to the left.

Adjacent to the River Wye in Symonds Yat West is the picturesque **Ye Olde Ferrie Inne**, surrounded by some of the most beautiful scenery in Herefordshire. This traditional country inn dates back in parts to the 1500s with the inn thriving on the busy river trade that passed by the door. The original building has been much extended over the centuries resulting in the characterful establishment you see today.

Food is served in the bar and restaurant from a carefully selected menu of meals and snacks. All dishes are freshly prepared to order and are reasonably priced. To accompany your meal, behind the bar there is a good choice of beer, lager and cider, including the house special, Olde Ferrie Inne ale. Food and drink can be enjoyed outside on the patio area, overlooking the river, in summer months.

If you are in need of somewhere to stay, Ye Olde Ferrie Inne is also able to offer accommodation, with a total of six en-suite double and twin rooms. All rooms are comfortably furnished and provided with TV and tea and coffee making facilities. Some rooms enjoy views across the river. This inn really does have everything the visitor could wish for; excellent food and drink, wonderful accommodation and magnificent character. It is well worth a visit.

Approached by a narrow road, the inn is located at the river's edge from which a hand-pulled ferry can be taken across the Wye to Symonds Yat East. This is the only direct crossing of the river, with the route by road involving a four mile trip!

Opening Hours: Mon-Sun 11.00-23.00

Food: Bar meals and snacks.

Credit Cards: Visa, Access, Delta, Switch.

Accommodation: Six en-suite rooms.

Facilities: Pool, Darts, Patio, Beer garden, Car Park.

Local Places of Interest/Activities: Jubilee Maze, Symonds Yat, Forest of Dean, Goodrich Castle 4 miles, Pembridge Castle 8 miles.

PLACES OF INTEREST:

Alfrick 89
Belbroughton 89
Bewdley 89
Bromsgrove 90
Callow Hill 91
Clifton 91
Droitwich 91
Great Witley 92
Hagley 92
Hanbury 92
Hartlebury 92
Harvington 93

Inkberrow 93
Kidderminster 93
Leigh 93
Lower Broadheath 94
Redditch 94
Shatterford 94
Spetchley 94
Stourport-on-Severn 94
Wichenford 94
Worcester 95
Wythall 96

PUBS AND INNS:

The Albion, Worcester   97
The Bell, Pensax   98
The Bridge Inn, Stourport-on-Severn   99
The Bridge Inn, Tibberton   100
The Butchers Arms, Stoke Prior   101
The Crown Inn, Worcester   102
The Fountain Inn, St. Michaels   103
The Horn and Trumpet, Bewdley   104
The Plough Inn, Lower Broadheath   105
The Red Lion, Bradley Green   106
The Rising Sun, Stourport-on-Severn   107
The Vernon Arms, Hanbury   108

The Hidden Inns of the Welsh Borders

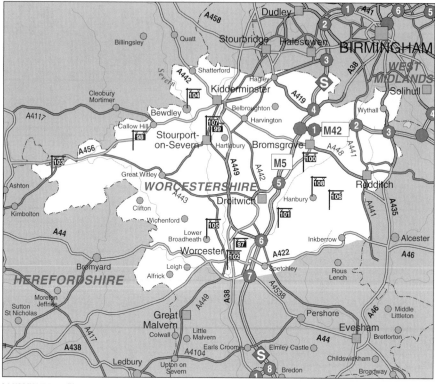

© MAPS IN MINUTES ™ (2000)

97	**The Albion**, Worcester	103	**The Fountain Inn**, St. Michaels
98	**The Bell**, Pensax	104	**The Horn and Trumpet**, Bewdley
99	**The Bridge Inn**, Stourport-on-Severn	105	**The Plough Inn**, Lower Broadheath
100	**The Bridge Inn**, Tibberton	106	**The Red Lion**, Bradley Green
101	**The Butchers Arms**, Stoke Prior	107	**The Rising Sun**, Stourport-on-Severn
102	**The Crown Inn**, Worcester	108	**The Vernon Arms**, Hanbury

Most of Worcestershire's industry was centred in the northern part of the county, and there are numerous examples of industrial archaeology to interest the historian. Salt and scythes, carpets, porcelain and needles all contributed to the local economy, along with ironworks and corn mills, and many fine old buildings survive as monuments to industries which have dwindled or disappeared.

Canals here were once as important as roads, and in this part of the county the Worcester & Birmingham Canal, the Staffordshire & Worcester Canal and the Droitwich Canal were a quicker means of transport than the Severn and more reliable than the roads. They themselves lost a good deal of their practical advantages when the railways arrived. The railway network has shrunk considerably over the last 40 years, so it's back to the roads for most local communications. The Severn Valley Railway, from Kidderminster to Bridgnorth, has survived and flourished, and today people come from far and wide for the chance to ride behind a steam engine through some incredibly beautiful scenery. Enthusiasts have also ensured that much of the canal system has survived, finding a new role as a major leisure and tourist attraction.

PLACES OF INTEREST

ALFRICK

Charles Dodgson (Lewis Carroll) once preached at the village Church of St Mary Magdalene, which enjoys a delightful setting above the village green. In the vicinity are two major attractions for nature-lovers. A little way to the north-west is **Ravenshill Woodland Nature Reserve** with waymarked trails through woodland that is home to many breeding birds, while a mile south of Alfrick is the **Knapp and Papermill Nature Reserve**, with 25 hectares of woodland and meadows rich in flora and fauna.

BELBROUGHTON

This village was once a centre of the scythe-making industry. Holy Trinity Church occupies a hillside site along with some pleasing Georgian buildings.

A little to the north are the village of **Clent** and the **Clent Hills**, an immensely popular place for walking and drinking in the views. On the top are four large upright stones which could be statement-making modern art but for the fact that they were put there over 200 years ago by Lord Lyttleton of Hagley Hall. Walton Hill is over 1,000 feet above sea level.

BEWDLEY

On the western bank of the Severn, linked to its suburb Wribbenhall by a fine Thomas Telford Bridge, Bewdley was once a flourishing port, but lost some of its importance when the Staffordshire & Worcestershire Canal was built. It's a quiet, civilised but much visited little town with some good examples of Georgian architecture, and has won fame with another form of transport, the **Severn Valley Railway**.

Guaranteed to excite young and old alike, the Severn Valley Railway operates a full service of timetabled trains hauled by a variety of steam locomotives. The service runs from Kidderminster to Bridgnorth, home of the railway since 1965, and the route takes in such scenic attractions as the Wyre Forest and the Severn Valley Country Park and Nature Reserve. Each of the six stations is an architectural delight, and there are buffets at Bridgnorth and Kidderminster, and a tea room at Bewdley.

Bewdley Museum, which also incorporates the Tourist Information Centre, is a great place for all the family, with exhibitions themed around the River Severn and the **Wyre Forest**. Crafts depicted include charcoal-burning, coopering and brass-making. Bewdley was the birthplace of Stanley Baldwin, three times Prime Minister between the Wars.

Signal Box, Bewdley

BROMSGROVE

A visit to the **Avoncraft Museum of Historic Buildings**, just south of Bromsgrove, is a walk through seven centuries of English history, with each building providing a snapshot of life in its particular period. The first building, a timber-framed merchant's house from Bromsgrove, was brought to the site in 1967, since when over 20 more have been installed. In addition to the buildings themselves, the Museum has regular demonstrations of such crafts as wood-turning, windmilling, racksawing, brick-making, chain-making and nail-making. There's also a shop, refreshment area, picnic site, a children's area, horse-drawn wagon rides and farm animals wandering around freely. One of the most treasured exhibits is the original 14th-century

beamed roof of Guesten Hall from Worcester Cathedral, now covering a modern brick building. In an area behind the shop is another unique collection, the **BT National Telephone Kiosk Collection**.

Bromsgrove Museum, near the town centre, has displays of local crafts and industry, including the Bromsgrove Guild, an organisation of craftsmen founded in 1894. The Guild of highly skilled craftsmen had its finest hour when commissioned to design and make the gates and railings of Buckingham Palace. Another popular exhibit is a street scene of Victorian shops.

Besides the museums, there is plenty to see, including some very handsome timber-framed buildings in the High Street, where stands a statue of A E Housman, the town's most famous son. Alfred Edward Housman was born one of seven children at Fockbury, Bromsgrove, in 1859, and spent his schooldays in the town. After a spell at Oxford University and some time teaching at his old school, he entered the Civil Service in London, where he found time to resume his academic studies. He was appointed Professor of Latin at University College, London, in 1892 and soon afterwards he published his first and best-known collection of poems - *A Shropshire Lad*. His total output was not large, but it includes some of the best-loved poems in the English language. He died in 1936 and is buried in the churchyard of St Lawrence in Ludlow. The forming in 1972 of a Housman Society brought his name to the forefront of public attention and in the region of Bromsgrove walking and driving trails take in the properties and places associated with him.

Bromsgrove has a prestigious annual **music festival** held during the month of May, when the town plays host to a wide range of musical entertainment from orchestral concerts to jazz, and featuring many well-known artists. Another annual event is the revival of the Court Leet, an ancient form of local administration. A colourful procession moves through the town and there's a lively Elizabethan street market.

The **Church of St John the Baptist** - see his statue over the south porch entrance - contains some superb 19th-century stained glass and an impressive collection of monuments, notably to members of the Talbot family. Side by side in the churchyard are tombs of two railwaymen who were killed in 1840 when their engine exploded while climbing the notorious

Lickey Incline. This stretch of railway, near the village of **Burcot** three miles northeast of Bromsgrove, is, at 1 in 37.7, the steepest gradient on the whole of the British rail network. One specially powerful locomotive, no. 58100, spent its days up until the late 1950s helping trains up the bank, a task which was later performed by massive double-boilered locomotives that were the most powerful in the then BR fleet. The steepness of the climb is due to the same geographical feature that necessitated the construction of the unique flight of **locks at Tardebigge**, between Bromsgrove and Redditch. In the space of 2½ miles the canal is lifted by no fewer than 30 locks. In the actual village of Tardebigge, on the A448, the Church of St Bartholomew enjoys a lovely setting with views across the Severn lowlands.

5 miles north of Bromsgrove lies **Wasely Hill** where open hillside and woodland offers great walking and spectacular views from the top of Windmill Hill. There is also a visitor centre. Just to the east there is more great walking and views in a varied landscape around the **Lickey Hills** which also has a visitor centre.

CALLOW HILL

The **Wyre Forest Visitor Centre** is set among mature oak woodland with forest walks, picnic area, gift shop and restaurant. Wyre Forest covers a vast area starting northwest of Bewdley and extending into Shropshire. The woodland, home to abundant flora and fauna, is quite dense in places. It was once inhabited by nomadic people who made their living from what was around them, weaving baskets and brooms, burning charcoal and making the little wooden whisks which were used in the carpet-making process. Just south of Callow Hill, the village of **Rock** has an imposing Norman church in a prominent hillside position with some lovely windows and carving.

CLIFTON

In lovely countryside near the River Teme, the village boasts a number of charming dwellings around the green and the Church of St Kenelm. Parts of the church go back to the 12th and 14th centuries.

There are other interesting churches at nearby **Shelsey Beauchamp**, in red sandstone, and **Shelsey Walsh**, with many treasures including the tomb of Sir Francis Walsh. The name of Shelsey Walsh will be familiar to fans of motor sport as the location of a very famous hill climb.

91

DROITWICH

"Salinae", the place of salt, in Roman times. Salt deposits, a legacy from the time when this area was on the seabed, were mined here for 2,000 years until the end of the 19th century. The natural Droitwich brine contains about 2 1/2 pounds of salt per gallon - ten times as much as sea water - and is often likened to the waters of the Dead Sea. The brine is pumped up from an underground lake which lies 200 feet below

Droitwich Heritage Centre

the town. Visitors do not drink the waters at Droitwich as they do at most other spas, but enjoy the therapeutic properties floating in the warm brine. The first brine baths were built in the 1830s and were soon renowned for bringing relief to many and effecting seemingly miraculous cures. By 1876, Droitwich had developed as a fashionable spa, mainly through the efforts of John Corbett, known as the "Salt King".

This typical Victorian businessman and philanthropist introduced new methods of extracting the brine and moved the main plant to Stoke Prior. The enterprise was beset with various problems in the 1870s and Corbett turned his attention to developing the town as a spa resort. He was clearly a man of some energy, as he also served as an MP after the 1874 General Election. Many of the buildings in present-day Droitwich were owned by Corbett, including the Raven Hotel (a raven was part of his coat of arms) in the centre. His most remarkable legacy is undoubtedly **Chateau Impney**, on the eastern side of town at Dodderhill. It was designed by a Frenchman, Auguste Tronquois, in the style of an ornate French chateau, with soaring turrets, mansard roof and classical French gardens. It was intended as a home for Corbett and his wife Anna, but she apparently didn't like the place; their increasingly stormy marriage ended in 1884, nine years after the completion of the flamboyant chateau, which is now a high-class hotel and conference centre.

The **Heritage and Information Centre** includes a local history exhibition (Salt Town to Spa) and a historic BBC radio room.

In the centre of the town is St Andrew's Church, part of whose tower was removed because of subsidence, a condition which affected many buildings and which can be seen in some fairly alarming angles. One of the chapels, dating from the 13th century, is dedicated to St Richard de Wyche, the town's patron saint, who became Bishop of Chichester. On the southern outskirts of Droitwich is the **Church of the Sacred Heart**, built in Italianate style in the 1930s and remarkable for its profusion of beautiful mosaics made from Venetian glass. Many of these mosaics also commemorate the life of St Richard.

One of Droitwich's most famous sons is Edward Winslow, born the eldest of eight children in 1595. He was one of the pilgrims who set sail for the New World to seek religious freedom and he later became Governor of the colony. A bronze memorial to Edward Winslow can be seen in St Peter's Church, Droitwich.

Salwarpe on the southwest fringes of Droitwich, is truly a hidden hamlet, approached by a stone bridge over James Brindley's Droitwich Canal. Opened in 1771, the canal linked the town to the River Severn at Hawford. The Church of St Michael, by the edge of the canal, has several monuments to the Talbot family, who owned nearby Salwarpe Court. Salwarpe Valley Nature Reserve is one of very few inland sites with salt water, making it ideal for a variety of saltmarsh plants and very well worth a visit.

Five miles south of Droitwich off the A449 at **Hawford** there's another amazing dovecote, this one half-timbered, dating from the 16th century and owned by the National Trust.

Great Witley

Great Witley Church, almost ordinary from the outside, has an unbelievable interior of Baroque flamboyance that glows with light in a stunning ambience of gold and white. Masters of their crafts contributed to the interior, which was actually removed from the Chapel of Canons in Edgware: Joshua Price stained glass, Bellucci ceiling paintings, Bagutti plasterwork. Next to the church are the spectacular and hauntingly beautiful remains of **Witley Court**, a palatial mansion funded by the riches of the Dudley family. Destroyed by fire in 1937, it stood a neglected shell for years, until English Heritage took over these most splendid of ruins and started the enormous task of making them safe and accessible. If you only see one ruin in the whole county, this should be it.

Hagley

George, 1st Lord Lyttleton, commissioned, in 1756, the creation of what was to be the last great Palladian mansion in Britain, **Hagley Hall**. Imposing without, exotic and rococo within; notable are the Barrell Room with panelling from Holbeach Hall, where two of the Gunpowder Plotters - the Wintour brothers - were caught and later put to death in the favourite way of hanging, drawing and quartering. Temples, cascading pools and a ruined castle are some of the reasons for lingering in the park, which has a large herd of deer.

Another attraction at Hagley is the **Falconry Centre** on the A4565, where owls, hawks, falcons and eagles live and fly.

Hanbury

Hanbury Hall is a fine redbrick mansion in William & Mary style, completed by Thomas Vernon in 1701. Internal features include murals by Sir James Thornhill, known particularly for his Painted Hall in the Royal Naval Hospital, Greenwich, and frescoes in the dome of St Paul's. See also a splendid collection of porcelain, the Long Gallery, the Moorish gazebos at each corner of the forecourt and the formal gardens with orangery and 18th-century ice house.

Hartlebury

Hartlebury Castle, a historic sandstone castle of the Bishops of Worcester and a prison for captured Royalist troops in the Civil War, now houses the **Worcester County Museum**. In the former servants' quarters in the north wing numerous permanent exhibitions show the past lives of the county's inhabitants from Roman times to the 20th century. Visitors can also admire the grandeur of the three Castle State Rooms.

On Hartlebury Common, **Leapgate Country Park** is a nature reserve in heath and woodland, with the county's only acid bog.

HARVINGTON

Harvington Hall is a moated medieval and Elizabethan manor house with a veritable maze of rooms. Mass was celebrated here during times when it was a very dangerous thing to do, and that is perhaps why the Hall has more priest holes than any other house in the land.

INKBERROW

A very pleasant and pretty spot to pause awhile, with the Church of St Peter (note the alabaster of John Savage, a High Sheriff of Worcester who died in 1631), the inn and other buildings round the village green, some in red brick, others black and white half-timbered. The **Old Bull Inn** has two claims to fame, one that William Shakespeare stayed there in 1582, the other that it is the original of The Bull at Ambridge, home of *The Archers*. Photographs of the cast adorn the walls, and the inn has become a place of pilgrimage for fans of the programme.

The Old Vicarage, a handsome 18th-century building in the Tudor style, was host in an earlier guise to King Charles 1, who stayed there on his way to Naseby; some maps he left behind are kept in the church.

At nearby **Dormston**, a timber-framed dovecote stands in front of the Moat farmhouse.

One mile south of Inkberrow is the village of **Abbots Morton**, whose dwellings are mainly 17th-century yeomen's houses. The village was once the site of the Abbot of Evesham's summer residence, but only some mounds and fishponds now remain.

KIDDERMINSTER

Known chiefly as a centre of the carpet-making industry, which began here early in the 18th century as a cottage industry. The introduction of the power loom brought wealth to the area and instigated the building of carpet mills. Standing on the River Stour, the town has a variety of mills, whose enormous chimneys dominate the skyline and serve as architectural monuments to Kidderminster's heritage. St Mary's Church, on a hill overlooking the town, is the largest parish church in the county and contains some superb tomb monuments. The Whittall Chapel, designed in 1922 by Sir Charles Gilbert Scott, was paid for by Matthew Whittall, a native of Kidderminster who went to America and made a fortune in carpets. Three beautiful windows depicting the Virgin Mary, Joan of Arc and Florence Nightingale, were given by his widow in his memory. Kidderminster's best-known son is Rowland Hill, who founded the modern postal system and introduced the penny post; he was also a teacher, educationalist and inventor. His statue stands outside the Town Hall. By the station on the Severn Valley Railway is the **Kidderminster Railway Museum** with a splendid collection of railway memorabilia. Run by volunteers, it is housed in an old GWR grain store.

Just outside town, at **Stone**, on the A448, is Stone House Cottage Garden, a lovely walled garden with towers. Unusual wall shrubs, climbers and herbaceous plants are featured, most of them for sale in the nursery.

In the Stour Valley just north of Kidderminster is the village of **Wolverley**, with charming cottages and pretty gardens, the massive Church of St John the Baptist, and the remains - not easy to see - of prehistoric cave dwellings in the red sandstone cliffs.

LEIGH

The **Church of St Eadburga** is very fine indeed, with some imposing monuments and a marvellous 15th-century rood screen. A curious legend attaches to the church. A man called Edmund Colles is said to have robbed one of his colleagues who was returning from Worcester and known to be carrying a full purse. It was a dark, gloomy night, and as Colles reached out to grab the man's horse, holding on to the bridle, the other struck at him with a sword. When he visited Edmund the next day, the appalling wound testified to the man's guilt; although forgiven by his intended victim, Colles died shortly after and his ghost once haunted the area. A phantom coach pulled by four fire-breathing steeds would appear and race down the hill to the church by Leigh Court, where they would leap over the tithe barn and disappear beneath the waters of the River Teme. A midnight service attended by 12 clergymen

94

eventually laid the ghost to rest. Leaping over the **tithe barn** was no mean feat (though easier of course if you're a ghost), as the 14th-century barn is truly massive, with great cruck beams and porched wagon doors. Standing in the grounds of Leigh Court, a long gabled mansion, the barn is open for visits on summer wekends.

Leigh Brook is a tributary of the Teme and wends its way through a spectacular valley cared for by Worcestershire Nature Conservation Trust. The countryside here is lovely, and footpaths make the going easier. Up on Old Storridge Common, birch, ash, oak and bracken have taken a firm hold, and there is a weird, rather unearthly feel about the place. Nearby, the hamlet of **Birch Wood** is where Elgar composed his *Dream of Gerontius*.

Lower Broadheath

The **Elgar Birthplace Museum** is a redbrick cottage that is crammed with items from the great composer's life. He was born here in 1857 and, despite long periods spent elsewhere, Broadheath remained his spiritual home. The violin was his first instrument, though he eventually succeeded his father as organist at St George's Church in Worcester. He played at the Three Choirs Festival and began conducting locally. He married in 1889 and was soon devoting almost all his time to composing, making his name with *The Enigma Variations* (1899) and *Dream of Gerontius* (1900). He was knighted in 1904 and when in 1931 he was made a baronet by King George V he took the title 1st Baronet of Broadheath. Various Elgar Trails have been established, the one in Worcester city taking in the statue and the *Dream of Gerontius* window in the Cathedral.

Redditch

A "New Town" from the 1960s, but there is plenty of history here, as well as some great walking. The **Arrow Valley Country Park**, a few minutes walk from the town centre, comprises a vast expanse of parkland with nature trails, picnic areas and lovely walks. Sailing, canoeing, windsurfing and fishing are popular pastimes on the lake.

Housed in historic buildings in the beautiful Arrow Valley, **Forge Mill Needle Museum & Bordesley Abbey Visitor Centre** offers a unique glimpse into a past way of life. The Needle Museum threads its way through the fascinating history of the Redditch needle-making industry, with the original water-powered machinery and re-created scenes showing vividly how needles were made in the 19th century. The link with needles has established the museum as a leading centre for textile-lovers, with exhibitions, workshops and a shop selling unusual needles and sewing accessories.

Shatterford

Shatterford Wildlife Sanctuary is home to Sika deer, red deer, goats, sheep, wild boar, pot-bellied pigs and koi carp.

Two miles further north, off the A442, **Kingsford Country Park** covers 200 acres of heath and woodland that is home to a wide variety of birdlife. It extends into Kinver Edge, across the border into Staffordshire, and many waymarked walks start at this point.

Spetchley

All Saints Church, 14th-century with a 16th-century chapel, is home to a fine collection of monuments to the Berkeley family, who owned adjoining **Spetchley Park**. The park, which extends over 12 hectares, has lovely formal gardens, wooded areas, lawns and a lake with an ornamental bridge.

Stourport-on-Severn

At the centre of the Worcestershire waterways is the unique Georgian "canal town" of Stourport, famous for its intricate network on canal basins. There was not much trade, nor even much of a town, before the canals came, but prosperity came quickly once the *Staffordshire & Worcestershire Canal* had been dug. The commercial trade has gone, but the town still prospers, the barges laden with coal, timber, iron and grain having given way to pleasure craft. Many of the old barges have been renovated and adapted to this new role.

Wichenford

A famous landmark here is the National Trust's **Wichenford Dovecote**, a 17th-century timber-framed construction with a lantern on top of its steeply sloping roof. There are lots of scenic walks in the vicinity.

Wichenford Dovecote

WORCESTER

Set on either side of the curving River Severn, Worcester is a bustling county capital and cathedral city. Its architecture spans many centuries and there are some marvellous examples from all of them. In the heart of England, this is an area characterised by red earth, apple orchards, hopyards, quiet inns, stone farmhouses and black-and-white timbered dwellings. As a visible legacy of the ancient forest that once surrounded Worcester, the half-timbered buildings lend colour and variety to the villages around this historic city.

The Cathedral, with its 200 foot tower, stands majestically beside the Severn. The 11th-century crypt is a classic example of Norman architecture and was built by St Wulstan, who is remembered in a stone carving. He was the only English bishop not to be replaced by a Norman after the Conquest. To many of the local people the task of building the Cathedral must have seemed endless; the central tower collapsed in 1175 and a fire destroyed much of the building in 1203. The Cathedral had only just been re-dedicated after these disasters when Bishop Blois began pulling it down again, only to re-build it in the fashionable Gothic style. The nave was rebuilt in the 14th century under the auspices of Bishop Cobham, but the south side was not completed until much later, and in a

far less elaborate style. King John requested that he be buried in the choir, and his tomb stands near the high altar. It is a masterpiece of medieval sculpture, showing the King flanked by the Bishops Oswald and Wulstan. Prince Arthur, elder brother of Henry VIII, is also entombed near the high altar.

There's a great deal more to see than the Cathedral, of course, and in the **City Museum and Art Gallery** are contemporary art and archaeological displays, a 19th-century chemist's shop and the military collections of the Worcestershire Regiment and the Worcestershire Yeomanry Cavalry. Friar Street has many lovely old timber houses. **Greyfriars**, in the care of the National Trust, is a medieval house that has managed to survive right in the heart of the city, and passing through its archway visitors will come across a pretty walled garden. The imposing Guildhall in the High Street is a

Worcester Cathedral

marvelous example of Queen Anne architecture, designed by a local man, Thomas White. The **Commandery Civil War Centre** is a stunning complex of buildings behind a small timber-framed entrance. At the Battle of Worcester in 1651 the Commandery was used as the Royalist headquarters, and today period rooms offer a fascinating glimpse of the architecture and style of Tudor and Stuart times while acting as the country's only museum devoted to the story of the Civil War. The story takes in the trial of Charles I, visits a Royalist encampment on the eve of the battle and enacts the last battle of

96

the war narrated by Charles II and Oliver Cromwell.

The **Royal Worcester Porcelain Visitor Centre** is an absolute must on any sightseer's list. Royal Worcester is Britain's oldest continuous producer of porcelain and is world famous for its exquisite bone china. The factory was founded in 1751 by Dr John Wall with the intention of creating "a ware of a form so precise as to be easily distinguished from other English porcelain". The collection in the Museum contains some of the finest treasures of the factory, and visitors can take a guided tour of the factory to observe the many stages of production and the premises include a shop and a restaurant, where the food is naturally served on Royal Worcester china. In the 1930s the company was acquired by (Charles William) Dyson Perrins, the grandson of William Perrins, founder of the Worcester Sauce company.

The **Museum of Local Life** reflects the history of Worcester and its people, with displays covering the past 700 years. There's a Victorian kitchen scene, a turn-of-the-century schoolroom and a variety of changing exhibitions throughout the year. The site is a 16th-century timber-framed building in wonderful Friar Street.

Famous sons of Worcester, where the **Three Choirs Festival** was first held in 1717, include Sir Edward Elgar, born at nearby Broadheath; his statue is a notable landmark opposite the Cathedral.

At the southwestern edge of the city, on the Malvern road, **Bennett's Park Farm**, overlooking the River Teme, is a working farm, open daily in summer, with a museum, farm shop, tea shop and nature trail.

WYTHALL

Right on the other side of Redditch, and well on the way to Birmingham, is the **Birmingham and Midland Museum of Transport**. Founded in 1977, the Museum's two large halls house a marvellous collection of some 100 buses and coaches, battery vehicles and fire engines, many having seen service in Birmingham and the West Midlands. Open Saturday and Sunday in summer.

The Albion

97

48 Bath Road,
Worcester
WR5 3EW
Tel: 01905 359943
Fax: 01905 764193

Directions:

From Worcester City Centre follow the A44 towards Evesham. Just after the bridge over the canal, turn right on the A38 towards Tewkesbury. The Albion is about 200 metres along this road, on the right

The Albion is a very impressive building, 3 storeys high, which was built in 1798 as a hotel to serve the nearby Diglis Locks and Basin. At that time, the docks here were the largest inland waterway docks in Britain and even today it's possible to walk along the canal all the way to Birmingham with only slight deviations. Chris and Geraldine Watts have been mine hosts at The Albion since 1987 and have a well-established reputation for providing good food and drink. Chris is the chef and his extensive menu offers a wide selection of home-made dishes such as Tipsy Steak & Mushroom Pie, made with Guinness, or Cottage Pie with a tasty cheese topping, as well as fish and poultry choices. For smaller appetites, there's also a range of hot butties, beefburgers, filled fresh baps and jacket potatoes. Real ale is available as well as wine by the glass. Enjoy your meal either in the lounge bar dining area or, in good weather, on the terrace. The Albion has a games room with darts, pool and dominoes available and on Fridays hosts a folk music evening. For special occasions, there's a function room on the first floor which has its own dance floor and can accommodate up to 70 guests.

Opening Hours: Mon-Fri: 12.00-14.30; 17.00-23.00. Sat: 11.30-15.00; 17.30-23.00; Sun: 12.00-15.00; 19.00-22.30

Food: Home cooked dishes available every lunchtime & evening; takeaway service

Credit Cards: Not accepted

Facilities: Terrace; Function room with dance floor; small car park on street

Entertainment: Pool table; darts; dominoes; folk music evening, Friday

Local Places of Interest/Activities: Canalside walk, Diglis Locks & Basin, Worcester Cathedral, Royal Worcester Porcelain Visitor Centre, City Museum & Art Gallery, Commandery Civil War Centre, Fort Royal Park, all within walking distance; Elgar Birthplace Museum, Lower Broadheath, 3 miles

Internet/Website: www.albion.pubworcs@virgin.net

98

The Bell

Pensax
Abberley
Worcestershire
WR6 6AE
Tel: 01299 896677

Directions:

Leave the M5 at junction 5 and pick up the A38 towards Droitwich. After about three miles leave the A38 at a large junction and head west on the A4133, which will shortly join the A443, heading towards Tenbury Wells. After 10 miles you will pass Abberley Hall on the left and the village of Pensax will be signposted to the right, two miles further on.

The Bell can be found in the village of Pensax, not far from the village of Abberley, and both are delightful villages surrounded by hills. Nearby Abberley Hall, which is privately owned, is a handsome 17th-century red-brick house with a landmark tower which can be clearly seen from the A443. In fact The Bell was built in 1883 by John Joseph Jones as a hunting and shooting lodge for Abberley Hall and the original half brick, half timbered structure is an imposing sight. The large interior is divided into a number of different areas - the main bar, a snug and a non-smoking dining room. Each area has a open fire which creates a warm, cosy atmosphere in cold weather.

Food is offered from a blackboard menu which is regularly updated to make the most of seasonal produce. All dishes are freshly prepared using locally sourced ingredients wherever possible, and everyone is sure to find something to suit their taste and appetite. To accompany your meal there is a good selection of real ales on offer behind the bar, with guest bars being regularly rotated.

This cosy establishment has recently been taken over by John and Trudy Greaves and there is no doubt that they are going to do well here. The friendly relaxed atmosphere means that families with children are most welcome. There are plenty of good walks in the surrounding countryside, as well as fishing, golf, horse riding and cycling. There are also a number of attractive towns, villages and stately homes that are worthy of a visit.

Opening Hours: Mon 17.00-23.00; Tues-Sat 12.00-14.30, 17.00-23.00; Sun 12.00-22.30.

Food: Bar meals and snacks.

Credit Cards: Visa, Access, Delta, Switch.

Facilities: Beer garden, Car Park.

Local Places of Interest/Activities:
Stourport-on-Severn 9 miles, Burford House, Tenbury Wells 11 miles, Worcester 15 miles, Hartlebury Castle 11 miles, Witley Court 4 miles, Wyre Forest 6 miles, West Midlands Safari Park 10 miles.

The Bridge Inn

99

Bridge Street,
Stourport-on-Severn,
Worcestershire
DY13 8UX
Tel: 01299 877475

Directions:

Stourport-on-Severn is on the A451, about 4 miles south of Kidderminster. The Bridge Inn is in the town centre by the bridge and overlooking the park

A handsome Georgian building of around 1770, **The Bridge Inn** stands on the site of an even earlier pub dating back to the 1600s. At one time the inn had stabling not only for coach horses but also for the horses that towed barges along the nearby canal. The inn is an impressive 3-storeyed structure, its cream-washed walls set off in summer by hanging baskets and tubs of flowers. Inside, the low ceilings, old beams and the friendly landlady, Katharine Moore, create a really welcoming atmosphere.

Traditional pub food is served, all home made and freshly prepared, with a Carvery every Sunday lunchtime. Meals can be enjoyed anywhere in the inn itself, in the non-smoking flagstoned conservatory overlooking the gardens, or on the patio picnic tables. The extensive choice of beverages includes 2 real ales along with all the popular brews. Children are welcome and the inn has good wheelchair access. The Bridge is a lively place, with a regular quiz night each week, as well as live music and karaoke evenings. The pub also supports it own netball team, and not just one but two football teams.

Opening Hours: Mon-Sat: 11.00-23.00; Sun: 12.00-22.30

Food: Traditional pub food every lunchtime & evening; Carvery, Sun lunchtime

Credit Cards: All major cards except Amex & Diners

Facilities: Beer garden; parking nearby

Entertainment: Darts, cribbage, cards; quiz nights; live music & karaoke

Local Places of Interest/Activities: Staffordshire & Worcestershire Canal, nearby; Aston Vineyards, 3 miles; Severn Valley Railway, Bewdley, 3 miles; Wyre Forest Visitor Centre, 5 miles

100   The Bridge Inn

Tibberton,
Droitwich,
Worcestershire
WR9 7NQ
Tel: 01905 345874
Fax: 01905 345793

Directions:

From Exit 6 of the M5, take the A4538 towards Evesham. At the first roundabout (1 mile) turn left on minor road to Tibberton (1.5 miles). You will see The Bridge Inn on your left

Enjoying a splendid position beside the Worcester & Birmingham Canal, **The Bridge Inn** is a handsome old building dating back to the late 1800s. Inside, there's a welcoming traditional atmosphere, complete with open fire and with not a juke box, games machine or dart board to be seen. Proprietor Mark Young's priority is for the inn to be "just a pub serving quality food in comfortable surroundings". Mark bought the inn in the autumn of 2000 and has introduced a new menu offering a wide selection of dishes using fresh, local produce. The choice ranges from a Prime Hereford beef & ox kidney pie, through Red Thai Chicken Curry or Grilled Fillets of Cornish Plaice, to game in season and an ever expanding selection of vegetarian options. Complement your meal with one of the 3 real ales on tap or with a choice from the extensive wine list. The traditional Sunday Lunch offers a choice of 3 roasts, accompanied by 4 fresh vegetables, roast and new potatoes - booking is essential. The inn can cater for functions for up to 70 guests, and Mark is also happy to cater for private parties at your own home or office. In good weather, customers can enjoy their refreshments in the attractive garden beside the canal where the inn has mooring for up to 14 narrowboats.

Opening Hours: Mon-Fri: 11.30-15.00; 18.00-23.00. Sat: 11.30-23.00. Sun: 12.00-22.30

Food: Home cooked food available every lunchtime & evening; Cream Teas in summer

Credit Cards: All major cards except Amex & Diners

Facilities: Beer garden; canalside garden; mooring for 14 narrowboats; large car park

Local Places of Interest/Activities: Worcester & Birmingham Canal, adjacent; Spetchley Park Garden, 3.5 miles; Worcester Cathedral, Royal Worcester Porcelain Visitor Centre, City Museum & Art Gallery, Commandery Civil War Centre, all in Worcester, 4 miles

The Butchers Arms | 101

Shaw Lane,
Stoke Prior,
Bromsgrove,
Worcestershire
B60 4EQ
Tel: 01527
832372

Directions:

From Exit 5 of the M5, take the A38 towards Bromsgrove. After about half a mile, at Wychbold, turn right on a minor road. This passes over a railway line (1 mile), then under another. The road bears left and you will see The Butchers Arms on your right, beside the canal.

The Butchers Arms stands beside the Worcester & Birmingham Canal about halfway along the famous Tardebigge Flight. Here, over the course of 2.5 miles, the canal is raised onto the Midlands plateau with the help of no fewer than 30 locks. Running almost parallel with the canal is another engineering marvel, the Lickey Incline, which with a gradient of 1 in 37.1 is the steepest on the whole of the British rail network.

Susan Wilkins' welcoming old hostelry was built in the 1800s when the canal was still busy with commercial traffic but today customers at the Butcher's Arms can watch colourful narrow boats and other craft passing by as they enjoy their drinks in the pleasant beer garden. There's also a safe play area for children outside, while inside you'll find 3 separate bars, plus a pool room, with lots of old beams, gleaming brass - and some fascinating characters! This is a "wet pub", (no food is served), offering a choice of 3 real ales, one of them a rotating guest ale, along with a range of Thatcher's ciders. Dogs are welcome. From the pub there are some delightful walks, either alongside the canal or through parkland to Hanbury Hall, a lovely William & Mary house set within a 400-acre estate.

Opening Hours: Mon-Sat: 12.00-23.00. Sun: 12.00-22.30

Food: Not available

Credit Cards: Not accepted

Facilities: Beer garden; children's play area; large car park; dogs welcome

Entertainment: Pool table; darts; weekly quiz night; occasional live entertainment

Local Places of Interest/Activities: Worcester & Birmingham Canal, on the doorstep; Tardebigge Lock Flights, nearby; Jinney Ring Craft Centre, 3 miles; Hanbury Hall (NT), 4 miles

102   The Crown Inn

St Johns, Worcester,
Worcsestershire
WR2 4EP
Tel: 01905 421041

Directions:

From Exit 7 of the M5
follow the signs on the
ring road to Malvern.
At the Malvern turn-
off, the A449, turn
right towards Worces-
ter. At the Jet service
station bear left, then
after the Citroen garage
on the left, turn left
and The Crown Inn is
on the right

Built in the 1800s, **The Crown Inn** is an attractive old building with a patio area and picnic tables to the front. Since 1999 the inn has been run by Colin Robinson, a friendly host with a passion for music - especially brass bands. He has provided his hostelry with some interesting decor. One bar is decked with flags, another has a varied collection of hats arrayed on the ceiling behind the bar, and there are areas designated with names such as The Library and Thespians' Corner. During the week, The Crown doesn't serve food but puts on an impressive show for Sunday lunchtime when there's a choice of 4 kinds of roast and no fewer than 10 different vegetables. To complement your meal, choose from the 2 real ales, a traditional cider, a range of other popular beverages, and a small selection of wines. In good weather, enjoy your drink on the patio. Cribbage and shove ha'penny are popular here, and Colin also arranges live music once or twice a week. St John's itself will be of interest to collectors of church curiosities. In the churchyard here, one of the elaborate gravestones is dedicated to John Gormston Hopkins who died at the age of 13 in 1871. Remarkably, his parents had a photograph taken of him in his shroud and this is incorporated into the tomb.

Opening Hours: Mon-Fri: 12.00-15.00; 17.00-23.00. Sat: 12.00-23.00. Sun: 12.00-22.30

Food: Sunday lunchtime only

Credit Cards: Not accepted

Facilities: Patio; barbecue area; functions catered for; off road parking

Entertainment: Cribbage, shove ha'penny; live music once or twice a week

Local Places of Interest/Activities: St John's churchyard, nearby; Worcester Cathedral, Royal Worcester Porcelain Visitor Centre, City Museum & Art Gallery, all at Worcester, 1 mile; Elgar Birthplace Museum, Lower Broadheath, 2 miles

The Fountain Inn 103

Oldwood, St. Michaels, Tenbury Wells
Worcestershire WR15 8TB
Tel: 01584 810701
Fax: 01584 819080

Directions:

Leave the M5 at Junction 3 and pick up the A456 which will take you round Kidderminster and on to Tenbury Wells, a total journey of 29 miles. From Tenbury Wells, head southwest on the A4112, signposted for Leominster. The Fountain Inn can be found 1 mile on the right.

The Fountain Inn dates back to the 17th century and was originally built as a farmhouse with an orchard. In 1855 it became a Beer and Cider house and was originally called The Hippodrome, meaning 'the racetrack'. This referred to the horse racing that used to take place on Oldwood Common, not far from the pub. As a coach house and cider mill, it served the Welsh drovers who travelled through the village with their herds of animals to the markets in England. It is also home to Mr Thomas, a somewhat mischevious ghost!

Today this is a popular establishment, both with the locals from the surrounding area and with visitors to this delightful part of the Welsh borders. The interior comprises a large bar which has been divided into three cosy snug areas and a separate restaurant, all of which are kept cosy with open fires. Boasting the motto "Weary and thin they stagger in, happy and stout they waddle out", it is not surprising to find a tasty menu of delicious-sounding dishes which includes Mediterranean Lamb, Baked Atlantic Tuna and many vegetarian options. This free house boasts a well-established organic vegetable and herb garden which is put to good use in the main menu and the daily specials board. Food is served throughout the day from 9am with the selection ranging from sandwiches through to hearty steak dishes. With your meal you could enjoy a bottle of wine chosen from the wine cellar, or behind the bar they stock a selection of 4 real ales, including a home brew called Fountain Ale. Incidentally, in addition to its excellent food and drink, the inn also proudly boasts the UK's first Shark Tank! As we go to press, plans are under way to provide bed & breakfast accommodation at the inn - just ring for details.

Opening Hours: Mon-Sat: 11.00-23.00 Sun: 12.00-22.30.

Food: Open for food from 9am. Bar meals & snacks. Supper licence to 24.00

Credit Cards: Access, Delta, Diners, Visa, Switch

Facilities: Beer garden; function room; children's play area; disabled facilities; non smoking areas; coaches by appointment; lounge; car park

Local Places of Interest/Activities: St Michael's Church (EH), 0.5 miles; Burford House, 3 miles; Berrington Hall, 6 miles; Leominster, 8 miles; Croft Castle, 10 miles; Ludlow Racecourse, 13 miles; Hampton Court, 14 miles; Hereford, 18 miles;

Internet/Website:
e-mail: miamifountain@ukonline.co.uk

104 Horn & Trumpet

Dog Lane,
Bewdley,
Worcestershire
DY12 2EH
Tel: 01299 403774

Directions:

From Kidderminster, take the A456 to Bewdley (3 miles). In the centre of Bewdley go clockwise around the church, turn right and the Horn & Trumpet is on the left

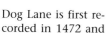

Dog Lane is first recorded in 1472 and it seems likely that there was already an alehouse in the lane, serving the medieval citizens of this popular little town. **The Horn and Trumpet** appears on the scene in 1840 when it was converted from a private residence into licensed premises. Today, it's a friendly, family run inn where landlady Linda Powell, who has been here since 1986, is assisted by her daughter Cheryl. An open fire in the lounge bar adds to the welcoming atmosphere and a separate games room provides some traditional pub entertainment.

The inn's menu is also in the traditional mould, offering a huge selection of light meals and snacks at extraordinarily good value-for-money prices. The choice ranges from home made Faggots to Fresh Fish, from Steak & Kidney Pie to more than 2 dozen varieties of sandwich, from Pizza to Jacket Potatoes. There are 2 real ales on tap along with traditional cider and a selection of wines. Children are welcome and have their own special choices. If you are looking for somewhere to stay in this attractive old town, the Horn & Trumpet has 6 comfortable guest bedrooms - 1 family room, 3 triples, and 2 twins. Four of the room have en suite facilities.

Opening Hours: Mon-Sat: 12.00-23.00 Sun: 12.00-22.30

Food: Available every lunchtime & evening

Credit Cards: Not accepted

Facilities: Games room; large public car park close by

Entertainment: Pool table; darts; Sky TV Sport

Accommodation: 6 rooms, (4 en suite)

Local Places of Interest/Activities: Riverside walks, Severn Valley Railway, nearby; West Midlands Safari Park, 1.5 miles; Wyre Forest, 1.5 miles; Kidderminster Railway Museum, 3 miles; Shatterford Wildlife Sanctuary, 5 miles

The Plough Inn **105**

Crown East Lane,
Lower Broadheath,
Worcestershire
WR2 6RH
Tel: 01905 333677

Directions:

From Worcester take the A44 west towards Leominster for about 3 miles. Then turn right on a minor road and follow the brown and white signs for Elgar's Birthplace Museum. The Plough Inn is next door to the museum

Built in the 1800s, **The Plough Inn** is an impressive building whose whitewashed frontage is a colourful sight in summer with its hanging baskets, tubs and creepers. Jean O'Hara arrived here in the autumn of 2000 after more than a decade in the hospitality business and has swiftly established The Plough as a place where you'll find good food, well-maintained ales and a welcoming atmosphere. The home cooked food is available every lunchtime and evening with a menu that offers a very wide choice of steaks, fish dishes and vegetarian options. The regular menu is supplemented by daily specials listed on the blackboard. Real ale lovers will be pleased to find a choice of 2 real ales, (1 permanent, 1 guest), and there's also a good selection of wines. Meals can be enjoyed in the spacious bar, which has both smoking and non-smoking areas, or if you are lucky with the weather in the pleasant beer garden where there's also a children's play area. The Plough is a very sociable pub with a regular weekly Quiz Night and also live entertainment. A visit to the Elgar Birthplace Museum, right next door and open throughout the season, is strongly recommended. It's a fairly modest redbrick house but Elgar remained strongly attached to this area throughout his life. When he was created a baronet in 1931 he assumed the title of 1st Baronet of Broadheath.

Opening Hours: Mon-Fri: 12.00-14.30; 18.00-23.00. Sat: 12.00-23.00. Sun: 12.00-22.30

Food: Wide selection of home cooked food every lunchtime & evening

Credit Cards: All major cards except Amex & Diners

Facilities: Beer garden; children's play area; large car park

Entertainment: Darts; quiz night, live entertainment weekly

Local Places of Interest/Activities: Elgar Birthplace Museum, next door; Worcester Cathedral, Royal Worcester Porcelain Visitor Centre, City Museum & Art Gallery, Commandery Civil War Centre, canalside walks, all in Worcester, 4 miles

106

The Red Lion

Droitwich Road
Bradley Green
Worcestershire
B96 6RP
Tel: 01527 821376
Fax: 01527 821376

Directions:

Leave the M5 at junction 5 and follow the A38 towards Droitwich. In just under a mile pick up the B4090 road for Alcester and Stratford-upon-Avon. After six miles the village of Bradley Green will be signposted on the right.

The Red Lion is a large, white painted building set slightly back from the road at Bradley Green. To the front is a large car park and there are also some tables where drinks can be enjoyed in warm weather. At the back is a large beer garden and a children's play area. Dating back to the 1800s The Red Lion probably originally served the many travellers heading towards Droitwich, which was a popular spa town during the 19th century. Much of this area was also forested at one time but the trees were felled for fuelling the salt pans and there is no evidence of it today.

The Red Lion is popular with modern day travellers too and the large interior is divided up into smaller areas making it cosy and welcoming. There is a separate non-smoking dining room, which is candlelit in the evenings to add to the intimate atmosphere, while open fires keep the whole place warm in cold weather. The restaurant serves an a la carte menu and there is a separate selection of bar meals and snacks served in the lounge bar. There is a daily specials board and traditional Sunday lunch is served for which advance reservations are recommended. The menu caters to all tastes and appetites, including vegetarian, and other special requirements can be accommodated on request. To enjoy with your meal there is an extensive wine list, carefully selected from wine growing regions around the world. For something else refreshing, the bar stocks a good range of beer and lager with a couple of real ales as well.

Opening Hours: Mon-Fri 12.00-14.30, 18.00-23.00; Sat 12.00-15.00, 18.00-23.00; Sun 12.00-15.30, 19.00-22.30. Supper License until 24.00.

Food: Bar meals and snacks, A la Carte, Traditional Sunday Lunch.

Credit Cards: Visa, Access, Delta, Switch.

Facilities: Beer garden, Children's Play Area, Function Room, Car Park.

Local Places of Interest/Activities: Hanbury Hall 6 miles, Droitwich Spa Baths 8 miles, Avoncroft Museum of Buildings 8 miles, Ragley Hall 8 miles, Stratford-upon-Avon 15 miles.

The Rising Sun

50 Lombard Street, Stourport-on-Severn, Worcestershire DY13 8DU
Tel: 01299 822530

Directions:

Stourport-on-Severn is on the A451, about 4 miles south of Kidderminster. The Rising Sun is beside the canal, opposite the Tesco superstore

Occupying a pleasant position beside the Staffordshire & Worcestershire Canal, **The Rising Sun** is a very popular "local", well-known for its good food, well-maintained ales and welcoming atmosphere. Originally just a canalside cottage, the inn first opened as a pub in 1835 and is now run by your friendly host, Robert Hallard, who has a lifetime of experience in the hospitality business. He is assisted by his equally friendly and courteous staff.

The emphasis here is on home-cooked and freshly prepared wholesome food. The regular menu offers a lot of variety - traditional steaks and home-made Steak & Kidney Pie, chicken and fish dishes, along with "Sizzling Skillets" of Cajun Chicken or Prawn Cantonese Style, "Mr Dave's Balti Meals", salads and a Children's Choice of meals. There also a wide selection of hot and cold sandwiches, basket meals, jacket potatoes, ploughman's and other light meals. In addition to the regular menu there are Specials listed on the board which change every month. Complete your meal with a delicious dessert, Apple Pie perhaps, or a liqueur coffee of your choice. The extensive range of beverages includes hand-pulled beers from Banks', Fosters, Kronenburg, a guest beer that changes each month, cider, Scrumpy, Guinness and more.

Opening Hours: Mon-Sat: 10.30-23.00; Sun: 12.00-22.30

Food: Home-cooked food available lunchtime & evening, Mon-Sat & Bank Holiday Mondays

Credit Cards: Not accepted

Facilities: Car park nearby

Entertainment: Dominoes; cribbage; Sky

TV; quiz night; live music, Sat evening

Local Places of Interest/Activities:
Staffordshire & Worcestershire Canal, nearby; Aston Vineyards, 3 miles; Severn Valley Railway, Bewdley, 3 miles; Wyre Forest Visitor Centre, 5 miles

108   The Vernon Arms

Droitwich Road,
Hanbury,
Bromsgrove,
Worcestershire
B60 4DB
Tel: 01527 821236

Directions:

The Vernon Arms is on the B4090, about 4 miles east of Droitwich

The Vernon Arms is an attractive old building which is believed to date back to the 1600s. The interior is replete with ancient beams, lots of gleaming brass and an open fire, all helping to create a welcoming, traditional atmosphere. Jayne Cummings is the landlady here, a friendly host who only took over here in the autumn of 2000 but has several years experience in the hospitality business.

The fare on offer provides a wide choice of traditional pub food - steaks and fish dishes for example, as well as vegetarian options and specialities of the house such as Grilled Cajun Chicken, Lamb & Mint Pudding and Beef Madras with rice & nan bread. Beverages include 2 real ales, plus a rotating guest ale, and a small selection of wines. Enjoy your meal either in the bar or in the two restaurants, one of which is non-smoking. In addition to the pool table and darts, Jayne also organises twice-weekly live entertainment.

For special occasions, the inn has 2 function rooms: the upstairs one can accommodate up to 180 guests, the downstairs one, 80. The inn's name, incidentally, honours the Vernon family whose fine red brick mansion, Hanbury Hall, set in formal gardens and parkland and open to the public, stands little more than mile away.

Opening Hours: Mon-Fri: 11.30-15.00; 18.00-23.00. Sat: 11.30-23.00. Sun: 12.00-22.30

Food: Available every lunchtime & evening

Credit Cards: All major cards except Amex

Facilities: Beer garden; children's play area; 2 function rooms; 36-acre caravan site; large car park

Entertainment: Pool table; darts; live entertainment twice weekly

Local Places of Interest/Activities: Mere Hall, 1 mile; Jinney Ring Craft Centre, 1.5 miles; Hanbury Hall (NT), 1.5 miles; Avon Croft Museum, 2 miles; Birmingham & Worcester Canal, 3 miles

6 South Worcestershire

PLACES OF INTEREST:

Bredon 111
Bretforton 111
Broadway 111
Childswickham 112
Colwall 112
Earls Croome 112
Elmley Castle 112
Evesham 113

Great Malvern 113
Honeybourne 114
Little Malvern 114
Middle Littleton 114
Pershore 115
Rous Lench 115
Upton-on-Severn 116

PUBS AND INNS:

The Boot Inn, Flyford Flavell 117

The Brewers Arms, Lower Dingle 118

The Chequers Inn, Fladbury 119

The Crown Inn, Evesham 120

The Kings Head's, Upton-upon-Severn 121

The Plough and Harrow, Guarlford 122

The Plume of Feathers,
    Castlemorton Common 123

The Talbot, Pershore 124

The Hidden Inns of the Welsh Borders

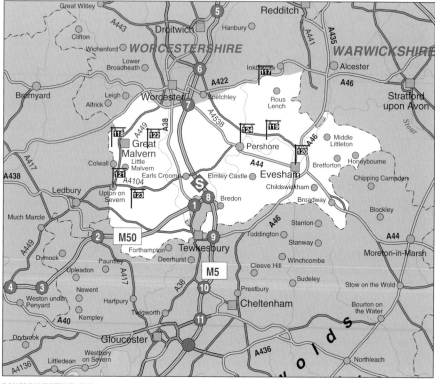

© MAPS IN MINUTES ™ (2000)

17 **The Boot Inn**, Flyford Flavell

18 **The Brewers Arms**, Lower Dingle

19 **The Chequers Inn**, Fladbury

20 **The Crown Inn**, Evesham

21 **The Kings Head's**, Upton-upon-Severn

22 **The Plough and Harrow**, Guarlford

23 **The Plume of Feathers**, Castlemorton Common

24 **The Talbot**, Pershore

Please note all cross references refer to page numbers

This chapter takes in the southern part of the county, which takes in the spectacular ridge of the Malvern Hills in the west, with marvellous walking and breathtaking views, to Upton-upon-Severn, Pershore and Evesham, along with many charming villages and ancient sites in the eastern part of the region. The Vale of Evesham, through which the Warwickshire countryside wanders, is one of the country's most important and prolific horticultural regions, and in springtime the Vale is alive with colour from the blossom of the fruit trees. High-quality fruit and vegetables are distributed from here throughout the land, and motorists will come across numerous roadside stalls selling a wonderful array of produce, At the eastern edge of this part of the county lies Broadway, a quintessential Cotswold village of outstanding beauty, beloved of tourists and not to be missed on any visit to this most delightful county.

PLACES OF INTEREST

BREDON

Plenty to see in this sizeable village, notably the Church of St Giles with its 14th-century stained glass and some very elaborate stone monuments; an Elizabethan rectory with stone figures on horseback on the roof; and some fine 18th-century stables. **Bredon Barn**, owned by the National Trust, is a huge 14th-century barn built of local Cotswold stone. 132 feet in length, it has a dramatic aisled interior, marvellous beams and two porches at the wagon entrances. Open April-November.

BRETFORTON

A pub in the care of the National Trust is a rarity indeed, and it's well worth a trip to Bretforton to visit the **The Fleece Inn**, a medieval half-timbered that was originally a farmhouse. It has changed very little since being first licensed in 1848, and an interesting feature is the Witches' Marks carved in the hearth to prevent witches coming down the chimney. The Church of St Leonard boasts a number of interesting and intricate carvings, notably a scene depicting St Margaret emerging (through a hole she made with her cross) from the side of the dragon who has just swallowed her.

BROADWAY

One of the most beautiful villages in England, and a magnet for tourists throughout the year,

this is the quintessential Cotswold village, its eponymous broad main street is lined with houses and cottages built of golden Cotswold stone. Broadway was settled as far back as 1900 BC, and later the Romans came and occupied the hill above the village. Broadway was probably re-established after the Battle of Dyrham in 557AD by conquering Saxons advancing towards Worcester. The parish records tell of hospitality being offered at a Broadway hostelry as early as 1532. This the time of the ad-

Broadway Tower

112

vent of the horse-drawn carriage, when Broadway became an important staging post. A journey from London to Worcester took about 17 hours including stops and a change of horse, and at one time Broadway boasted an incredible 33 public houses.

One of the must-sees on any trip to Broadway is the enchanting **Teddy Bear Museum**, housed in a picturesque 18th-century shop in the High Street. The atmosphere within is of an Edwardian carnival, with music playing, rides revolving and many other surprises. The hall of fame tells of celebrity bears, including Paddington, Pooh and the three who came upon Goldilocks. Bears of all ages and sizes are kept in stock, and some bears and dolls are made on the premises. Old bears and dolls are lovingly restored at - wait for it - St Beartholomew's Hospital.

In the centre of Broadway is a wide village green from where the main street continues gently upwards for nearly a mile, with the surrounding hills always in view. The gradient increases at Fish Hill then rises to more than 1,000 feet above sea level at **Broadway Beacon**. At the top of the Beacon is **Broadway Tower**, standing in a delightful country park with something to interest all ages, from animal enclosures and adventure playground to nature walks and barbecue sites. The tower was built as a folly by the 6th Earl of Coventry at the end of the 18th century as part of the great movement of the time towards picturesque and romantic landscapes. James Wyatt designed the tower, which now contains various displays and exhibitions.

Broadway's St Michael's Church (1839) boasts an intricate Elizabethan pulpit which came from the nearby St Eadburga's Church and was installed in a thanksgiving service marking the end of the First World War.

CHILDSWICKHAM

The **Church of St Mary the Virgin**, its tall, slender spire a prominent landmark, is a good place to start a walk round the old part of the village. Close by, on the Broadway roda, is the **Barnfield Cider Mill Museum**, where visitors can see a display of cider-making down the years before sampling cider, perry or one of the wines produced from local plums and berries.

COLWALL

On the west side of the Malverns, Colwall lies just across the border in Herefordshire. Its chief claim to fame is the enormous lump of limestone which stands at its centre. How it got there no one knows, but the Devil and a local giant are among the suspects. Less mysterious are the attractions of the **Picton Garden**, which contains a National Collection of Michaelmas daisies, which flower in September/October. William Langland, author of *Piers Ploughman*, lived at Colwall.

EARLS CROOME

There are several attractions in the area of Earls Croome. **Croome Landscape Park**, under the care of the National Trust, was Capability Brown's first complete landscape, which made his reputation and set a pattern for parkland design that lasted half a century. The buildings have equally distinguished pedigrees, with Robert Adam and James Wyatt as architects.

The **Hill Croome Dovecote** is a very rare square building next to the church in Hill Croome. **Dunstall Castle** folly at **Dunstall Common** is a folly in the style of a Norman castle, put up in the 18th century and comprising two round towers and one square, connected by arches.

At **Croome d'Abitot**, a little way north of Earls Croome, the 18th-century Church of St Mary Magdalene is filled with memorials to the Coventry family - it stood on their estate.

ELMLEY CASTLE

Just one of the many enchanting villages around Bredon Hill, no longer boasting a castle but with this memorandum of 1540: "The late Castle of Elmley standing on high and adjoining the Park, compassed in with wall and ditch is uncovered and in decay."

The village's main street is very wide and lined with trees, with a little brook flowing to one side. Picturesque cottages with thatched roofs lead up to a well-preserved 15th-century cross, then to St Mary's Church with its handsome tower and battlements. Inside are some of the finest monuments to be found anywhere in England, most notably the 17th-century alabaster tomb of William Savage, his son Giles and Giles's wife and children.

EVESHAM

A bustling market town at the centre of the Vale of Evesham, an area long known as the Garden of England, with a prolific harvest of soft fruits, apples, plums and salad vegetables. **The Blossom Trail**, which starts in the town, is a popular outing when the fruit trees burst into blossom. The Trail follows a signposted route from the High Street to Greenhill, where the Battle of Evesham took place. The River Avon performs a loop round the town, and the Abbey park is a good place for a riverside stroll; it is also the start point for boat trips. The magnificent bell tower (110 feet is the only major building remaining of the **Abbey**, which was built around 700 by Egwin, Bishop of Worcester, and was one of the largest and grandest in the whole country. It was knocked down by Henry VIII's men at the time of the Dissolution of the Monasteries. The story of the town is told in vivid detail at the **Almonry Heritage Centre**, which was formerly the home of the Abbey Almoner and was built around 1400. It now houses a unique collection of artefacts as well as exhibitions showing the history of the Abbey, and the defeat of Simon de Montfort at the Battle of Evesham in 1265 (the Leicester Tower stands

Stocks and Almonry

on the site of the Battle). The Almonry also houses Evesham's Tourist Information Centre.

There are many other interesting buildings in Evesham, including the neighbouring churches of All Saints and St Lawrence. The former is entered through a porch built by Abbot Lichfield in the 16th century, and the Lichfield Chapel, with a lovely fan-vaulted ceiling, contains his tomb. Much of the building, as well as the stone pulpit, dates from Victorian times, when major restoration work was

carried out. The latter, declared redundant in 1978, was also the subject of extensive restoration, in the 1830s and again in the 1990s. In the market

The Round House

place is a grand old timbered building called the **Round House** - a curious name, because it is actually square.

GREAT MALVERN

Beneath the northeastern slopes of the Malvern Hills, Great Malvern is known for its porcelain, its annual music and drama festivals, Malvern water and Morgan cars. Though invaded by tourists for much of the year, Great Malvern has retained its dignity and elegance, with open spaces, leafy avenues and handsome houses. Close to the start of the Malvern walking trail, on a path leading up from the town, is a Regency cottage housing one source of the water - **St Anne's Well** - where one can sample the water and drink in the views. Great Malvern was for many centuries a quiet, little-known place with a priory at its heart, and even when the curative properties of its spring waters were discovered, it took a long time for it to become a fashionable spa resort. Hotels, baths and a pump room were built in the early 19th century, and the arrival of the railway provided easy access from the middle of the century. The station is one of many charming Victorian buildings, and with its cast-iron pillars, stone ornaments and beautifully painted floral designs, is a tourist attraction in its own right.

The Priory **Church of St Mary and St Michael** is a dominant feature in the centre of the town. Its windows, the west a gift from Richard III, the east from Henry VII, contain a wonderful collection of 15th-century stained glass, and another unique feature is a collection of more than 1,200 wall tiles on the chancel screens. These also date from the 15th century. Among many interesting graves in the cemetery is that of Jenny Lind, "The Swedish Nightingale" who was born in Stockholm in 1820 and died at Wynd's Point, Malvern which she used as a summer retreat, in 1887. In the churchyard at West Malvern, Peter Mark Roget (the Thesaurus man) is buried (interred, entombed, coffined, laid to rest, consigned to earth). The 14th-century **Abbey Gateway**, whose huge wooden gateposts can be seen in the archway, houses the **Malvern Museum**. Open Easter to October, it displays include the geology of the Malvern Hills, the history of Malvern spring water and the development of Morgan cars. In Tanhouse Lane stands the factory of Boehm of Malvern, where the remarkable American Edward Marshall Boehm (call it 'Beam') founded the centre which has become known worldwide for the quality of its porcelain. Great Malvern has a distinguished tradition of arts and culture, much of it the legacy of Sir Edward Elgar and George Bernard Shaw, and the **Victorian Winter Gardens** are an exciting setting for performances of music and drama. Malvern is the home of the excellent English Symphony Orchestra, formed in 1980 by William Boughton.

Great Malvern is the largest of six settlements that make up the Malverns: to the south are Malvern Wells and Little Malvern, to the north North Malvern and to the northeast Malvern Link. A permanent site on low ground below Great Malvern is the venue for the **Three Counties Show**, one of England's premier agricultural shows.

The whole area is glorious walking country, with endless places to discover and explore. British Camp, on Herefordshire Beacon 2 miles west of Little Malvern, is one of the most important Roman settlements in Britain, and a little way south is Midsummer Hill, site of another ancient settlement. Six miles south of Great Malvern on the B4208 is the Malvern Hills Animal and Bird Garden, whose collection of animals includes snakes, monkeys and wallabies.

HONEYBOURNE

The **Domestic Fowl Trust and Honeybourne Rare Breeds** is a conservation centre for pure breeds of poultry and rare breeds of farm animals. All are in labeled breeding paddocks, and visitors are welcome to "stroke the sheep and say hello to the cows". Books, gifts and animal equipment and feedstuffs are available from the shop, and the centre also has a tea room.

LITTLE MALVERN

At Little Malvern stands the **Church of St Wulstan**, where a simple headstone marks the grave of Sir Edward Elgar and his wife Caroline. Their daughter is buried next to them.

Little Malvern Court, off the A4104, enjoys a glorious setting on the lower slopes of the Malvern Hills. It stands next to **Little Malvern Priory**, whose hall, the only part that survived the Dissolution, is now incorporated into the Court. Of the priory church, only the chancel tower and south transept remain. The Court was once a Catholic safe house, with a chapel reached by a secret staircase. The Court and gardens are open Wednesday and Thursday afternoons from mid-April to mid-July.

Just to the north at **Malvern Wells**, where the first medicinal wells were discovered, stands St Peter's Church, dating from 1836 and notable for some original stained glass and a William Morris window of 1885.

MIDDLE LITTLETON

The Littletons - North, Middle and South - lie close to each other and close to the River Avon. In Middle Littleton is a huge and wonderful **tithe barn**, built in the 13th century and once the property of the Abbots of Evesham. Now owned by the National Trust, it is still in use as a farm building, but can be visited.

Nearby, a bridleway leads off the B4510 to **Windmill Hill Nature Reserve**, an area of fertile limestone which continues up to Cleeve Prior, where the Church of St Andrew is well worth a visit.

PERSHORE

A gem of a market town, with fine Georgian architecture and an attractive setting on the banks of the Avon. Its crowning glory is **the Abbey**, combining outstanding examples of Norman and Early English architecture. The Abbey was founded by King Oswald in 689, and in 972 King Edgar granted a charter to the Benedictine monks. Only the choir remains of the original church, but it is still a considerable architectural treasure. The south transept is the oldest part, while among the most impressive features is some superb vaulting in the chancel roof.

Pershore Abbey

Pershore Bridge, a favourite picnic spot, still bears the marks of damage done during the Civil War. A mile east of town on the A44 is Pershore College of Architecture. Originally part of the Wyke Estate, the college has been developed round an early 19th-century mansion and is the Royal Horticultural Society's Centre for the West Midlands. The ground contains many unusual trees and shrubs, and in the glasshouses are tropical, temperate and cool decorative plants.

The area south of Pershore towards the boundary with Gloucestershire is dominated by **Bredon Hill**, which is surrounded by charming villages such as Great and Little Comberton and Elmley Castle on the north side, and

Bredon, Overbury and Kennerton to the south. Bredon Hill is almost circular, a limestone outcrop of the Cotswolds covering 12 square miles, accessible from many of the villages that ring it, and

Pershore

rising to over 900 feet. On the crest of its northern slope, best accessed from Great Comberton, are the remains - part of the earthworks - of the pre-Roman settlement known as Kennerton Camp. Much more visible on the top is a curious brick tower called Parsons Folly, built by a Mr Parsons in the 18th century.

ROUS LENCH

The Lenches are attractive little villages in an area known for its particularly rich soil. Rous Lench church has a chapel with monuments to the Rous family and an oil painting of Jesus in the house of Simon the Pharisee. The road to the hilltop village of **Church Lench** (a mile south), with the church at the very top of the hill, passes by Rous Lench Court,the seat of the Rous family for many centuries from 1382. The

116

Court is a splendid half-timbered mansion with a tall Italianate tower in the beautiful gardens.

UPTON-ON-SEVERN

An unspoilt town which gained prominence as one of the few bridging points on the Severn. The first records indicate that it was a Roman station, and it is mentioned in the Domesday Book. It became an important medieval port, and its strategic position led to its playing a role in the Civil War. In 1651, Charles sent a force to Upton to destroy the bridge, but after a long and bloody struggle the King's troops were routed and Cromwell regained the town. A Dutch gabled building used for stabling during the War still stands. The medieval church, one of the most distinctive buildings in the whole county, is affectionately known as "**the Pepperpot**", because of its handsome tower with its copper-covered cupola, the work the 18th-century architect Keek. This former place

The Church of St Peter and St Paul, built in 1879, has an interesting talking point in a large metal abstract hanging above the altar. The Tudor House, which contains a museum of Upton past and present, is open daily on summer afternoons. The **White Lion Hotel**, in the High Street, has a history going back to 1510 and was the setting for some scenes in Henry Fielding's *Tom Jones*. The commecial trade has largely left the Severn, replaced by a steady stream of summertime pleasure craft.

The Pepperpot

of worship is now a heritage centre, telling of the Civil War battles and the town's history.

The Boot Inn 117

Radford Road
Flyford Flavell
Nr. Worcester
WR7 4BS
Tel: 01386 462658
Fax: 01386 462547

Directions:

Leave the M5 at junction 6 and follow the A4538 south. At the junction with the A422 turn left towards Alcester. After five miles, the village of Flyford Flavell will be signposted off to the right.

The Boot Inn is a traditional country coaching inn and can be found just off the A422 in the village of Flyford Flavell. Parts of the inn date back to the 13th century though most of the present structure is much later. The interior retains much of its traditional character with plenty of exposed beams and wooden furniture. Open fires add to the cosy atmosphere and keep the inside nice and warm out of season. The restaurant is divided into two areas, one part is non-smoking and adjoins the lounge bar while the other section, where smoking is permitted, is located with the conservatory. The menu offers a selection of classic dishes, all freshly prepared and home cooked, and caters to all tastes and appetites. The regular menu is complemented by a blackboard of daily specials. Meals can be enjoyed with some fine wines and traditional beers which are kept in tip top condition behind the bar. There is no live entertainment here, but the traditional pursuits of pool, darts and crib are available. Outside there is a small beer garden which can be enjoyed in fine weather.

If you are in need of somewhere to stay, adjoining the inn is a converted coach house which is where you will find the highest standard of accommodation. There are five en-suite rooms, all non-smoking, and one is suitable for disabled or less mobile guests. Each room is also provided with a colour TV and coffee and tea making facilities.

Opening Hours: Mon-Fri 11.30-15.00, 18.30-23.00; Sat 11.00-15.00, 18.00-23.00; Sun 12.00-15.00, 19.00-22.30.

Food: Bar meals and snacks.

Credit Cards: Visa, Access, Delta, Switch, Amex.

Accommodation: 5 en-suite rooms.

Facilities: Pool table/games room, Beer garden, Car Park.

Local Places of Interest/Activities: Stratford-upon-Avon 15 miles, Inkberrow 4 miles, Wylde Moor Nature Reserve 6 miles, Ragley Hall 10 miles, Coughton Court 13 miles

118 Brewers Arms

Lower Dingle
West Malvern
Worcestershire
WR14 4BQ
Tel: 01684 568147

Directions:

From the centre of Great Malvern, follow the B4232 signposted for West Malvern for two and a half miles and you will see a parade of shops on the left. The Brewers Arms is opposite, on the right, below the level of the road.

Like many of the best places, **The Brewers Arms** is a bit tricky to find, although it is signposted off the road through West Malvern, heading towards Colwall. Parking is available on the road and the pub can be found a little further on, a short walk down an unmade track, and well worth the trouble of seeking out!

There has been a pub on the site for over 150 years and before that there was probably an alehouse. Unfortunately the original building burnt down some years ago leaving just the four stone walls still standing. It has since been completely rebuilt with the aim being to recreate its former, traditional feel. This has been admirably accomplished with the charming and quaint interior now featuring the original fireplaces, exposed stone walls, wood panelling and quarry tiled floors. Outside there is a large beer garden which can be enjoyed at its best in summer.

Food can be selected from a comprehensive menu, each lunchtime and early evening, with an excellent range of sandwiches, snacks and meals catering to all tastes and appetites. All dishes are freshly prepared and are well-priced. With your meal why not sample one of the three real ales? Or there is the usual selection of wines, lager, spirits and soft drinks behind the bar. Your hosts George and Vanessa have helped to make this a friendly and welcoming establishment where locals and visitors are made to feel very welcome. Entertainment is provided for customers in the form of occasional, impromptu folk music and regular quiz nights.

Opening Hours: Mon-Sat 12.00-15.00, 18.00-23.00; Sun 12.00-15.00, 19.00-22.30.

Food: Bar meals and snacks.

Credit Cards: None.

Facilities: Function Room.

Entertainment: Occasional Folk Music, Regular Quiz night.

Local Places of Interest/Activities: Great Malvern 2 miles, Little Malvern Court 4 miles, Malvern Hills, Eastnor Castle and Arboretum 8 miles.

The Chequers Inn 119

Chequers Lane, Fladbury
Nr. Pershore
Worcestershire WR10 2PZ
Tel: 01386 860276
Fax: 01386 861286

Directions:

From the M5, take exit 7 following the A44 to Pershore. Continue through Pershore towards Evesham. After about 4 miles, there will be a small turning on the left for the village of Cropthorne. Continue along these small roads north for about a mile and you will find the village of Fladbury.

The Chequers Inn is a long established feature of the charming, riverside village of Fladbury. Dating back to 1372, this delightfully presented inn is built in a traditional style of stone with a slate roof. The neat exterior is decorated with flower beds and hanging baskets which add a dash of colour all year round. Inside there is a large bar with an inglenook fireplace, and features exposed beams and polished brasses throughout. The warm and welcoming atmosphere of the bar attracts regular visitors from the surrounding villages, Evesham and Pershore, as well being popular with tourists and holiday makers staying in the area. The quality of the food served at The Chequers is another of the main attractions. The restaurant, which can seat 40 diners, serves a daily changing menu of delicious dishes using the best of local and seasonal produce. Dishes on offer could range from the classic Carbonade of Beef and Rack of Welsh Lamb, to the more exotic Louisiana Chicken Gumbo and Monkfish with Sweet and Sour vegetables. You can also be assured that they taste as delicious as they sound! To accompany your meal there is an extensive wine list, catering to all palates, featuring some delicious new world wines as well some from more familiar territories. Behind the bar there are also three real ales one of which is regularly changed.

This sizeable establishment also incorporates eight en-suite rooms which are available for bed and breakfast and short breaks. The rooms, which are of varying sizes, are comfortably furnished and provided with colour TV and hot drinks facilities. There is also a telephone point with internet access in each room.

Opening Hours: Mon-Sat 11.00-15.00, 18.00-23.00; Sun 12.00-15.00, 19.00-22.30.

Food: Bar meals and snacks, A la carte.

Credit Cards: Visa, Access, Delta, Switch, Amex.

Accommodation: 8 en-suite rooms.

Facilities: Function room, Car Park.

Entertainment: None.

Local Places of Interest/Activities:
Fladbury Water Mill, Stratford-upon-Avon 18 miles, Evesham 4 miles, Worcester 12 miles, Cheltenham 19 miles.

Internet/Website: e-mail:
chequers_inn_fladbury@hotmail.com

120   The Crown Inn

53 Waterside
Evesham
WR11 6JZ
Tel: 01386 446151
Fax: 01386 446175

Directions:

Entering the town of Evesham from Worcester along the A44 go straight through the first set of lights. The Crown Inn will be found shortly on the right.

Enjoying a prime position on the banks of the river Avon, in the heart of Evesham, is **The Crown Inn**. Easily located on the busy through road there is ample parking for visitors. Dating back to the late 18th century it opened as a pub in 1807 and has continued to be a popular drinking spot for locals ever since.

A warm reception is extended to all visitors by the managers Rob and Chris and, being animal lovers, well behaved dogs are also welcome. Children will also enjoy their visit here with the garden at the back having a large play area. Adults can keep a eye on their charges while enjoying a drink in the beer garden and in summer months food can be eaten out here as well. Inside there are two bars with pool and darts in the public bar area. Attached to the lounge bar is a non-smoking dining room which can seat up to 20. Meals and snacks are available each lunchtime from a small, select menu with all dishes freshly prepared and cooked on the premises. Being a free house there is a wide range of beers and lagers, both local and continental, all kept and served in the best of condition. There are four real ales on tap, with three regularly rotated, and an extensive wine list.

Being an establishment of some size, bed and breakfast accommodation is also available with a total of 10 rooms. All are comfortable and cosily furnished and this would make an ideal base for a short break in the area.

Opening Hours: Mon-Tue 17.30-23.00; Wed-Fri 12.00-14.30, 17.30-23.00; Sat 12.00-23.00; Sun 12.00-22.30.

Food: Bar meals and snacks, Traditional Sunday Lunch.

Credit Cards: Visa, Access, Delta, Switch.

Accommodation: Ten rooms.

Facilities: Pools/Games room, Beer garden, Children's Play Area, Car Park.

Entertainment: Disco on Saturdays.

Local Places of Interest/Activities: Evesham Abbey, Broadway 6 miles, Broadway Tower Country Park 7 miles, The Fleece Inn, Bretforton 3 miles, Middle Littleton Tithe Barn 3 miles.

The Kings Head 121

Riverside,
Upton-upon-Severn,
Worcestershire WR8 0HF
Tel: 01684 592621
Fax: 01684 594256

Directions:

From Exit 1 of the M50, take the A38 towards Worcester. About 3 miles along this road, turn left on the A4104 to Upton upon Severn (2 miles). After crossing the river, turn left after 20 yards, and left again. The Kings Head is on your left

What could be more pleasant on a summer's day than to settle down at a table on **The Kings Head's** spacious riverside terrace and just watch the world glide by? If you are travelling in your own boat, you can even moor here. This inviting old hostelry was built in the late 1700s as a coaching inn and the old beams, tiled floor and polished brass items all testify to the inn's long tradition of hospitality. Mine hosts are Claire and Grahame Bunn, both of whom are very experienced in the hospitality business. Indeed, Grahame has more than a quarter of a century's knowledge and practice in the trade.

A trained chef, Grahame offers his customers an extensive menu in which traditional pub food co-exists happily with brasserie style dishes. Meals and snacks can be enjoyed either in the two bars or in the elevated, non-smoking dining room. To complement your meal, make a selection from the interesting wine list, choose one of the 3 real ales on tap, or take your pick from the wide range of other beers, spirits and soft drinks available. The inn also has a function room which Claire and Grahame are planning to extend to provide an even more spacious dining room. Upton village is a historic little town which in medieval times was an important port and later played a significant role in the Civil War. The story is vividly told in the nearby Heritage Centre, formerly a medieval church and known to locals at The Pepperpot because of its distinctive tower crowned by a copper-covered cupola.

Opening Hours: Mon-Sat: 11.00-23.00 Sun: 12.00-22.30

Food: Meals and bar snacks available every lunchtime & evening

Credit Cards: All major cards except Amex & Diners

Facilities: Riverside terrace; function room for 50; car park

Entertainment: Darts; pool table; games night weekly; live entertainment every 2 weeks

Local Places of Interest/Activities: "The Pepperpot" Heritage Centre, nearby; Croome Landscape Park (NT), 3 miles; Tewkesbury Abbey, 6 miles; Three Counties Showground, Great Malvern, 6 miles; Eastnor Castle, 9 miles

122   The Plough and Harrow

Rhydd Road
Guarlford
Malvern
Worcestershire
WR13 6NY
Tel: 01684 310453

Directions:

From junction 7 of the M5 follow the A422 round to the west for 3 miles. Turn left onto the A449 very quickly turning left again at the village of Powick onto the B4424. Follow this road for a little over 4 miles before turning right onto the B4211. The village of Guarlford can be found just over a mile along this road and the pub is on the right just before the village.

Set slightly back from the road, just on the outskirts of the village of Guarlford, stands **The Plough and Harrow**. This single storey stone-built inn has origins in the mid-17th century and has provided refreshment for the local community for over 250 years. Drawing a loyal following from locals, the pub is also popular with the many tourists visiting nearby Great Malvern. Cosy and welcoming within, the two bar areas feature many traditional features with exposed wooden beams and a open fire.

Food is served from a classic menu of bar meals and snacks catering to all tastes and appetites. The menu is complemented by a daily specials board which features fresh local produce wherever possible. There are discounts available at lunch time on each weekday for pensioners. If you enjoy a drink, on its own or with your meal, there is a good range of wines and two real ales on tap, as well as the usual selection of soft drinks, lager and spirits.

Outside there is parking to the front and rear and children can make use of their own special play area. There is also a beer garden which is popular in summer. Adding to the lively atmosphere, the new owners have planned a programme of regular live events, with karaoke twice a week and occasional live music. The restaurant can seat up to 47 people is available for private hire for parties and functions.

Opening Hours: Mon-Fri 12.00-14.30, 18.00-23.00; Sat 11.00-14.30, 18.00-23.00; Sun 12.00-15.00, 19.00-22.30

Food: Bar meals and snacks.

Credit Cards: Visa, Access, Delta, Switch.

Facilities: Beer garden, Children's Play Area, Function room, Car Park.

Entertainment: Regular Karaoke nights and quiz nights. Occasional live music.

Local Places of Interest/Activities:

Great Malvern 2 miles, Upton upon Severn 5 miles, Little Malvern Court 7 m.

Plume of Feathers | 123

Castlemorton Common
Malvern
Worcestershire
WR13 6JB
Tel: 01684 833554

Directions:

From the M5 leave at exit 7 taking the A422 towards Great Malvern. After 2 miles pick up the A38 heading south towards Upton upon Severn. After seven miles turn right onto the A4104 signposted to Upton upon Severn and Welland. Follow the road all the way to Welland where you turn left onto the B4208. Castlemorton Common can be found a mile and half along this road.

Located on the B4208 just south of Welland, you will find the **Plume of Feathers**. This traditional country inn has been serving the local community since Tudor times and continues to enjoy a loyal following from the surrounding area. The convenient location also makes this establishment popular with passers by and tourists while from all sides fine views to the surrounding hills can be enjoyed.

The sizeable property incorporates a large car park, gardens at the front and rear and a children's play area. The fact that the present owners are keen gardeners is also apparent from the profusion of colourful hanging baskets that decorate the front of the property. Customers are made welcome in the bar and the non-smoking dining room, both of which feature exposed wooden beams and are decorated with polished brasses and a collection of walking sticks. In cooler weather the open fire is lit to add to the warm and cosy ambience. Food is served at every session from menus offering bar snacks, starters and main dishes. The style is traditional English fayre with the well-priced dishes being freshly served in hearty portions. To accompany your meal there is a good wine list and no less than six real ales on tap, of which five are changed regularly. Occasional live music is featured with singers and small bands catering to popular tastes. Parties and functions can also be catered for in a large marquee on the back lawn. This cosy, country inn is conveniently located and well worth a stop.

Opening Hours: Mon-Sat 11.00-23.00; Sun 12.00-22.30.

Food: Bar meals and snacks, A la carte.

Credit Cards: None.

Facilities: Marquee available for functions, Car Park, Children's Play Area.

Entertainment: Occasional live music.

Local Places of Interest/Activities: Little Malvern Court 3 miles, Eastnor Castle and Arboretum 6 miles, Great Malvern 7 miles.

124 Talbot Inn

52 Newlands
Pershore
Worcestershire
WR10 1BP
Tel: 01386 553575

Directions:

In the centre of Pershore on Newlands, which runs from the A4104 into the centre of the town. The inn can be found on the left.

Newlands was once the main road from Worcester serving the Norman Abbey in the centre of Pershore and the town grew from the settlement that surrounded the Abbey. The Talbot was built in the early 17th century, at a time when Newlands was still a busy road, and is one of the oldest pubs in the town. Originally called The Malthouse the name was later changed to that of **The Talbot**, referring to a now extinct breed of dog. Some stories about the town, and the role the pub played in its history, are celebrated in a number of prints that are on display in the bar. There are also tales of a Royalist soldier's ghost, nicknamed "Sam", wandering round the back of the Talbot!

Recently taken over by Dennis and Irene Spencer, the Talbot is undergoing some refurbishments and improvements to enhance the high quality of welcome and service visitors already receive. The comfortable, cosy interior has been retained with a large lounge bar extending to over 40 feet. A separate snug is ideal for a cosy drink and is also offered as a small function room. Food is available - every day except Mondays - freshly prepared and cooked to order in the newly fitted kitchen. The menu offers some tasty choices of traditional English and Continental cuisine with Steak, Venison when in season and Chicken in Stilton Sauce being the specialities. Vegetarians have not been forgotten with some interesting options available. If you enjoy a glass of wine with your meal there is a small wine list, or alternatively there are two real ales on tap at the bar together with the usual selection of lager, spirits and soft drinks. Parties can be catered for and in the summer the garden at the back of the pub can be used for barbecues.

Opening Hours: Mon 17.00-23.00; Tue-Wed 12.00-15.00, 17.00-23.00; Thu-Sat 11.00-23.00; Sun 12.00-22.30.

Food: Bar meals and snacks.

Credit Cards: None.

Facilities: Car Park.

Entertainment: Occasional live music

Local Places of Interest/Activities: Pershore Abbey, Pershore Bridge, St. Andrew's Church, Evesham 7 miles, Bredon Barn 6 miles.

7 Gloucester and East Gloucestershire

PLACES OF INTEREST:

Bibury 127
Blockley 127
Bourton-on-the-Water 127
Cheltenham 128
Chipping Campden 129
Cirencester 129
Cleeve Hill 130
Deerhurst 130
Edge 130
Fairford 130
Forthampton 130
Gloucester 130
Hartpury 132
Lechlade 132

Moreton-in-Marsh 133
Northleach 133
Painswick 133
Pauntley 134
Prestbury 134
Slad 135
Stanton 135
Stanway 135
Stow-on-the-Wold 135
Sudeley 136
Tewkesbury 136
Toddington 137
Twigworth 137
Winchcombe 137

PUBS AND INNS:

The Bell Inn, Moreton-in-Marsh 139

The Black Bear Inn , Moreton-in-Marsh 140

The Black Swan Inn, Gloucester 141

The Hollow Bottom, Guiting Power 142

The Horse & Groom, South Cerney 143

The Kings Head Inn, Bledington 144

The Kingsholm Inn, Gloucester 145

The Plaisterers Arms, Winchcombe 146

The Plough Inn, Stratton 147

Riverside Lechlade Ltd, Lechlade 148

The Snowshill Arms, Snowshill 149

The Swan Inn, Moreton-in-Marsh 150

The Hidden Inns of the Welsh Borders

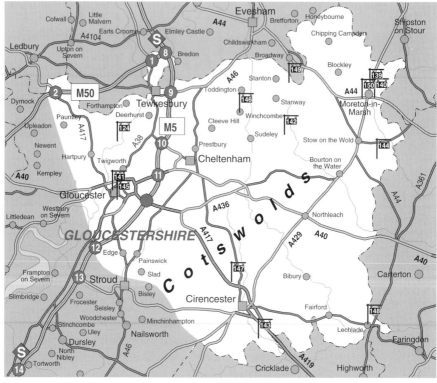

© MAPS IN MINUTES ™ (2000)

139	The Bell Inn, Moreton-in-Marsh	**145**	The Kingsholm Inn, Gloucester
140	The Black Bear Inn , Moreton-in-Marsh	**146**	The Plaisterers Arms, Winchcombe
141	The Black Swan Inn, Gloucester	**147**	The Plough Inn, Stratton
142	The Hollow Bottom, Guiting Power	**148**	Riverside Lechlade Ltd, Lechlade
143	The Horse & Groom, South Cerney	**149**	The Snowshill Arms, Snowshill
144	The Kings Head Inn, Bledington	**150**	The Swan Inn, Moreton-in-Marsh

Please note all cross references refer to page numbers

Laurie Lee's Slad Valley is just one of the many scenic delights of the Central Cotswolds in eastern Gloucestershire. These limestone hills sweep across the county from Wotton-under-Edge to Chipping Campden. In this chapter the major centres of Gloucester, Cheltenham and Cirencester reveal their historic and cultural attractions on a tour that also includes some of the most glorious scenery and the prettiest villages in the whole of Britain.

PLACES OF INTEREST

BIBURY

William Morris, founder of the Arts & Crafts Movement, described Bibury as "the most beautiful village in England" and, apart from the tourists, not a lot has changed since he made the claim. The Church of St Mary, with Saxon, Norman and medieval parts, is well worth a visit, but the most visited and most photographed building in Bibury is **Arlington Row**, a superb terrace of medieval stone cottages built as a woolstore in the 14th century and converted three centuries later into weavers' cot-

Arlington Mill

tages and workshops. Fabric produced here was supplied to nearby **Arlington Mill** for fulling, a process in which the material was cleaned in water and beaten with mechanically-operated hammers. Today the mill, which stands on the site of a corn mill mentioned in the Domesday Book, is a museum with a collection of industrial artefacts, crafts and furniture, including pieces made in the William Morris workshops.

BLOCKLEY

Silk-spinning was the main industry here, and six mills created the main source of employment until the 1880s. As far back as the Domes-

day book water mills were recorded here, and the village also once boasted an iron foundry and factories making soap, collars and pianos. The mills have now been turned into private residences and Blockley is a quieter place. One of the chief attractions for visitors is **Mill Dene Garden**, set around a mill in a steep-sided valley. The garden has hidden paths winding up from the mill pool, and at the top there are lovely views over the Cotswolds. Also featured are a grotto, a potager, a trompe l'oeil and dye plants.

BOURTON-ON-THE-WATER

Probably the most popular of all the Cotswold villages. The willow-lined Windrush flows through the centre, crossed by several delightful low-arched pedestrian bridges, two of which date from the late 18th century. The golden stone cottages are pretty as a picture, and among the notable larger buildings are St Lawrence's Church, with its 14th century chancel and rare domed Georgian tower, and a manor house with a 16th century dovecote. In the High Street, **Miniature World - The Museum of Miniatures** is a unique exhibition of miniature scenes and models that took the country's leading master miniature makers 3 1/2 years to complete. Bourton is a great place for miniatures,

Bourton on the Water

128

as there is also the famous **Model Village** at the Old New Inn - in the grounds behind the inn is a wonderful 1/9th replica in local stone of the village, complete with the River Windrush, the Church of St Lawrence and the music of the actual church choir. The model was built by six local men and opened on Coronation Day 1937 - and **Bourton Model Railway** with over 40 British and Continental trains running on three main displays in OO, HO and N gauge. The **Cotswold Motor Museum and Toy Collection**, in an 18th century water mill, has a fascinating collection of antique toys, a display of historic advertising signs and 30 or so (full-size!) cars and motorcycles. Bourton has Europe's only **Perfumery Exhibition**, a permanent attraction which explains the extraction and manufacturing processes and includes a perfume garden and a perfume quiz to test visitors' noses.

Two attractions outside the village are the Iron Age **Salmonsbury Camp** and **Folly Farm**, home to Europe's largest domestic waterfowl and wildlife conservation area, with over 160 rare breeds. Also at this major attraction off the A436 Cheltenham road are spectacular lavender fields, a garden centre and a coffee shop.

CHELTENHAM

Smart, fashionable Cheltenham: a small, insignificant village until a mineral spring was accidentally discovered in 1715 by a local man, William Mason, who built a pump room and began Cheltenham's transformation into one of Europe's leading Regency spa towns. Mason's son-in-law was the astute Captain Henry Skillicorne, who added a meeting room, a ballroom and a network of walks and carriageways, and called it a spa. A number of other springs were soon discovered, including one in the High Street around which the first Assembly Rooms were built. In 1788 the Royal seal of approval came in the shape of King George III, who spent five weeks taking the waters with his family and made Cheltenham a highly fashionable resort.

An entirely new town was planned based on the best features of neoclassical Regency architecture, and as a result very few buildings of any antiquity still stand. One of these is the Church of St Mary, with parts going back to the 12th century and some very fine stained glass.

Skillicorne's walks and rides are now the tree-lined Promenade, one of the most beautiful boulevards in the country, its crowning glory the wonderful Neptune's Fountain, modelled on the Fontana di Trevi in Rome and erected in 1893. Housed in Pittville Park in the magnificent Pump Room overlooking gardens and lakes north of the town centre is the **Pittville Pump Room Museum**, which uses original period costumes to bring alive the story of Cheltenham from its Regency heyday to the 1960s. Special exhibitions are held throughout the year. **Cheltenham Art Gallery and Museum** has an acclaimed collection of furniture and silver, much of it made by Cotswold craftsmen and inspired by William Morris's Arts and Crafts Movements. Also Oriental porcelain, English ceramics, fine paintings and changing special exhibitions. Gustav Holst was born in 1874 in a terraced Regency house in Clarence Road which is now the **Holst Birthplace Museum and Period House**. The original piano of the composer of *The Planets* is the centrepiece of the story of the man and his works, and there's a working kitchen, a Regency drawing room and a nursery.

Cheltenham Ladies College, where the pioneering Miss Beale was principal, was founded in 1854. Two remarkable modern pieces of public art take the eye in the centre of town. The **Wishing Fish Clock** in the Regent Arcade is a work in metal by the famous artist and craftsman Kit Williams: below the clock, from which a mouse pops out when disturbed by the arrival of an egg laid by a duck on high, is suspended a 12 foot fish which celebrates the hour by swishing its tail and blowing bubbles, to the delight and fascination of shoppers below. The mechanical parts of the clock are the work of the renowned local clockmaker Michael Harding. Off the High Street are the **Elephant Murals**, which portray an event that occurred in 1934 when three elephants from a travelling circus escaped and raided a provision shop stocked with corn - an incident which older locals with long memories still recall. **Cheltenham Racecourse**, two miles north of town, is the home of National Hunt Racing, staging numerous top-quality races highlighted by the March Festival when the Gold Cup and the Champion Hurdle find the year's best steeplechaser and best hurdler. Several other festivals have their home in Cheltenham, including the International Jazz Festival (April), the International Festival of Music (July) and the International Festival of Literature (October).

The village of **Badgeworth**, virtually a suburb of Cheltenham, boasts what is probably the smallest nature reserve in the world, some 350 square yards that are home to the exceptionally rare Adder's-Tongue Spearwort.

CHIPPING CAMPDEN

The "Jewel of the Cotswolds", full of beautifully restored buildings in golden Cotswold stone. It was a regional capital of the wool trade between the 13th and 16th centuries and many of the fine buildings date from that period of prosperity. In the centre of town is the Jacobean Market Hall, built in 1627 and one of many buildings financed by the noted wool merchant and financier Sir Baptist Hicks. He also endowed a group of almshouses and built Old Campden House, at the time the largest residence in the village; it was burnt down by Royalists to prevent it falling into the hands of the enemy, and all that survives are two gatehouses and the old stable block. The 15th century Church of St James was built on a grand scale and contains several impressive monumental brasses, the most impressive being one of William Grevel measuring a mighty 8 by 4 feet.

Dover's Hill, a natural amphitheatre above the town, is the scene of the **Cotswold Olympics**, founded in the 17th century by Captain Robert Dover, whom we met at Stanway House. The Games followed the traditions of ancient Greece and added some more down-to-earth ac-

tivities such as shin-kicking and bare-knuckle boxing. The lawlessness and hooliganism that accompanied the games led to their being closed down in 1852 but they were revived in a modern form in 1951 and are still a popular annual attraction on the Friday following the spring Bank Holiday.

Almshouses

CIRENCESTER

The "Capital of the Cotswolds", a lively market town with a long and fascinating history. As Corinium Dobonnorum it was the second largest Roman town in Britain (Londinium was the largest). Few signs remain of the Roman occupation, but the award-winning **Corinium Museum** features one of the finest collections of antiquities from Roman Britain, and reconstructions of a Roman kitchen, dining room and garden give a fascinating and instructive insight into life in Cirencester of almost 2,000 years ago.

The main legacy of the town's medieval wealth is the magnificent **Church of St John the Baptist**, perhaps the grandest of all the Cotswold "wool churches", its 120 foot tower dominating the town. Its greatest treasure is the Anne Boleyn Cup, a silver and gilt cup made for Henry VIII's second wife in 1535, the year before she was executed for adultery. Her personal insignia - a rose tree and a falcon holding a sceptre - is on the lid of the cup, which was given to the church by Richard Master, physician to Queen Elizabeth I. The church has a unique three-storied porch which was used as the Town Hall until 1897. Cirencester today has a thriving crafts scene, with workshops in the Brewery Arts House, a converted Victorian brew-

Market Hall

ery, and regular markets in the Corn Hall. **Cirencester Open Air Swimming Pool**, next to the park, was built in 1869 and is one of the oldest in the country. Both the main pool and the paddling pool use water from a private well.

CLEEVE HILL

The Cotswolds rise to their highest point, 1083 feet above sea level, at **Cleeve Cloud** above Prestbury and a mile from the village of Cleeve Hill. The view from this high point on the ridge is well worth the exercise, with Tewkesbury Abbey, the Herefordshire Beacon and the distant Brecon Beacons visible on a clear day. Also worth the climb is a massive neolithic long barrow known as **Belas Knap**, where excavations in Victorian times and in the 1920s revealed the bones of more than 30 people. It is very unusual in having a false entrance at the north end apparently leading to no chambers; most of the bodies were found in small chambers at the side and south end, but behind the false entrance were found the bones of a man and five children, perhaps killed in some ancient sacrificial rite.

DEERHURST

On the eastern bank of the Severn, a village whose current size and status belies a distinguished past. The church, with a distinct Celtic feel, is one of the oldest in England, with parts dating back to the 7th century, and its treasures include a unique double east window, a 9th century carved font, a Saxon carving of the Virgin and Child and some fine brasses dating from the 14th and 15th centuries. One depicts St Anne teaching the Virgin to read, another the Cassey family, local landowners, and their dog.

Another Saxon treasure, 200 yards from the church, is **Odda's Chapel**, dedicated in 1056 and lost for many centuries before being gradually rediscovered after 1885 under an unsuspecting half-timbered house. The connection was then made with a stone inscribed with the date of consecration discovered in 1675 and now on view in the Ashmolean in Oxford.

EDGE

Straddling a hilltop across the Spoonbed Valley, Edge has two delightful village greens and the mid 19th century Church of St John the

Baptist with an ornate spire. To the west of the village lies **Scottsquarr Common**, an area of Special Scientific Interest with an abundance of wild flowers and butterflies and spectacular views.

FAIRFORD

A welcoming little town in the valley of the River Coln, with many fine buildings of the 17th and 18th centuries and an abundance of inns as evidence that this was an important stop

Church of St Mary

on the London-Gloucester coaching run. John and Edmund Tame, wealthy wool merchants, built the superb late-Perpendicular **Church of St Mary**, whose greatest glory is a set of 28 medieval stained glass windows depicting the Christian faith in picture-book style. John Tame's memorial stone, along with those of his wife and son, are set into the floor of the church.

FORTHAMPTON

An unspoilt Severn Vale village dominated by the ancient Church of St Mary with a rare original stone altar, and **Forthampton Court**, sometime home to the abbots of Tewkesbury and still retaining its fine 14th century banqueting hall, the chapel and a medieval wood-based picture of Edward the Confessor. Near the churchyard can be seen a couple of relics of harsher times - a set of stocks and a whipping post complete with manacles.

GLOUCESTER

The capital city of Gloucestershire first gained prominence under the Romans, who in the 1st century AD established a fort to guard what was then the lowest crossing point on the Severn. A much larger fortress soon followed, and the

Gloucester Cathedral

tle head rather than a crown.

The old area of the city around Gloucester Cross boasts some very fine early buildings, including St John's Church and the Church of St Mary de Crypt. Just behind the latter, near the house where Robert Raikes of Sunday School fame lived, stands an odd-looking tower built in the 1860s to honour Hannah, the wife of Thomas Fenn Addison, a successful solicitor. The tower was also a memorial to Raikes.

Three great inns were built in the 14th and 15th centuries to accommodate the scores of pilgrims who came to visit Edward II's tomb, and two of them survive. The galleried New Inn, founded by a monk around 1450, doubled as a theatre and still retains the cobbled courtyard. It was from this inn that Lady Jane Grey was proclaimed Queen. Equally old is The Fleece Hotel in Westgate Street, which has a 12th-century stone-vaulted undercroft. In the same street is **Maverdine House**, a four-storey mansion reached by a very narrow passage. This was the residence and headquarters of Colonel Massey, Cromwell's commander, during the Civil War siege of 1643. Most of the region was in Royalist hands, but Massey survived a month-long

settlement of Glevum became one of the most important military bases, crucial in confining the rowdy Celts to Wales. William the Conqueror held a Christmas parliament and commissioned the Domesday Book in Gloucester, and also ordered the rebuilding of the abbey, an undertaking which included the building of a magnificent church that was the forerunner of the superb Norman Cathedral. The elaborate carved tomb of Edward II, murdered at Berkeley Castle, is just one of many historic monuments in **Gloucester Cathedral**; another, the work of the Wedgwood designer John Flaxman, remembers one Sarah Morley, who died at sea in 1784, and is shown being delivered from the waves by angels. The exquisite fan tracery in the cloisters is the earliest and among the finest in existence, and the great east window, at 72 feet by 38 feet, is the largest surviving stained-glass window in the country. It was built to celebrate the English victory at the Battle of Crécy in 1346 and depicts the coronation of the Virgin surrounded by assorted kings, popes and saints. The young King Henry III was crowned here, with a bracelet on his lit-

Gloucester Cathedral

132

assault by a force led by the King himself and thus turned the tide of war.

Gloucester Docks were once the gateway for waterborne traffic heading into the Midlands, and the handsome Victorian warehouses are always in demand as location sites for period films. The docks are now home to several award-winning museums. The National Waterways Museum, on three floors

Gloucester Docks

of a beautiful warehouse, is entered by a lock chamber with running water and tells the fascinating story of Britain's canals with films, displays and historic boats.

The **Robert Opie Collection** at the **Museum of Advertising and Packaging** takes a nostalgic look at the 40s, 50s, 60s and 70s with the aid of toys and food, fashions, packaging and a continuous screening of vintage TV commercials. **Soldiers of Gloucestershire** uses archive film, photographs and life-size reconstructions to tell the history of the county's regiments.

Elsewhere in the city **Gloucester City Museum and Art Gallery** houses treasures from all over the county to reveal its history, from dinosaur bones and Roman remains to antique furniture and the decorative arts. Among the highlights are the amazing **Birdlip Mirror**, made in bronze for a Celtic chief just before the Roman conquest, two Roman tombstones and a section of the Roman city wall revealed under the cut-away gallery floor. English landscape painting is represented by Turner, Gainsborough and Richard Wilson. Timber-framed Tudor buildings house **Gloucester Folk Museum**, where the exhibits include farming, fishing on the Severn, the port of Gloucester,

the Civil War, a Victorian schoolroom, a dairy, an ironmongery and a wheelwright's workshop. **Gloucester Transport Museum** has a small collection of well-preserved vehicles and baby carriages housed in a 1913 former fire station. The **House of the Tailor of Gloucester**, in College Court, is the house sketched by Beatrix Potter in 1897 and used in her tale *The Tailor of Gloucester*. It now brings that story to life, complete with Simpkin the Cat and an army of helpful mice.

In the southwestern suburbs of Gloucester are the ruins of **Llanthony Abbey**. The explanation of its Welsh name is an interesting one. The priory of Llanthony was originally founded in the Black Mountains of Wales at the beginning of the 12th century, but the inmates were so frightened of the local Welsh that they begged the Bishop of Hereford to find them a safer place. The Bishop passed their plea to Milo, Earl of Hereford, who granted this plot of land for a second priory bearing the same name as the first. Llanthony Secunda was consecrated in 1136. On a nearby hill the monks built St Ann's Well, whose water was - is - believed to cure eye problems.

In Hangar 7 Meteor Business Park at Gloucestershire Airport (entrance opposite Down Hatherley Road on the B4063 north of Gloucester) is the **Jet Age Museum**, whose exhibits include a Meteor and a Javelin. Visitors can sit in a Vulcan, Canberra, Buccaneer and Harrier cockpit. Two miles south of the city, off the A4173, is Robinswood Hill Country Park, 250 acres of pleasant walks, views and trails with a Rare Breeds farm.

HARTPURY

Two very unusual Grade II listed buildings here: a rare medieval set of bee hives in an outbuilding known as a bee bole, and, in the churchyard, a Soper stone tomb with a shroud-wrapped body on the top. At nearby **Ashleworth** is a magnificent 14th century tithe barn with a stone-tiled roof, projecting porches and elaborate interlocking roof timbers.

LECHLADE

Lechlade stands at the junction of the A417 and A361 where the Rivers Leach and Coln join the Thames. A statue of Old Father Thames looks over **St John's Lock**, the highest navigable point on the river, where barges loaded with building stone bound for Oxford and London have given way to pleasure craft. Halfpenny Bridge, which crosses the Thames in the town centre, has a tollhouse at its eastern end. The market place is dominated by the Church of St Lawrence with a tall, slender spire visible for miles around across the low-lying water meadows. The churchyard is said to have inspired Shelley to write his *Stanzas in a Summer Evening Churchyard*. The verse can be seen inscribed on a stone at the churchyard entrance.

At **Kelmscott**, about 4 miles east of Lechlade, **Kelmscott Manor** was the country home of William Morris from 1871 to 1896. Built near the Thames in the 16th century, it is the most evocative of all his houses and he loved it dearly; it is the scene of the end of his utopian novel *News From Nowhere*. Morris is buried in the village churchyard under a tombstone designed by his associate Philip Webb.

MORETON-IN-MARSH

A bustling market town at the junction of the A44 and the A429 Fosse Way, once an important stop on the coaching route between London and the West Midlands. One of the main coaching inns was the White Hart, where Charles I took refuge during the Civil War. Its broad main street is lined with handsome 17th and 18th century buildings, while from earlier days the old town gaol and the Curfew Tower are well worth a visit; the latter still has its original clock and bell dated 1633. In Bourton Road, the **Wellington Aviation Museum** has a collection of Second World War aircraft paintings, prints and models and a detailed history of the Wellington bomber. A mile east of town on the

Chastleton Manor

A44 stands the Four Shires Stone marking the original spot where the counties of Gloucestershire, Oxfordshire, Warwickshire and Worcestershire met. Moreton-in-the-Marsh is the scene, every Tuesday, of the biggest open-air street market in the Cotswolds.

NORTHLEACH

A traditional market town with some truly magnificent buildings. It was once a major wool-trading centre that rivalled Cirencester in importance and as a consequence possesses what now seems a disproportionately large church. The Church of St Peter and St Paul, known as 'the Cathedral of the Cotswolds', is a fine example of Cotswold Perpendicular, built in the 15th century with pinnacled buttresses, high windows and a massive square castellated tower. Treasures inside include an ornately carved font and some rare monumental brasses of which rubbings can be made (permits obtainable from the Post Office). An old country prison is now home to the **Cotswold Heritage Centre**, with displays telling the story of social history and rural life in the Cotswolds. **Keith Harding's World of Mechanical Music**, located in a 17th century merchant's house in the High Street, is a living museum of antique self-playing musical instruments, music boxes, automata and clocks, all maintained in perfect working order in the world-famous workshops on the premises.

At **Yanworth**, a couple of miles west of Northleach off the A429 Fosse Way, is the National Trust's **Chedworth Roman Villa**, a large, well-preserved Romano-British villa discovered by chance in 1864 and subsequently excavated to reveal more than 30 rooms and buildings, including a bath house and hypocaust. Some wonderful mosaics are on display, one depicting the four seasons, another showing nymphs and satyrs.

PAINSWICK

This beautiful little town, known as the "Queen of the Cotswolds", prospered with the wool trade, which had its peak in the second half of the 18th century. At that time 30 mills provided power within the parish, and the number of fine houses and farms in and around the town are witness to those days. Many of them are built of the pale grey limestone that was quar-

134

ried at Painswick Hill.

St Mary's Church, which dates from around 1380, contains some rare corbels

Painswick

thought to represent Richard ll and his queen. The church tower rises to 172 feet and can be seen for miles around. The church was the site of one of many local skirmishes in the Civil War when a party of Parliamentary soldiers came under cannon fire, which did considerable damage to the building. In 1643 King Charles I spent the night at Court House before the siege of Gloucester. In the grounds of **Painswick House**, on the B4073 at the northern edge of town, **Painswick Rococo Garden**, hidden away in magnificent Cotswold countryside, is a unique 18th century garden with plants from around the world and a maze planted in 1999 with a path structure in the shape of "250" to commemorate the garden's

Painswick Rococo Garden

250th anniversary. Other attractions are a specialist nursery, a children's nature trail, a gift shop and a restaurant.

A little further north, at Cranham, **Prinknash Abbey Park** (call it Prinnage) comprises an active monastery, chapel, working pottery, gift shop and tearoom. The Benedictine monks of Caldey Island moved here in 1928 when the old house was made over to them by the 20th Earl of Rothes in accordance with the wishes of his grandfather. They no longer occupy the old house, having moved into the impressive new monastery in 1972. The abbey chapel is open daily for solitude and contemplation. Visitors can have a guided tour round the pottery and buy a hand-made Prinknash pot. Part of the abbey gardens are given over to the **Prinknash Bird & Deer Park**, where visitors can feed and stroke the fallow deer and see the waterfowl, the peacocks and the African pygmy goats. By the lake is a charming two-storey Wendy House.

PAUNTLEY

The penniless orphan boy who in the pantomime fable was attracted by the gold-paved streets of London and who became its Lord Mayor was born at **Pauntley Court**. Richard Whittington, neither penniless nor an orphan, was born here about 1350, one of three sons of landowner Sir William de Whittington and Dame Joan. He became a mercer in London, then an important financier and was three times Mayor (not Lord Mayor - that title had not been invented). He married Alice Fitzwarren, the daughter of a wealthy landowner from Dorset. The origin of the cat connection is unclear, but an event which could have contributed to the myth was the discovery in 1862 of the carved figure of a boy holding a cat in the foundations of a house in Gloucester. The carving can be seen in Gloucester Museum.

PRESTBURY

Racing at Cheltenham started at Cleeve Hill but moved to land belonging to **Prestbury Park** in 1819, since when all the great names of steeplechasing have graced the Prestbury turf. The village has an abundance of timber-framed buildings, several ghosts and, alas, no trace at all of the medieval bishop's palace that once stood here. Prestbury's greatest son was not a steeplechasing jockey but the amazing Fred Archer, undisputed champion of flat race jockeys, born in the village in 1857. In the King's Arms a shoe from Archer's first mount hangs proudly in the bar, along with a plaque with this inscription:

> *At this Prestbury Inn*
> *lived FRED ARCHER the jockey*
> *Who trained upon toast,*
> *Cheltenham water & coffee.*
>
> *The shoe of his pony*
> *hangs in the bar*
> *where they drink to his prowess*
> *from near and from far*
>
> *But the man in the street*
> *passes by without knowledge*
> *that twas here Archer*
> *swallowed his earliest porridge.*

SLAD

Immortalised by Laurie Lee in his autobiographical *Cider With Rosie*, the sprawling village of Slad in the valley of the same name was for centuries a centre for milling and the production of fruit. A Roman villa was found in the Valley, and the votive tablets found there - one was dedicated to Romulus in his guise of fertility god and protector of crops - are now in Gloucester Museum.

STANTON

One of the prettiest spots in the Cotswolds, an attractive village of steeply-gabled limestone cottages dating mainly from the 16th and 17th centuries. The whole village was restored by the architect Sir Philip Scott in the years before the First World War; his home between 1906 and 1937 was **Stanton Court**, an elegant Jacobean residence built by Queen Elizabeth I's Chamberlain. The village church, dedicated to St Michael and All Angels, has many interesting features, including some stained glass from Hailes Abbey and a number of medieval pews with scarred ends caused perhaps by the leashes of dogs belonging to local shepherds. The architect Sir Ninian Comper added several features as World War l memorials. John Wesley is said to have preached in the church. Beyond Stanton, on the road to Broadway, the National Trust-owned **Snowshill Manor** is an elegant

manor house dating from Tudor times; once the home of Catherine Parr, it contains a fascinating collection of crafts and artefacts assembled by the last private owner, Charles Paget Wade.

STANWAY

A charming village clustered round one of the finest Jacobean manor houses in the region. Built of mellow golden stone, **Stanway House** has much to interest the visitor, including fine paintings, two superb Broadwood pianos, a

Stanway House

shuffleboard table and a Chippendale exercising chair on which keep-fit enthusiasts of the time would bounce for half an hour a day. In the grounds are a 14th century tithe barn, water mill, ice house, brewery, dog's cemetery and a pyramid erected on a hill behind the house in honour of John Tracy, one of the owning family. Another resident was Thomas Dover, the sea captain who rescued Alexander Selkirk from a desert island, an event which gave Daniel Defoe the inspiration for *Robinson Crusoe*. Also on note in Stanway is a thatched cricket pavilion resting on mushroom-shaped stones. The pavilion was a gift from JM Barrie, the author of *Peter Pan*, who was a frequent visitor to the village.

STOW-ON-THE-WOLD

At 800 feet above sea level, this is the highest town in the Cotswolds, and the winds sometimes prove it. At one time twice-yearly sheep fairs were held on the Market Square, and at one such fair Daniel Defoe records that over 20,000 sheep were sold. Those days are remembered today in **Sheep Street** and **Shepherds Way**. The square holds another reminder of the past in the town stocks, used to punish minor offenders. The sheep fairs continued until they were replaced by an annual horse fair, which

Tewkesbury Abbey

was held until 1985. The Battle of Stow, in 1646, was the final conflict of the Civil War, and after it some of the defeated Royalist forces made their way to St Edward's Church, while others were cut down in the market square. The church, which suffered considerable damage at this time, has been restored many times down the centuries, not always to its advantage, but one undoubted treasure is a painting of the Crucifixion in the south aisle, thought to be the work of the 17th century Flemish artist Gaspard de Craeyer. The church is dedicated to King Edward the Martyr, who was murdered at Corfe Castle by his stepmother Elfrida. Other buildings of note in the town are the 15th century Crooked House and the 16th century Masonic Hall. In Park Street is the **Toy and Collectors Museum**, housing a charming display of toys, trains, teddy bears and dolls, along with textiles and lace, porcelain and pottery.

SUDELEY

Southeast of Winchcombe lies the village of Sudeley and **Sudeley Castle**, a restored medieval stately home that was the last home, and burial place, of Catherine Parr, Henry VIII's sixth and last wife. She outlived Henry and married her former lover Sir Thomas Seymour, Baron of Sudeley, but died in childbirth; her tomb (not the original but a 19th century replacement designed by Sir Gilbert Scott) can be seen in St Mary's Chapel. The castle was the garrison headquarters of Charles I's nephew Prince Rupert during the Civil War and was besieged in 1643 and 1644. The conflict left the castle severely damaged (Catherine Parr's tomb was destroyed) and a large gap in the wall of the Octagon Tower is evidence of the bombardment. The interior of the castle, restored by the Dent family in sumptuous Victorian style, is a treasure house of old masters, tapestries, period furniture, costumes and toys, and the beautiful grounds include a lake, formal gardens and a 15 foot double yew hedge. Open daily April to October.

TEWKESBURY

A town of historic and strategic importance at the confluence of the Severn and Avon rivers. Those rivers also served to restrict the lateral expansion of the town, which accounts for the unusual number of tall buildings. Its early prosperity was based on the wool and mustard trades, and the movement of corn by river also contributed to its wealth. Tewkesbury's main thoroughfares, High Street, Church Street and Barton Street, form a Y shape, and the area between is a marvellous maze of narrow alleyways and small courtyards hiding many grand old pubs and medieval cottages. At the centre of it all is **Tewkesbury Abbey**, the cathedral-sized parish church of St Mary. One of the largest parish churches in the country, it was founded in the 8th century and completely rebuilt in the 11th. It was once the church of the Benedictine Abbey and was among the last to be dissolved by Henry VIII. In 1540, it was saved from destruction by the townspeople, who raised £453 to buy it from the Crown. Many of its features are on a grand scale - the colossal double row of Norman pillars; the six-fold arch in the west front; and the vast main tower, 132 feet in height and 46 foot square, the tallest surviving Norman main tower in the world. The choir windows have stained glass dating from the 14th century, and the abbey has more medieval monuments than any besides Westminster.

Among the most interesting memorials is a tomb which might be that of John Wakeman, the last abbot, who became the first Bishop of Gloucester in 1541. His tomb depicts the decaying corpse of a monk being nibbled at by vermin. A less dramatic monument by the south transept remembers Dinah Maria Mulcock, who, as Mrs Craick, wrote *John Halifax, Gentleman*, which features Tewkesbury under the name of Nortonbury. (This famous Victorian novelist visited the town in 1825 and took lunch at The Bell, as did her creation John Halifax. When Charles Dickens' Mr Pickwick came, he stayed at the Hop Pole Hotel, an occasion celebrated by a plaque outside the inn.)

Two other outstanding features in the Abbey are the high altar, a massive slab of Purbeck marble over 13 feet in length, and the renowned **Milton Organ**, built for Magdalen College, Oxford. Cromwell had it moved into the chapel of his Hampton Court residence, where the young John Milton, his Latin secretary at the time and later to become a great poet, played it to entertain the boss. It later returned to Magdalen, from where it was brought to Tewkesbury in 1737. Its 17th century pipes are thought to be among the oldest still in use. The half-timbered town is full of old and interesting buildings, among them the House of Nodding Gables on the High Street and Mythe Bridge, designed by Thomas Telford and built in a single cast-iron span in the 1820s, with a charming little tollhouse at each end.

Three museums tell the story of the town and its environs: the Little Museum, laid out like a typical old merchant's house; Tewkesbury Museum, with displays on the social history and archaeology of the area; and the **John Moore Countryside Museum**, a natural history collection displayed in a 15th century timber-framed house. The museum commemorates the work of John Moore, a well-known writer, broadcaster and naturalist, who was born in Tewkesbury in 1907.

The **Battle of Tewkesbury** was one of the fiercest in the Wars of the Roses. It took place in 1471 in a field south of the town which has ever since been known as Bloody Meadow. Following the Lancastrian defeat, those who had not been slaughtered in the battle fled to the Abbey, where the killing began again. Abbot Strensham intervened to stop the massacre, but the survivors, who included the Duke of Somerset, were handed over to the King and executed at Market Cross. The 17-year-old son of Henry VI, Edward Prince of Wales, was killed in the conflict and a plaque marking his final resting place can be seen in the Abbey. Tewkesbury was again the scene of military action almost two centuries later during the Civil War. The town changed hands several times during this period and on one occasion Charles I began his siege of Gloucester by requisitioning every pick, mattock, spade and shovel in Tewkesbury.

TODDINGTON

Toddington Manor, a magnificent Gothic pile built in the 1820s by Sir Charles Hanbury-Tracy, has stood deserted for many years, but the **Gloucestershire-Warwickshire Railway** has been very much better cared for. The northern terminus is the restored Toddington Station,

from where trains run on a six-mile return trip through some truly delightful countryside. The station, in pristine GWR condition, is open all year round and includes a signal box and a goods shed.

TWIGWORTH

Twigworth is the home of **Nature in Art**, a renowned museum of wildlife art housed in 18th century Wallsworth Hall. The collection depicts many aspects of nature in a variety of media, from life-size sculptures to Picasso, David Shepherd to ethnic art, tapestries to ceramics. Artists in residence. Changing temporary exhibitions. Art courses. Evening events.

WINCHCOMBE

The Saxon capital of Mercia, where in medieval times the shrine of St Kenelm, martyred here by his jealous sister in the 8th century, was second only to that of Thomas à Becket as a destination for pilgrims. Winchcombe grew in importance into a walled town with an abbot who presided over a Saxon parliament. The abbey was destroyed in 1539 after the Dissolution of the Monasteries and all that remains today is a section of a gallery that is part of the George Inn. As well as pilgrims, the abbey gave rise to a flourishing trade in wool and sheep.

One of the most famous townsmen of the time was Jack Smallwood, the Jack o' Newbury who sponsored 300 men to fight at Flodden Field in 1513 and was a leading producer of woollen goods. Silk and paper were also produced, and for a few decades tobacco was grown locally - a fact remembered in place names such as Tobacco Close and Tobacco Field. This activity ceased in 1670 when a law was passed banning home-produced tobacco in favour of imports from the struggling colony of Virginia.

The decline that followed had the effect of stopping the town's development, with for us the happy result that many of the old buildings have survived largely unaltered. These include St Peter's Church, built in the 1460s and known particularly for its 40 grotesques and gargoyles, the so-called Winchcombe Worthies. **Winchcombe Folk and Police Museum**, in the Tudor-style Town Hall by the Tourist Information Centre, tells the history of the town from neolithic times to the present day and also keeps a collection of British and international police uniforms and equipment.

138 A narrow passageway by an ordinary-looking house leads to **Winchcombe Railway Museum and Garden**, a wonderland full of things to do: the railway museum contains one of the largest collections of railway equipment in the country, and visitors can work signals and clip tickets and generally get misty-eyed about the age of steam. The Cotswold garden is full of old and rare plants.

A couple of miles north of Winchcombe lies the village of **Gretton**, near the western terminus of the Gloucestershire-Warwickshire Railway and the renowned **Prescott Hillclimb**, scene of hillclimb championships and classic car meetings.

A mile or so north of Winchcombe stand the ruins of **Hailes Abbey**, founded in 1246 by Richard, Earl of Cornwall, who built it on such an ambitious scale that the Cistercian monks were hard pressed to maintain it. But after a wealthy patron donated a phial said to contain the blood of Christ the abbey soon became an

Hailes Abbey, Nr Winchcombe

important place of pilgrimage; it was even mentioned in Chaucer's *Canterbury Tales*. The authenticity of the phial was questioned at the time of the Dissolution and it was destroyed, and with it the abbey's main source of income. The abbey fell into disrepair and the only significant parts to survive are the cloister arches. Some of the many artefacts found at the site, including medieval sculptures and decorated floor tiles, are on display in the abbey's museum. National Trust.

The Bell Inn   139

High Street, Moreton-in-Marsh,
Gloucestershire GL56 0AF
Tel: 01608 651688
Fax: 01608 652195

Directions:

From Oxford take the A44 to Moreton-in-Marsh (26 miles). As you come to the T-junction with the A429 in Moreton you will see The Bell Inn across the road, just to the right.

A striking Georgian building in honey-coloured local stone, **The Bell Inn** stands at the heart of this delightful Cotswold town. Moreton's High Street, where a colourful market has been held every Tuesday for generations, is one of the broadest in the country and was once part of the Roman Fosse Way running from Devon to the northeast. Originally built as a coaching inn, The Bell is a picture-postcard hostelry which offers everything one could hope for from a traditional English inn.

The restaurant serves an excellent selection of home cooked food, lighter meals, snacks and sandwiches, as well as vegetarian options, and is also open for morning coffee and afternoon teas. In good weather, meals can be taken in the charming courtyard, surrounded by flowers and mementoes of the days of stagecoach travel. A recent addition is the beer garden where customers can drink or dine in the tranquil setting of a lovely, flower-filled walled garden. The Bell is also noted for its exceptional accommodation which has received several prestigious awards. There are 5 beautifully furnished rooms, all en suite, where the old beams and Cotswold stone features take guests back in time. Two of the rooms have disabled access and all are well-equipped with colour television and tea/coffee-making facilities. For those who prefer self-catering, the inn has a self-contained adjoining cottage which sleeps up to 5 people.

Opening Hours: Mon-Sat: 10.00-23.00 Sun: 12.00-22.30

Food: Mon-Thu: 12.00-20.30 Fri-Sat: 12.00-21.00 Sun: 12.00-17.00

Credit Cards: All major cards except Diners

Facilities: Restaurant/function room; courtyard seating; beer garden; children's play area

Entertainment: Traditional pub games; live entertainment weekly during the season, occasionally out of season

Accommodation: 5 rooms, all en suite; self-catering cottage

Local Places of Interest/Activities: Curfew Tower, Redesdale Hall, Wellington Aviation Museum, all nearby; Falconry Centre & Arboretum, Batsford Park, 1.5 miles; Sezincote Water Garden, 2.5 miles; Chastleton House (NT), 4.5 miles; Stratford-on-Avon, 23 miles; Cheltenham, 23 miles; City of Oxford, 26 miles

Internet/Website:
www.bellinncotswold.com

140   The Black Bear Inn

High Street
Moreton-in-Marsh
Gloucestershire
GL56 0AX
Tel: 01608 652992

Directions:

From junction 15 of the M40, follow the A429 south. It will be signposted for Moreton-in-Marsh and will bring you directly into the centre of the town after 21 miles.

Moreton-in-Marsh is a bustling market town which stands at the busy junction of the A44 and A429. In its time, the town has been an important stopping place for stage-coaches and it was also a leading linen-weaving centre. The present-day centre is full of 18th and 19th-century buildings which give it a great deal of character.

On the busy main street you will find **The Black Bear Inn**, a traditional stone-built structure, fronting a small square. Popular with locals there is a busy public bar and quieter lounge bar which also serves as the dining room. There is an excellent menu offering a wide range of bar meals and snacks, complemented by a specials board. The menu features a range of traditional and more unusual dishes utilising fresh local produce such as trout from the nearby Donnington Trout Farm. The traditional Sunday Lunches prove very popular so it would be advisable to arrive early if you intend to eat, and the bars can get busy in the main tourist season and on market days when there will be a influx of visitors from the surrounding villages. To enjoy with your meal, the bar stocks a selection of beer and lager including some locally produced real ales and cider.

If you would like to stay a while in this popular area of the Cotswolds then you need look no further, as The Black Bear can offer two double rooms for bed and breakfast accommodation.

Opening Hours: Mon-Sat 11.00-23.00; Sun 12.00-22.30.

Food: Bar meals and snacks, Traditional Sunday Lunch.

Credit Cards: Visa, Access, Delta, Switch.

Accommodation: 2 double rooms.

Facilities: Patio Beer garden, Car Park.

Local Places of Interest/Activities:
Batsford Park Arboretum 2 miles, Sezincote 3 miles, Chastleton House 4 miles, Stow-on-the-Wold 5 miles, Motor Museum, Bourton-on-the-Water 10 miles, Cotswold Farm Park 11 miles.

The Black Swan Inn | 141

68-70 Southgate St,
Gloucester
Gloucestershire
GL1 2DR
Tel: 01452 523642
Fax: 01452 308840

Directions:

Entering Gloucester on
the A38 from Bristol, follow the signs for Central
Gloucester until you have
to turn left. Then take the
first right, and you will
see the inn's car park on
the left

An imposing Victorian
structure in the Classical style, **The Black Swan Inn** enjoys the status of a Grade II
Listed Building. The interior is equally impressive with its high ceilinged rooms and
Victorian fittings. Pictures with an equine theme and paintings of the city by local
artists adorn the walls, along with a blackboard listing the day's menu. All the food on
offer here is home made and freshly prepared, vegetarian options are available and
other special diets can also be catered for. Lovers of real ales will be in their element
here. The inn received CAMRA's Gloucester Pub of 2000 award and there are always 6
real ales on tap, all of which are constantly rotated. There's also a wide range of other
popular beverages and an extensive wine list. Your welcoming "mine hosts" are Dan
and Lucy Sulyma who have been here since 1999 and took over as managers in June,
2000. Their grand old hostelry has 18 guest bedrooms, - 8 twins, 4 doubles, 3 singles
and 3 family rooms. All of them have en suite facilities and are attractively and comfortably furnished. Southgate Street runs into the pedestrianised centre of the city and
it's a short walk from the inn to the glorious Cathedral, Beatrix Potter's House of the
Tailor of Gloucester, and many of the city's other major visitor attractions.

Opening Hours: Mon-Sat: 11.00-23.00
Sun: 12.00-22.30

Food: Available every lunchtime &
evening

Credit Cards: All major cards except
Diners

Facilities: Function room; parking for 15
cars & street parking nearby

Entertainment: Live music every Tuesday,
and every 3rd Saturday

Accommodation: 18 rooms, all en suite

Local Places of Interest/Activities:
Gloucester Cathedral, Gloucester Docks,
Robert Opie Collection, Transport Mu-
seum, Folk Museum, Jet Age Museum, all
within walking distance; Robinswood Hill
Country Park, 2 miles; Cheltenham Art
Gallery & Museum, Cheltenham Race-
course, Holst Birthplace Museum, Pittville
Pump Room Museum, all at Cheltenham,
10 miles

142 Hollow Bottom

Guiting Power
Nr. Winchcombe
Gloucestershire
GL54 5UX
Tel: 01451 850392
Fax: 01451 850392

Directions:

Leaving the M5 at junction 11, follow the A40 through Cheltenham. At Andovers-ford, pick up the A436 signposted for Stow-on-the-Wold. After 4 miles bear left onto the B4068 and the village of Guiting Power will be signposted on the left after about 2 miles.

In the centre of the charming village of Guiting Power is the unusually named inn, **The Hollow Bottom**. Sited right on the road the inn has a small seating area at the front and there is also a car park and garden to the rear. The building blends in with the rest of the village, being built of honey-coloured Cotswold Stone with a slate roof. The frontage is covered with Virginia Creeper and the patio is decorated with flowering tubs which are a mass of colour in season. Inside, the cosy atmosphere is enhanced by the beamed ceilings and open fire in the bar.

This is a popular pub with the locals and also with the many visitors to the village. There is a good selection of wines, beers and lagers on tap, with one guest real ale, as well as the usual selection of spirits and soft drinks. There is a good choice of food served each lunch time and evening with all the dishes home cooked and freshly prepared to order. The wide ranging menu includes an excellent range of starters, a choice of main dishes to suit all appetites and some delicious home made desserts. There is a separate dining room and dishes can also be enjoyed in the bar where there is a TV showing Sky Sports and The Racing Channel. If you would like to linger a while in this delightful part of the Cotswolds, there are three rooms available for bed and breakfast. Each room has its own private bathroom and is provided with a colour TV and tea and coffee making facilities.

Opening Hours: Mon-Sat 11.00-23.00; Sun 12.00-22.30.

Food: Bar meals and snacks. Bookings taken for the dining room.

Credit Cards: Visa, Access, Delta, Switch.

Accommodation: 3 rooms.

Facilities: Garden, Car Park.

Entertainment: Sky TV.

Local Places of Interest/Activities: Cotswold Farm Park 1 mile, Sudeley Castle, Winchcombe 5 miles, Cheltenham 13 miles, Stow-on-the-Wold 8 miles, Folly Farm Conservation Centre 3 miles, Birdland, Bourton-on-the-Water 6 miles.

The Horse & Groom Inn | 143

**Cricklade Road, South Cerney,
Cirencester,
Gloucestershire
GL7 5QE
Tel: 01285 860236**

Directions:
From Cirencester take the A419 towards Swindon. The Horse & Groom is about 3 miles along this road, adjacent to the dual carriageway

Located on the edge of the village, just off the A419, **The Horse & Groom** is a former coaching inn, dating back some 300 years, which has been carefully restored and extended. The twin visitor attractions of the Cotswold Water Park and the Keynes Country Park are only a mile or so away, and there are good road links to Cheltenham, Gloucester and the M4 and M5 motorways. The Horse & Groom is a traditional family run hostelry where the owner, Ernie Lucker, is assisted by his daughter Elizabeth and son Jonathan who has been heavily involved with the restoration work and works behind the bar in the evenings.

Elizabeth is the chef and her menu offers a good choice of dishes which are almost entirely home made. A traditional roast is served on Sundays and to accompany your meal there's a choice of 2 real ales, a wide range of all the popular beverages and a comprehensive wine list. Enjoy your meal in the bar or in the refurbished restaurant (which is also available for private functions). The 12 guest bedrooms at the Horse & Groom are all purpose built and contained within a traditional building replicating the Cotswold stone barn that formerly occupied the site. The tastefully furnished comfortable rooms are all en suite and provided with colour television and tea/coffee-making facilities.

Opening Hours: Mon-Sat: 10.00-23.00
Sun: 12.00-22.30

Food: Mon-Sat: 12.00-15.00; 18.30-22.00
Sun: 12.00-15.00

Credit Cards: All major cards except Amex & Diners

Facilities: Restaurant; beer patio; large car park

Accommodation: 12 rooms, all en suite

Local Places of Interest/Activities:
Riverside walk, 0.5 miles; Cotswold Water Park & Keynes Country Park, 1 mile; Church of St John the Baptist, Corinium Museum, both at Cirencester, 3 miles; Barnsley House Garden, 8 miles

Internet/Website:
e-mail: ernie@lucker.fsbusiness.co.uk
website: www.horsegroom.co.uk

144 The Kings Head Inn

*The Green,
Bledington
Gloucestershire
OX7 6XQ
Tel: 01608 658365*

Directions:

From junction 15 of the M40, follow the A429 south. From the centre of Stow-on-the-Word turn left onto the A436 and after a mile bear right onto the B4450 signposted for Chipping Norton. The village of Bledington will be found about 3 miles further on.

The Kings Head is a lovely old village inn and can be found in the centre of the small village of Bledington on the B4450. Superior in every way this characterful inn is built of traditional Cotswold Stone and features beamed ceilings throughout the interior. There is a great lively atmosphere as this hostelry is very popular at all times, even weekday lunch times, with visitors enjoying the comfortable bars and friendly service. Food is served at every session and the quality is outstanding. The menu is mainly a la carte which is available in the restaurant, and there is also an extensive specials board. All dishes are freshly prepared and cooked to order and utilise locally sourced ingredients where possible. The restaurant can get very busy so to be sure of getting a table, advance booking is recommended. This is perfect for a special night out or for a celebratory meal, and to make any occasion extra special, why not stay for the night?

There are twelve double rooms, with one featuring a four poster bed, and all are en-suite. The quality and standard of the furnishings are exceptional and every small detail has been attended to. Don't expect to be able to stay here on the spur of the moment though, the bed and breakfast is as popular as the restaurant and booking well in advance is strongly advised. This would certainly make an ideal base for a short stay or romantic weekend break.

Opening Hours: Mon-Sat 11.00-15.00, 18.00-23.00; Sun 12.00-15.00, 18.30-22.30.

Food: Bar meals and snacks, Traditional Sunday Lunch.

Credit Cards: Visa, Access, Delta, Switch, Amex, Diners.

Accommodation: 12 rooms.

Facilities: Car Park.

Local Places of Interest/Activities: Stow-on-the-Wold 4 miles, Chastleton House 8 miles, Donnington Trout Farm 7 miles, Birdland, Bourton-on-the-Water 9 miles, Upper Slaughter Manor House 8 miles

Kingsholm Inn 145

8 Kingsholm Road,
Gloucester GL1 3AT
Tel: 01452 530222

Directions

From Gloucester city centre, take the A38 towards Tewkesbury. You will see the Gloucester Rugby Club on your left; the Kingsholm Inn is opposite, on the right

Located just across the road from the Gloucester Rugby Club ground, the **Kingsholm Inn** celebrates its near neighbour with an interior decor devoted to the popular sport. Walls are covered with photographs, jerseys, ties and other rugby-related paraphernalia. (Another advantage of the ground being so near is that patrons of the Kingsholm can use its car park in the evenings).

The Kingsholm is a spacious 3-storeyed building with two bars: the larger bar contains the dining area, the smaller is where you'll find the popular skittle alley. Apart from Sunday evening, a tasty selection of traditional pub food is available every lunchtime and evening, - steak & chips, ploughman's, jacket potatoes, filled baps and baguettes, chicken or scampi in a basket. Sunday lunch also features traditional fare with a choice of three different roasts served with roast and boiled potatoes along with 3 other vegetables. Mine host, Keith Bryon, keeps 2 real ales on tap and also offers a small selection of wines as well as all the most popular pub beverages. And if you are looking for accommodation in this historic city, the inn has 4 comfortable guest bedrooms, three of them doubles and one single.

Opening Hours: Mon-Fri: 12.00-14.30; 18.00-23.00 Sat: 11.00-23.00 Sun: 12.00-22.30

Food: Available every lunchtime & evening, except Sunday evening

Credit Cards: Not accepted

Facilities: Beer garden; functions for 80-100 guests; parking on street and in Rugby Club in the evenings

Entertainment: Skittle alley; pool; large screen TV; Quiz Night, Sunday

Accommodation: 4 rooms, (3 doubles, 1 single)

Local Places of Interest/Activities: Gloucester Cathedral, Gloucester Docks, Robert Opie Collection, Transport Museum, Folk Museum, Jet Age Museum, all within walking distance; Robinswood Hill Country Park, 2 miles; Cheltenham Art Gallery & Museum, Cheltenham Racecourse, Holst Birthplace Museum, Pittville Pump Room Museum, all at Cheltenham, 10 miles

146   The Plaisterers Arms

Abbey Terrace,
Winchcombe
Gloucestershire GL54 5LL
Tel: 01242 602358
Fax: 01242 602360

Directions:

Leave the M5 at junction 9 and follow signs for Evesham along the A438. At the second large junction carry straight on to the B4077 signposted for Stow-on-the-Wold. After 4 miles Winchcombe is signposted to the right on the B4632. The Plaisterers Arms can be found in the centre of the town, opposite the parish church.

Winchcombe is an attractive small town that was once the regional capital of Saxon Mercia. One of the town's most enduring legends concerns Kenelm, a popular child king who is said to have been martyred here by his jealous sister, Quendrida, in the 8th century. In medieval times St Kenelm's shrine grew to rank second only to Thomas a Beckett's as a destination for pilgrims, a factor which made the town one of the wealthiest tourist attractions in the country. Winchcombe grew to become a walled town with an abbot who presided over a Saxon parliament; however in 1539 the abbey was destroyed by Thomas Seymour of Sudeley following Henry VIII's Dissolution of the Monasteries. Nothing remains of the abbey today, except for a few features which have been incorporated into later buildings.

In the centre of Winchcombe is a fine inn, **The Plaisterers Arms**. This impressive establishment dates from the 15th century and inside has oak-beamed ceilings and a wonderfully traditional atmosphere. Here they serve an excellent selection of hand-pulled ales, a range of delicious home-cooked bar meals and a traditional roast lunch on Sundays. There are also five comfortable letting rooms available which are all pleasantly appointed and equipped with en-suite facilities. The land to the rear of the inn slopes away sharply to form a delightful beer garden. An attractive patio area has been created here and in spring and summer the whole area overflows with spectacular floral displays. The garden enjoys fine views over the surrounding landscape and also contains a children's play area.

Opening Hours: Winter - Mon-Sun 11.00-15.00, 17.00-23.00; Summer - Mon-Sun 11.00-23.00.

Food: Bar meals and snacks.

Credit Cards: Visa, Access, Delta, Switch.

Accommodation: 5 en-suite rooms.

Facilities: Beer garden.

Local Places of Interest/Activities: Sudeley Castle, Folk Museum, Winchcombe, Cheltenham 6 miles, Hailes Abbey 3 miles, Stanway House 5 miles, Broadway 9 miles, Snowshill 9 miles, Broadway Country Park 10 miles.

The Plough Inn
147

5 Gloucester Road,
Stratton,
Cirencester, Glos.
GL7 2LB
Tel: 01285 653422

Directions:

From Cirencester take the A417 towards Gloucester. The Plough Inn is on this road, on the left about 1 mile from the town centre.

When the original **Plough Inn** was built way back in the 1700s it stood on the busy main road to Gloucester. By the 1990s this thoroughfare had become horribly congested. To the relief of the good people of Stratton the A417 was diverted around the town and the Plough is now almost off the beaten track. It's a family-friendly place with a pleasant, convivial atmosphere, and the old beams, polished brass, Cotswold stone walls, flagstone floors and open fires all add to the charm. And do look out for the Jurassic element in the decor, - spectacular fossils some 165 million years old which are embedded in the window sills.

The inn still maintains the 100-year-old tradition of a festival for children on Hot Cross Bun day while year-round entertainment includes darts and skittles. Landlady Cherie Tancock also arranges live music entertainment once a month. The Plough enjoys an excellent reputation for its wholesome, home-made food, with vegetarian and other diets catered for, and there's also a special menu for children. Sunday lunch, when there's a choice of 3 different roasts complete with all the trimmings, is especially popular. There are 3 real ales on tap, a small selection of quality wines is available, and there's also a wide choice of other popular beverages. If you are planning to stay in this corner of the Cotswolds, the Plough has 3 attractive double rooms to let, all of them en suite and with their own entrance.

Opening Hours: Mon-Sat: 10.00-15.00; 17.00-23.00 Sun: 12.00-15.00; 19.00-22.30

Food: Restaurant & bar meals available every lunchtime & evening

Credit Cards: All major cards except Amex & Diners

Facilities: Restaurant; beer garden; adventure playground; large car park

Entertainment: Darts; skittles; live music monthly

Accommodation: 3 double rooms, all en suite

Local Places of Interest/Activities: Riverside walks, 0.5 miles; Golf, 1 mile; Church of St John the Baptist, Corinium Museum, both at Cirencester, 1 mile; Cotswold Water Park, 4.5 miles; Barnsley House Garden, 6 miles

148 Riverside Lechlade Ltd

*Park End Wharf,
Lechlade,
Gloucestershire
GL7 3AQ
Tel: 01367 252229
Fax: 01367 250003*

Directions:

Lechlade is on the A361, about 11 miles north of Swindon. Riverside Lechlade is on the southern edge of the town, just after the A361 crosses the River Thames, on the left

Occupying a superb position on the north bank of the Thames in this historic little town, **Riverside Lechlade Ltd** offers its customers a huge range of amenities. If you are travelling by boat, you can moor alongside or in the 100-berth marina, refuel with petrol or gas, and find all your boating necessities in the well-stocked chandlery. Boats are also available for hire, - as they have been at this spot for more than a hundred years.

If you are looking for some wholesome fare, there's an extensive choice of traditional pub food as well as around 10 daily, home made specials. Beverages on offer include 2 real ales, a lengthy and well-chosen wine list, and no fewer than 70 different lagers. In fine weather, customers can enjoy their refreshments in the spacious riverside beer garden where there's seating for up to 100. Children are welcome and so too are well-behaved dogs. And if you are looking for a place to stay in this attractive corner of the county, why not rent the traditional canal narrowboat which is moored alongside the pub. Riverside Lechlade is a fascinating complex which has been created by Tim and Nigel Lloyd over the past 20 years. The 250-year-old main building was once a wool warehouse and its outbuildings now house an interesting variety of antique and other shops.

Opening Hours: Mon-Sat: 08.30-23.00, Sun 08.30 - 22.30

Food: 08.30 - 20.30 (later by arrangement)

Credit Cards: All major cards except Amex & Diners

Facilities: Restaurant; café; function room; large car park; boat mooring; boat hire; chandlery

Entertainment: Pool table; pub games; live bands every Thu; karaoke every other Sat

Accommodation: In narrowboat moored alongside pub

Local Places of Interest/Activities: Thames Path passes close by; Halfpenny Bridge, nearby; Cotswold Water Park, 3 miles; Kelmscott Manor, 3.5 miles; Buscot Park (NT), 4 miles

Snowshill Arms 149

Snowshill, Nr. Broadway
Gloucestershire WR12 7JU
Tel: 01386 852653

Directions:

From the M5 leave at junction 9 following the A438 east towards Stow-on-the-Wold. At the second cross-roads (about 3 miles) carry straight on to the B4077. Continue for about 9 miles, passing through the village of Stanway, and then turn left signposted for Snowshill. The village will be found after 3 miles, and the Snowshill Arms is on the left in the centre of the village.

Snowshill is a pretty, picture post-card village in the heart of the Cotswolds which lies on the tourist trail and is popular with photographers. Not quite as well known as nearby Broadway, the village has grown around the church and features some delightful stone cottages and other interesting buildings. The old Manor House can be reached by a 500 metre walk along a country path and is well worth a visit. It is a charming Tudor building best known for Charles Paget Wade's collections of craftsmanship and design. The Manor House is preserved by the National Trust and open to the public from April to September.

The **Snowshill Arms** has an equally long history dating back to the 13th century. It retains the qualities of a real English Inn and its interior features many original features with exposed beamed ceilings, exposed stone walls and an open fire. There is one large bar behind which they serve two real ales, lager, soft drinks, spirits and a good selection of wines. A full menu of bar meals and snacks caters to hungry walkers, tourists and locals and there is a good choice catering to all tastes, the regular menu supplemented by a daily blackboard of specials. The Snowshill Arms has its own skittle alley which is popular with visitors and it is available both for the playing of skittles or occasionally used as a function room. The outdoor children's play area is well equipped and popular with younger children in summer months.

Opening Hours: Mon-Sat 11.00-14.30, 18.00-23.00; Sun 12.00-14.30, 19.00-22.30.

Food: Bar meals and snacks.

Credit Cards: None.

Facilities: Skittle Alley/Function Room, Darts, Car Park.

Entertainment: Skittle Alley.

Local Places of Interest/Activities: Snowshill Manor, Broadway Tower Country Park 1 mile, Broadway 3 miles, Sudeley Castle 10 miles, Cotswold Farm Park 6 miles.

150   The Swan Inn

High Street,
Moreton-in-Marsh,
Gloucestershire GL56 0LL
Tel: 01608 650711
Fax: 01608 650813
Directions:

From Oxford take the A44 to Moreton-in-Marsh (26 miles). In Moreton you will come to a T-junction with the A429 which is also Moreton's High Street. The Swan Inn is opposite the HSBC bank.

Occupying a prime position on Moreton's enormously wide main street, **The Swan Inn** is an enchanting 18th century building of local Cotswold stone which enjoys a Grade I Listed Building status. Inside, the old beams and exposed stone walls testify to the inn's long tradition of hospitality. There are 3 bars: - a friendly public bar, a lounge bar where there's an interesting beaten copper plaque more than a hundred years old hanging over the fireplace, and a third room which offers that great West Country entertainment, a skittle alley, and also doubles as a function room capable of accommodating up to 100 guests.

Mine hosts, Sandra and Bernard Edgeworth, have been at The Swan since 1987 and during that time have established the inn's outstanding reputation for good food, fine ales and top quality accommodation. The extensive menu includes main dishes, snacks and sandwiches, as well as vegetarian choices, children's meals and daily specials. Every couple of months or so, there are special Steak Nights and every Thursday lunchtime a value for money lunch for Senior Citizens. A perfect base for exploring the Cotswolds, The Swan has 7 beautifully appointed guest room. Two of them are en suite and one of these also boasts a magnificent 4-poster bed inscribed with the date "1724".

Opening Hours: Mon-Sat: 11.00-23.00 Sun: 12.00-22.30

Food: Available every lunchtime & evening; Senior Citizens' menu, Thu lunchtime

Credit Cards: All major cards except Amex & Diners

Facilities: Two small beer patios; function room for 100; small car park

Entertainment: Skittle Alley; pool table; darts; dominoes; crib

Accommodation: 7 rooms, (2 en suite & 1 with 4-poster bed)

Local Places of Interest/Activities: Curfew Tower, Redesdale Hall, Wellington Aviation Museum, all nearby; Falconry Centre & Arboretum, Batsford Park, 1.5 miles; Sezincote Water Garden, 2.5 miles; Chastleton House (NT), 4.5 miles; Stratford-on-Avon, 23 miles; Cheltenham, 23 miles; City of Oxford, 26 miles

---

PLACES OF INTEREST:

Badminton 154
Berkeley 154
Bisley 155
Blakeney 156
Cannop 156
Chipping Sodbury 156
Coleford 156
Drybrook 157
Dursley 157
Dymock 158
English Bicknormap 158
Frampton-on-Severn 158
Frocester 159
Horton 159
Kempley 159
Littledean 159
Lydney 159
Marshfield 160
Minchinhampton 160
Nailsworth 161
Newent 161

Newland 161
North Nibley 161
Ozleworth 162
Parkend 162
Ruardean 162
St Briavels 162
Selsley 163
Slimbridge 163
Staunton 163
Stinchcombe 163
Stroud 163
Tetbury 163
Tortworth 164
Uley 164
Upleadon 165
Westbury-on-Severn 165
Westonbirt 165
Woodchester 165
Wortley 165
Wotton-under-Edge 165

PUBS AND INNS:

The Bailey Inn, Yorkley 167
The Black Dog, Newent 168
The Cross Hands, Alveston 169
The Crown, Hambrook 170
The George Inn, Aylburton 171
The George Inn, Frocester 172
The Hedgehog, Bream 173
The Old Crown Inn, Uley 174
The Stagecoach Inn, Newport 175
The Vine Tree Inn, Randwick 176
The White Hart, Leonard Stanley 177
The White Hart Inn, Newnham on Severn 178
The Yew Tree, Clifford's Mesne 179

The Hidden Inns of the Welsh Borders

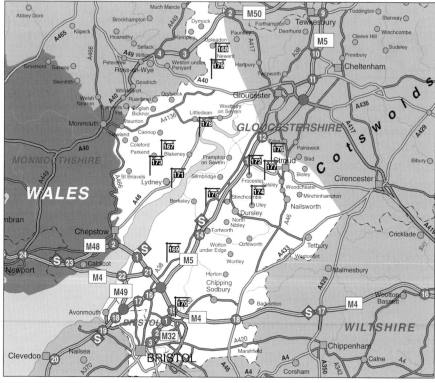

© MAPS IN MINUTES ™ (2000)

167	The Bailey Inn, Yorkley		174	The Old Crown Inn, Uley
168	The Black Dog, Newent		175	The Stagecoach Inn, Newport
169	The Cross Hands, Alveston		176	The Vine Tree Inn, Randwick
170	The Crown, Hambrook		177	The White Hart, Leonard Stanley
171	The George Inn, Aylburton		178	The White Hart Inn, Newnham on Severn
172	The George Inn, Frocester		179	The Yew Tree, Clifford's Mesne
173	The Hedgehog, Bream			

Please note all cross references refer to page numbers

Wild wood, royal hunting ground, naval timber reserve, important mining and industrial area. The Royal Forest of Dean, one of England's few remaining ancient forests, has been all these, and today its rich and varied landscape provides endless interest for walkers, historians and nature-lovers. Its geographical location in an area bordered by the Severn Estuary to the south and the Wye Valley to the west has effectively isolated it from the rest of England and Wales and as a result it has developed a character all its own. To the playwright Dennis Potter it was "This heart-shaped land". Following the last Ice Age an area of some 120,000 acres between the Rivers Severn, Wye and Leadon became covered with deciduous forest and remained so until around 4000 BC, when the farmers of the New Stone Age began clearing the land with their state-of-the-art flint axes, felling vast numbers of trees. Coppicing was started about this time, and the new shoots growing from the bases of the felled trees provided the timber of the future.

The Forest has long been home to a wide variety of wildlife, and it was the presence of deer that led Edmund Ironside to designate it a royal hunting forest in the 11th century. In the same century King Canute established the Court of Verderers with responsibility for everything that grew or lived in the Forest. Iron ore deposits were first discovered in the Forest 2,500 years ago; they were exploited by the Romans, but it was not until the 1600s that mineral began to be extracted on a grand scale.

The most ruinous development in the Forest was the demand for timber for the process of iron-smelting; at one time 72 furnaces were operating in the area, feeding on such enormous quantities of timber that by the 1660s only a few hundred trees remained. The severity of the situation was realised by the government, which in 1668 cancelled all the permits for extracting minerals and set about an extensive re-planting programme that was accelerated a long time later during the Napoleonic Wars. The Victorians exploited another of the Forest's natural resources, coal, and at one time up to a million tons were removed each year, mostly from open-cast workings. This industry came more or less to an end in the 1930s, although a few seams are still worked to this day. The centuries of mining inevitably left their mark, the Forest has gradually reclaimed the workings (known as scowles), often hiding them in a dense covering of moss, trees and lime-loving plants.

Today, the wooded area covers some 24,000 acres and has a large number of attractions for the visitor, including Dean Heritage Centre, Puzzlewood, Clearwell Caves, Hopewell Colliery and Dean Forest Railway. The Forest is a marvellous place for walking, whether it's a gentle stroll or an energetic hike. There are numerous waymarked walks in and around the forest, most of which are detailed in leaflets available at the visitor centres and Tourist Information Centres. Among them are the Wye Valley Walk; Offa's Dyke Path, which covers the Wye Valley between Chepstow and Ross-on-Wye; the Wysis Way, passing west to east; and the Gloucestershire Way, covering a route from Chepstow to Symonds Yat and then taking in the spectacular May Hill to the north. A tour down the eastern bank of the great River Severn takes in the meanderings of the river, the great tidal ranges of the estuary, the old and new bridges; natural history at Slimbridge, bricks and mortar history at Berkeley, industrial archaeology, glorious gardens and the charming towns of Tetbury and Stroud.

BADMINTON

The **Badminton Park** estate was founded by Edward Somerset, the son of the Marquis of Worcester, whose 25-foot monument stands in the little church next to the main house. The central section of the house dates from the 1680s and contains some marvellous carvings in lime wood by Grinling Gibbons. The rest of the house, along with the grounds and the many follies and gateways, is the work of the mid-18th century architect William Kent. The house contains an important collection of Italian, English and Dutch paintings. The game of badminton is said to have started here during a weekend party in the 1860s. The Duke of Beaufort and his guests wanted to play tennis in the entrance hall but were worried about damaging the paintings; someone came up with the bright idea of using a cork studded with feathers instead of a ball. In such a moment of inspiration was the game born, and it was one of the guests at that weekend bash who later took the game to Pakistan, where the first rules were formalised.

Many of the buildings on the estate, including the parish church and the estate villages of Great and Little Badminton, were designed in an ornate castellated style by Thomas Wright. The park is perhaps best known as the venue of the **Badminton Horse Trials**, which annually attract the best of the international riders, and spectators in their thousands.

BERKELEY

The fertile strip that is the Vale of Berkeley, bounded on the north by the Severn and on the south by the M5, takes its name from the small town of Berkeley, whose largely Georgian centre is dominated by the Norman **Berkeley Castle**. Said to be the oldest inhabited castle in Britain, and home to 24 generations of the Berkeley family, this wonderful gem in pink sandstone was built between 1117 and 1153 on the site of a Saxon fort. It was from here that the barons of the West met before making the journey to Runnymede to witness the signing of Magna Carta by King John in 1215. Edward II was imprisoned here for several months after being usurped from the throne by his wife

and her lover, and eventually met a gruesome death in the dungeons in the year 1327. Three centuries later the castle was besieged by Cromwell's troops and played an important part in the history of the Civil War. It stands very close to the Severn and once incorporated the waters of the river in its defences so that it could,

Berkeley Castle

in an emergency, flood its lands. Visitors passing into the castle by way of a bridge over a moat will find a wealth of treasures in the **Great Hall**, the circular keep, the state apartments with their fine tapestries and period furniture, the medieval kitchens and the dungeons. The Berkeley family have filled the place with objects from around the world, including painted glassware from Damascus, ebony chairs from India and a cypress chest that reputedly belonged to Sir Francis Drake. Security was always extremely important, and two remarkable signs of this are a four-poster bed with a solid wooden top (no nasty surprises from above in the night) and a set of bells once won by the castle's dray

Great Hall, Berkeley Castle

year. His beautiful Georgian house in Church Lane has a state-of-the-art display showing the importance of the science of immunology, and in the grounds of the house is a rustic thatched hut where Jenner used to vaccinate the poor free of charge and which he called the Temple of Vaccinia. The museum is open Tuesday to Sunday afternoons from April to September and on Sunday afternoons in October.

At **Sharpness**, a mile or so west of Berkeley, the world's first nuclear power station operated between 1962 and 1989. It marks the entrance to the Sharpness Canal. There are several interesting villages in the vicinity, including Breadstone, which has a church built entirely of tin.

BISLEY

Country roads lead across from Stroud or up from Oakridge Lynch to the delightful village of Bisley, which stands 780 feet above sea level and is known as "Bisley-God-Help-Us" because of the winter winds which sweep across the hillside. Bisley's impressive All Saints Church dates from the 13th century and was restored in the early 19th by Thomas Keble, after whose poet and theologian brother John Keble College, Oxford was named. The font has two carved fish inside the bowl and a shepherd and sheep on the base. In the churchyard is the Poor Souls' Light, a stone wellhead beneath a spire dating from the 13th century. It was used to hold candles lit for souls in purgatory. Below the church are the **seven wells of Bisley** (also restored by Thomas Keble), which are blessed and decorated with flowers each year on Ascension Day. At the top of the village is a double lock-up built in 1824, with two cells beneath an ogee gable.

The village's main claim to fame is the story of the Bisley Boy. When Bisley was a rich wool town it had a royal manor, Over Court, where the young Princess Elizabeth (later Queen Elizabeth I) often stayed. The story goes that during one of those visits the princess, then aged 10, caught a fever and died. Fearing the wrath of her father Henry VIII, her hosts looked for a substitute and found a local child with red hair and remarkably similar physical characteristics except for the rather important fact that the child was a boy called John Neville. Could this explain the Virgin Queen's reluctance to marry,

horses and now hanging in the dairy. Each horse wore bells with a distinctive chime so that if an outsider attempted to gain entrance as a carter his strange bells would betray him. The castle is surrounded by sweeping lawns and Elizabethan terraced gardens. Special features include a deer park, a medieval bowling alley, a beautiful lily pond and a butterfly farm with hundreds of exotic butterflies in free flight.

The parish church of St Mary, which contains several memorials to the Berkeley family, has a fine Norman doorway, a detached tower and a striking east window depicting Christ healing the sick. A curious piece of carving in the nave shows two old gossips with a giant toad sitting on their heads. Next to the castle and church is the **Jenner Museum**, once the home of Edward Jenner, the doctor and immunologist who is best known as the man who discovered a vaccine against smallpox. The son of a local parson, Jenner was apprenticed to a surgeon in Chipping Sodbury in 1763 at the tender age of 14. His work over several decades led to the first vaccination against smallpox, a disease which had killed many thousands every

156

her problem with hair loss and her "heart that beats like a man's", or was the story made up to fit those facts?

BLAKENEY

An attractive little village and a convenient base for exploring the heart of the Forest. Bed and Take the B4227 up from Blakeney to visit the **Dean Heritage Centre at Soudley**. The centre, open throughout the year, tells the story of the unique landscape of the Forest and its fiercely independent people. Attractions include displays of natural, industrial and social history, a Victorian cottage, a smallholding with animals, millpond and waterwheel, a charcoal stack, crafts shop and café.

At nearby **Awre**, an ancient crossing place of the Severn, is the Church of St Andrew, not much changed in the 700 years since it was built. Its most remarkable possession is the massive **Mortuary Chest**, carved from a single trunk and used down the years as a laying out place for bodies recovered from the river. In the churchyard are several examples of headstones depicting the local speciality of cherubs.

CANNOP

Cannop Valley has many forest trails and picnic site; one of the sites is at **Cannop Ponds**, picturesque ponds created in the 1820s to provide a regular supply of water for the local iron-smelting works. At Speech House Road, near Cannop, is **Hopewell Colliery**, a true Forest of Dean free mine where visitors can see mine workings dating back to the 1820s and some of the old tools of the trade. Open daily March to October.

CHIPPING SODBURY

A pleasant market town that was one of the earliest examples of post-Roman town planning, its settlement being arranged in strips on either side of the main street in the 12th century. The town once enjoyed prosperity as a market and weaving centre, and it was during that period that the large parish church was built.

A mile or so to the east, on a loop off the A432, is **Old Sodbury**, whose part-Norman church contains some exceptional tombs and monuments. One of these is a carved stone effigy of a 13th century knight whose shield is a

very rare wooden carving of a knight. Also in the church is the tomb of David Harley, the Georgian diplomat who negotiated the treaty which ended the American War of Independence. A tower just to the east of the church marks a vertical shaft, one of a series sunk to ventilate the long tunnel that carried the London-South Wales railway through the Cotswold escarpment. Opened in 1903, the 2 1/2 mile tunnel required its own brickworks and took five years to complete.

A lane leads south from Old Sodbury to **Dodington House**, built between 1796 and 1816 where previously an Elizabethan house stood. It was designed in lavish neo-Roman style by the classical architect James Wyatt, who was killed in a carriage accident before seeing his work completed. The house, whose interior is even more ornate than the facade, is open daily in the summer. Connected to the house by an elegant conservatory is the private Church of St Mary, also designed by Wyatt, in the shape of a Greek cross.

COLEFORD

A former mining centre which received its royal charter from Charles I in the 17th century in recognition of its loyalty to the Crown. It was by then already an important iron processing centre, partly because of the availability of local ore deposits and partly because of the ready local supply of timber for converting into charcoal for use in the smelting process. It was in Coleford that the Mushet family helped to revolutionise the iron and steel industry. Robert Forester Mushet, a freeminer, discovered how spiegeleisen, an alloy of iron, manganese, silicon and carbon, could be used in the reprocessing of "burnt iron" and went on to develop a system for turning molten pig iron directly into steel, a process which predated the more familiar one developed later by Bessemer.

Coleford, still regarded as the capital of the Royal Forest of Dean, is a busy commercial centre with an interesting church and a number of notable industrial relics. It is home to the **Great Western Railway Museum**, housed in an 1883 GWR goods station next to the central car park. Exhibits include several large-scale steam locomotives, railway relics and memorabilia, an engine shed and a miniature locomotive for children. Another treat for railway fans is the **Perrygrove Railway** on the B4228 just south of town. Designed as a family attraction, it offers unlimited trips on its narrow-gauge steam train, a village with secret passages and a treasure hunt in the woods.

Clearwell Caves are set in an area of special landscape value, just on the outskirts of the historic village of Clearwell, which boasts a

Clearwell Caves, Near Coleford

castle, pretty church, chapel and several good pubs. This is the only remaining working iron mine in the Forest of Dean out of the very many that once worked here. The mine produces ochres for use as paint pigments by artists or those wishing to decorate their homes using natural paints.

Before the 19th century only Free Miners were allowed to enter Forest of Dean mines; any Free Miner allowing access to non-members of the fellowship would be brought before the mine law court, their fellowship withdrawn, their tools broken or confiscated and the Miner never allowed to mine within the Forest of Dean again. Today such punishment is frowned upon and at Clearwell Caves nine impressive caverns have been opened to visitors, allowing you to descend over 100 feet underground, although the mine itself goes down over 600 feet. The Cave shop is a treat in itself with unusual gift ideas and a wide range of spectacular minerals and crystals to buy from all around the world.

Don't miss visiting the Tearoom, which contains some very interesting artefacts but particularly some exceptional paintings of local Free Miners; the two paintings of iron miners have been done using the ochres that they used to mine!

Complete a memorable visit by wandering down to see **Clearwell** village and the pretty surrounding countryside; there are several walks from the Caves that explore surface mining remains, some with spectacular views over the Welsh mountains and the Wye Valley.

Half a mile from Coleford, on the B4228 Chepstow road, **Puzzle Wood** is nearly 14 acres of pre-Roman open-cast iron ore mines (known locally as scowles) which have been left over the course of 2,700 years to slip back into the healing hands of nature. The result is a magical outdoor grotto of trailing vines, moss-covered rocks, fern and wild flowers. The paths were laid nearly 200 years ago and there are many dead-ends, circles, wooden bridges and passageways through the rocks, taking visitors through a most unusual maze of unique and spectacular scenery.

DRYBROOK

Hidden away at Hawthorn's Cross on the edge of the forest is a unique collection of mechanical music spanning the last 150 years. The **Forest of Dean Mechanical Organ Museum** is open Tuesday and Thursday afternoons in April, May, July and August. Drybrook has a very unusual black-and-white building with a five-storey square tower. This was once the Euroclydon Hotel (the name is still on the tower) and was originally built, in 1876, for a wealthy mine-owner to provide a look-out over his domain and his workers.

DURSLEY

A small town on the Cotswold Way that prospered as a cloth-making centre. It still has something of the feel of a "working town", and one of the old mills still operates at Cam. One of the notable buildings is the 18th century Market Hall standing on 12 pillars at a busy town-centre junction. It has a bell turret on its roof and a statue of Queen Anne facing the fine parish church. The Priory is a large 16th century house built for a family of Flemish weavers who settled here and, it is said, taught the people of Dursley how to weave. William Shakespeare reputedly spent some time in Dursley in hiding after being spotted poaching. There is a reference to a bailiff from Dursley in *Henry IV*.

Cloth is still produced in the mill at Cam on the northern edge of Dursley, continuing a tradition started in the 16th century. Local legend is rich in stories about **Cam Long Down**, a small, isolated peak on the edge of Cam. One story concerns the Devil, who decided one day

158

to cart away the Cotswolds and dam the Severn. On setting out with his first cartload he met a cobbler and asked him how far it was to the river. The cobbler showed him one of the shoes he was taking home to mend and replied, "Do you see this sole? Well, I've worn it out walking from the Severn." This persuaded the Devil, who was obviously a lazy devil, to abandon his task; he tipped out his cartload, creating the unusual hill to be seen today. The hill is also one of several sites claimed for King Arthur's last battle.

DYMOCK

At the heart of the village is the early Norman Church of St Mary, whose unusual collection of artefacts and memorabilia includes the last ticket issued at Dymock station, in 1959. Dymock boasts some fine old brick buildings, including the White House and the Old Rectory near the church, and outside the village, the Old Grange, which incorporates the remains of the Cistercian Flaxley Abbey. In the years before the First World War, Dymock became the base for a group of writers who became known as the Dymock Poets. The group, which included Rupert Brooke, Wilfred Gibson, Edward Thomas and Lascelles Abercrombie, and was later joined by Robert Frost, sent out its New Numbers poetry magazine from Dymock's tiny post office, and it was also from here that Brooke published his *War Sonnets*, including *The Soldier (If I should die, think only this of me.....)*. Brooke and Thomas died in the War, which led to the dissolution of the group. Two circular walks from Dymock take in places associated with the poets.

ENGLISH BICKNOR

The Church of St Mary, high above the Wye Valley, boasts some intriguing 14th century stone figures of females, one of them holding a round object that is thought by some to be a heart, by others an egg. Just by the church can be seen the earthworks of a **Norman motte and bailey castle**. Welsh Bicknor is, naturally, on the other side of the Wye.

FRAMPTON-ON-SEVERN

The 22-acre Rosamund Green, incorporating a cricket ground and three ponds, is one of the largest village greens in England, formed when the marshy ground outside the gates of

Frampton Court was drained in the 18th century. The court is an outstanding example of a Georgian country house, built in the Palladian style in the 1730s and the seat of the Clifford family ever since. Fine porcelain, furniture and paintings grace the interior, and in the peacock-strutted grounds an ornamental canal reflects a superb Orangery in Dutch-influenced strawberry gothic. A unique octagonal tower was built in the 17th century as a dovecote. The Court is open by appointment only.

On the other side of the green is **Frampton Manor**, the Clifford family's former home, built between the 12th and 16th centuries. This handsome timber-framed house is thought to be the birthplace of Jane Clifford, who was the mistress of Henry II and bore him two children. The manor, which has a lovely old walled garden with some rare plants, is open by written appointment. At the southern edge of the village stands the restored 14th century Church of St Mary with its rare Norman lead font. The church stands beside the **Sharpness Canal**, which was built to allow ships to travel up the Severn Valley as far as Gloucester without being at the mercy of the estuary tides. The canal has several swing bridges and at some of these, as at Splatt Bridge and Saul Bridge at Frampton, there are splendid little bridge-keeper's cottages with Doric columns.

To the west of Frampton, on a great bend in the river, is the Arlingham Peninsula, part of the **Severn Way Shepperdine-Tewkesbury long-distance walk**. The trail passes close to Wick Court, a 13th century moated manor house. The land on which the village of Arlingham stands once belonged to the monks of St Augustine's Abbey in Bristol who believed it to be the point where St Augustine crossed the Severn on his way to converting the heathen Welsh tribes. Nearby is **St Augustine's Farm** on the site of a monastic house. It is a 110-acre working farm and a popular venue for family outings.

The Severn naturally dominated life hereabouts and at **Saul**, a small village on the peninsula, the inhabitants decorated their houses with carvings of sailors, some of which, in bright, cheerful colours, can be seen today. The village lies at the point where two canals cross. Continuing round the bend in the river, **Epney** is the point from which thousands of baby eels are exported each year to the Netherlands and elsewhere to replenish their own stocks. A mile or so inland from Epney is the historic hamlet of **Moreton Valence**, whose 15th century church has an impressive Norman doorway with a depiction of the Archangel Michael thrusting a spear into a dragon's mouth. Also to be seen here are the ramparts of a 14th century castle, once the property of the De Valence family.

FROCESTER

The chapel in the centre of the village was built in 1680 using materials from nearby Frocester Court. In the grounds are a superb timber-framed gatehouse and the wonderful **Frocester Tithe Barn**, a massive 186 feet in length and substantially as it was when built on the instructions of Abbot John de Gamages between 1284 and 1306.

HORTON

On high ground northeast of the long, narrow village stands the National Trust's **Horton Court**, a part-Norman manor house rebuilt for William Knight, the man given the task of presenting Henry VIII's case to the Pope when the King was trying to divorce Catherine of Aragon. Among the many interesting features is a covered walkway, or ambulatory, which seems to have been modelled on a Roman cloister. The 12th century Great Hall survives from its earlier incarnation, and both the walkway and the hall can be visited. Next to the Court stands the little Church of St James, built between the 14th and 16th centuries and retaining many original features in spite of a Victorian makeover. It also holds memorials to the Paston family, lords of the manor in Jacobean times.

KEMPLEY

A village famous for its cider and also for having two churches, of very different age and significance. The Church of St Mary, easily the most popular church in the area, dates from the end of the 11th century and would be a gem even without its greatest treasure. That treasure, in the chancel, is an almost complete set of 12th century frescoes, the most renowned in the region and among the finest in the land. Their subjects include St Peter and the Apostles, Christ with his feet resting on a globe, and the de Lacy family, local lords of the manor. The red sandstone Church of St Edward the Confessor was built in 1903 by the 7th Earl Beauchamp in the style of the Arts and Crafts Movement using exclusively local materials.

This is the area of **Dymock Woods**, an area of Forestry Commission woodland famous for its daffodils.

Two miles further south, on National Trust land, stands **May Hill**. It rises to nearly 1,000 feet and its domed summit is planted with trees commemorating Queen Victoria's Golden Jubilee (1887), Queen Elizabeth II's Silver Jubilee (1977) and the Queen Mother's 80th birthday (1980). The reward for climbing to the top is a quite magnificent view that stretches over Gloucestershire, and, on a clear day, as far as Bristol.

LITTLEDEAN

Places of interest here include the 13th century church, the 18th century prison and, just south of the village, **Littledean Hall**, reputedly the oldest inhabited house in England. The house has Saxon and Celtic remains in the cellars and is thought to have originated in the 6th century. Highlights in the grounds, from which balloon flights launch, include a Roman temple site, a Victorian walled garden and a number of ancient chestnut trees.

LYDNEY

The harbour and the canal at Lydney, once an important centre of the iron and coal industries and the largest settlement between Chepstow and Gloucester, are well worth exploring, and no visit to the town should end without a trip on the **Dean Forest Railway**. A regular service of steam and diesel trains operates between Lydney Junction, St Mary's Halt and Norchard. At **Norchard Railway Centre**, headquarters of the line, are a railway museum,

Dean Forest Railway

160

souvenir shop and details of restoration projects, including the imminent extension of the line to Parkend. Air-conditioned classic coaches in the platform serve light snacks on steam days. The backbone of the locomotive fleet (this is for real railway buffs!) are 5541, a Churchwood-designed Prairie tank engine, and 9681, an 0-6-0 pannier tank built in 1948, when GWR was becoming BR.

One of the chief attractions in the vicinity is **Lydney Park Gardens and Museum**. The gardens, which lie beside the A48 on the western outskirts, are a riot of colour, particularly in May and June, and the grounds also contain the site of an Iron Age hill fort and the remains of a late-Roman temple excavated by Sir Mortimer Wheeler in the 1920s. The builders of this unusual temple were probably wealthy Romanised Celts; the mosaic floor, now lost, depicted fish and sea monsters and was dedicated to Nodens, the Roman-Celtic god of healing whose emblem was a reclining dog with curative powers. The nearby museum houses a number of Roman artefacts from the site, including the famous "Lydney Dog" and a number of interesting items brought back from New Zealand in the 1930s by the first Viscount Bledisloe after his term there as Governor General. Also in the park are traces of Roman iron-mine workings and Roman earth workings.

MARSHFIELD

This old market town was once the fourth wealthiest town in Gloucestershire, after Bristol, Gloucester and Cirencester, its prosperity based on the malt and wool industries. Its long main street has many handsome buildings dating from the good old days of the 17th and 18th centuries, but not many of the coaching inns remain that were here in abundance when the town was an important stop on the London-Bristol run. Among the many notable buildings are the **Tolzey market hall** and the imposing Church of St Mary, which boasts a fine Jacobean pulpit and several impressive monuments from the 17th and 18th centuries. Each Boxing Day brings out the **Marshfield Mummers**, who take to the streets to perform a number of time-honoured set pieces wearing costumes made from newspapers and accompanied by a town crier. On the northern edge of town is a folk museum at Castle Farm.

A lane leads south through a pretty valley to the delightful hamlet of **St Catherine's**, whose church contains a splendid 15th century stained-glass window with four lights depicting the Virgin Mary, the Crucifixion, St John and St Peter. The great manor house, St Catherine's Court, now privately owned, once belonged to the Benedictine priory at Bath.

Three miles northwest of Marshfield, on the A46, the National Trust-owned **Dyrham Park** stands on the slope of the Cotswold ridge, a little way south of the site of a famous 6th century battle between Britons and Saxons. This striking baroque mansion, the setting for the film *Remains of the Day*, houses a wonderful collection of artefacts accumulated by the original owner William Blathwayt during diplomatic tours of duty in Holland and North America (he later became Secretary of State to William III). Among the most notable are several Dutch paintings and some magnificent Delft porcelain. The west front of the house looks out across a terrace to lawns laid out in formal Dutch style; much of the estate is a deer park, which perhaps it was originally, as the word Dyrham means "deer enclosure" in Saxon. A charming little church in the grounds has a Norman font, a fine 15th century memorial brass and several memorials to the Winter and Blathwayt families.

MINCHINHAMPTON

A scattered community on the ridge between Golden Valley and Nailsworth Valley, Minchinhampton acquired its market charter as far back as 1213. Following the Dissolution of the Monasteries, Henry VIII presented Minchinhampton Manor to the 1st Baron Windsor in return for the baron's family estate near Windsor. The estate was later acquired by Samuel Sheppard, whose family was responsible for the building of Gatcombe Park and of Minchinhampton's **Market House**. There's good walking and good exploring hereabouts, with the old stone quarries at Ball's Green, the National Trust woodland and grassland at Minchinhampton and Rodborough Commons, the Iron Age defences of Minchinhampton Bulwarks and the Neolithic long barrow known as **Whitfield's Tump**, from whose summit the Methodist preacher George Whitfield gave a famous public address in 1743.

NAILSWORTH

This small residential and commercial town was once, like so many of its neighbours, a centre of the wool trade. Several of the old mills have been modernised, some playing new roles, others plying their original trades. **Ruskin Mill** is a thriving Arts & Crafts Centre. **Stokescroft** is an unusual 17th century building on Cossack Square. During restoration work in 1972 scribblings found on an attic wall suggested that soldiers had been billeted there in 1812 and 1815. Perhaps this is why it is known locally as "the Barracks". It is thought to have housed Russian prisoners during the Crimean War, which accounts for the name of the square.

NEWENT

Capital of the area of northwest Gloucestershire known as the Ryelands, and the most important town in the Vale of Leadon, Newent stands in the broad triangle of land called Daffodil Crescent. The rich Leadon Valley soil was traditionally used for growing rye and raising the renowned Ryelands sheep, an ancient breed famed for the quality of its wool. The town was one of the county's principal wool-trading centres, and the wealth produced from that trade accounts for the large number of grand merchants' houses to be seen here. The most distinctive house in Newent is the splendid timber-framed **Market House**, built as a butter market in the middle of the 16th century, its upper floors supported on 16 oak pillars that form a unique open colonnade. The medieval **Church of St Mary** has many outstanding features, including the shaft of a 9th century Saxon cross, the 11th century 'Newent Stone' and the 17th century nave. Royalist troops had removed the lead from the roof to make bullets, an act which caused the roof to collapse during a snowstorm in 1674. A new nave was started after Charles II agreed to donate 60 tons of timber from the Forest of Dean.

The **Shambles Museum of Victorian Life** is virtually a little Victorian town, a jumble of cobbled streets, alleyways and squares, with shops and trades tucked away in all corners, and even a mission chapel and a Victorian conservatory. At Nicholson House is the private collection Crime Through Time, often called the Black Museum of Gloucestershire.

There aren't too many windmills in Gloucestershire, but at **Castle Hill Farm** just outside town is a working wooden mill with great views from a balcony at the top.

161

A mile south of Newent is the **National Bird of Prey Centre** housing one of the largest and best collections of birds of prey in the world. Over 110 aviaries are home to eagles, falcons, owls, vultures, kites, hawks and buzzards. Between 20 and 40 birds are flown daily.

On the road north towards Dymock, set in 65 acres of rolling countryside, the **Three Choirs Vineyard** is the country's largest wine producer.

NEWLAND

Newland's Church of All Saints is often known as the **Cathedral of the Forest** because of its impressive size. Its aisle is almost as wide as its nave and its huge pinnacled tower is supported by flying buttresses. Like many churches in the county, it was built during the 13th and 14th centuries and remodelled by the Victorians. Inside, it has a number of interesting effigies, including an unusual brass relief of a medieval miner with a pick and hod in his hand and a candlestick in his mouth. Other effigies depict a forester in 15th century hunting gear with a hunting horn, a sword and knife; and, from the 17th century, an archer with wide-brimmed hat, bow, horn and dagger.

NORTH NIBLEY

This village is the birthplace, around 1494, of William Tyndale, who was the first to translate and print the Old and New Testaments. He used the original Greek and Roman sources instead of the approved Latin, as a result of which he was accused of heresy and burnt at the stake at Vivolde near Brussels in 1536. 350 years later the imposing **Tyndale Monument**, paid for by public subscription, was erected on the ridge above the village to commemorate his life and work. Standing 111 feet high on the 700 foot escarpment, it offers amazing views and is itself one of the most prominent landmarks on the Cotswold Way. Tucked away near the village, **Hunts Court** is a mecca for serious gardeners, a two-acre maze of exciting rare shrubs, frothy borders and a marvellous collection of old roses. North Nibley is also the site of the last "private" battle in England, which took place in 1471 between the rival barons William Lord Berkeley and Viscount de Lisle.

162

OZLEWORTH

A secluded hamlet with a very unusual circular churchyard, one of only two in England. The church itself has a rare feature in a six-sided Norman tower. Also at Ozleworth is the National Trust's **Newark Park**, built as a hunting lodge by the Poyntz family in Elizabethan times. James Wyatt later converted it into a castellated country house. Open by appointment only.

This is great walking country, and one of the finest walks takes in the **Midger Wood Nature Reserve** on its way up to **Nan Tow's Tump**, a huge round barrow whose tomb is said to contain the remains of Nan Tow, a local witch.

PARKEND

A community once based, like so many others in the area, on the extraction of minerals. New Fancy Colliery is now a delightful picnic area, with a nearby hill affording breathtaking views over the forestscape. Parkend is to be the northern terminus of Dean Forest Railway. The track is there, the signal box has been renovated and a replica station built. Off the B4431, just west of Parkend, is the RSPB's **Nagshead Nature Reserve**, with hundreds of nest boxes in a woodland site with footpaths, waymarked trails and a summer information centre.

RUARDEAN

A lovely old village whose **Church of St John the Baptist**, one of many on the fringe of the forest, has many interesting features. A tympanum depicting St George and the Dragon is a great rarity, and on a stone plaque in the nave is a curious carving of two fishes. These are thought to have been carved by craftsmen from the Herefordshire School of Norman Architecture during the Romanesque period around 1150. It is part of a frieze removed with rubble when the south porch was being built in the 13th century. The frieze was considered lost until 1956, when an inspection of a bread oven in a cottage at nearby Turner's Tump revealed the two fish set into its lining. They were rescued and returned to their rightful place in the church.

From Ruardean, country roads lead westward to the sister villages of **Upper and Lower Lydbrook**. These tranquil villages were once major producers of pig iron, rivals even for Shef-

field, and when the extraction of iron ore and coal was at its height their position on the northwest edge of the forest made then ideally suited for the processing of the ore. The first commercially viable blast furnace in the area was sited here at the beginning of the 17th century. For several centuries flat-bottomed barges were loaded at Lower Lydbrook with coal bound for Hereford, 25 miles upstream; this river trade continued until the 1840s, when it was superseded, first by the Gloucester-Hereford Canal and then by the Severn and Wye Railway. The actress Sarah Siddons lived in Lydbrook as a child.

ST BRIAVELS

A historic village named after a 5th century Welsh bishop whose name appears in various forms throughout Celtic Wales, Cornwall and Brittany, but nowhere else in England. In the Middle Ages St Briavels was an important administrative centre and also a leading manufacturer of armaments, supplying weapons and ammunition to the Crown. In 1223 it is believed that Henry III ordered 6,000 crossbow bolts (called quarrels) from here. The ample Church of St Mary the Virgin, Norman in origin, enlarged in the 12th and 13th centuries and remodelled by the Victorians, is the scene of a curious and very English annual custom, the St Briavels **Bread and Cheese Ceremony**. After evensong a local forester stands on the Pound Wall and throws small pieces of bread and cheese to the villagers, accompanied by the chant "St Briavels water and Whyrl's wheat are the best bread and water King John can ever eat." This ceremony is thought to have originated more than 700 years ago when the villagers successfully defended their rights of estover (collecting wood from common land) in nearby Hudnalls Wood. In gratitude each villager paid one penny to the churchwarden to help feed the poor, and that act led to the founding of the ceremony. Small pieces of bread and cheese were considered to bring good luck, and the Dean Forest miners would keep the pieces in order to ward off harm.

St Briavels Castle, which stands in an almost impregnable position on a high promontory, was founded by Henry I and enlarged by King John, who used it as a hunting lodge. Two sturdy gatehouses are among the parts that survive and they, like some of the actual castle buildings, are now in use as a youth hostel.

SELSLEY

All Saints Church was built in the 1860s by Sir Samuel Marling, one of a family of wealthy Stroud mill-owners. A distinctive landmark with its saddleback tower, it is modelled on a church seen by Sir Samuel on his travels around Europe and is notable for its exceptional stained glass. The glass was commissioned from William Morris and Company and the designers included Morris himself, Dante Gabriel Rossetti, Ford Madox Brown and Edward Burne-Jones.

Selsley Herb Farm is a small nursery specialising in herbs and selected garden plants, with a barn shop and plant sales area. Open Tuesday-Sunday in summer.

SLIMBRIDGE

The **Wildfowl and Wetlands Trust** was founded on the banks of the Severn in 1946 by the distinguished naturalist, artist, broadcaster and sailor Peter (later Sir Peter) Scott. He believed in bringing wildlife and people together for the benefit of both, and the Trust's work continues with exciting plans for the Millennium. Slimbridge has the world's largest collection of exotic wildfowl, with up to 8,000 wild winter birds on the 800-acre reserve. Viewing facilities are first-class, and there's a tropical house, pond zone, children's play area, restaurant and gift shop. Also in the long, rambling village is a fine 13th century church whose 18th century windows incorporate fragments of the original medieval glass.

*Slimbridge Wildfowl and
Wetlands Trust*

STAUNTON

Lots to see here, including a Norman church with two stone fonts and an unusual corkscrew staircase leading up past the pulpit to the belfry door. Not far from the village are two enormous mystical stones, the **Buckstone** and the **Suck Stone**. The former, looking like some great monster, used to buck, or rock, on its base but is now firmly fixed in place. The Suck Stone is a real giant, weighing in at many thousands of tons. There are several other stones in the vicinity, including the **Near Harkening** and **Far Harkening** down among the trees, and the **Long Stone** by the A4136 at Marion's Cross.

STINCHCOMBE

A picturesque village with several notable buildings, including 17th century **Melksham House**, seat of the Tyndale family for 300 years, and the 18th century **Piers Court**, home of the writer Evelyn Waugh. **Stancombe Park**, on the southern edge, is a handsome country house built in 1880 on the site of a Roman villa. The gardens are open occasionally under the National Gardens Scheme. The mosaic floor from the villa was recovered and moved to Gloucester Museum.

STROUD

The capital of the Cotswold woollen industry, an ideal centre on the River Frome at a point where five valleys converge. The surrounding hill farms provided a constant supply of wool, and the Cotswold streams supplied the water-power. By the 1820s there were over 150 textile mills in the vicinity; six survive, one of them specialising in green baize for snooker tables. A stroll round the centre of town reveals some interesting buildings, notably the **Old Town Hall** dating from 1594 and the **Subscription Rooms** in neo-classical style. An easy walk from the centre is Stratford Park, a large park containing dozens of trees both ordinary and exotic. Lots of ducks on the pond.

TETBURY

A really charming Elizabethan market town, another to have prospered from the wool trade. Its most famous building is the stone-pillared 17th century **Market House** in the heart of town, but a visit should also take in the ancient **Chipping Steps** connecting the market

The Hidden Inns of the Welsh Borders

164

house to the old trading centre, and the Church of St Mary, an 18th century period piece with high-backed pews, huge windows made from recovered medieval glass and slender timber columns hiding sturdy iron uprights. **Tetbury Police Museum**, housed in the original cells of the old police station, has a fascinating collection of artefacts, memorabilia and uniforms from the Gloucestershire Constabulary.

Two miles northwest of Tetbury, west of the B4104, stands **Chavenage House**, a beautiful Elizabethan mansion built of grey Cotswold stone on earlier monastic foundations in the characteristic E shape of the period. The elegant front aspect has remained virtually unchanged down the years, and the present owners, the

Chavenage House

Lowsley-Williams family, can trace their lineage back to the original owners. Two rooms are covered with rare 17th century tapestries, and the house contains many relics from the Cromwellian period. Cromwell is known to have stayed at the house, and during the Civil War he persuaded the owner, Colonel Nathaniel Stephens, a relative by marriage, to vote for the King's impeachment. According to the Legend of Chavenage the owner died after being cursed by his daughter and was taken away in a black coach driven by a headless horseman. The present owner, who conducts tours round the property, welcomes visitors to "Gloucestershire's second most haunted house" (Berkeley Castle is the most haunted!). In 1970 an astonishing find was made in the attic - a portfolio of watercolours by George IV of plans for the restoration of Windsor Castle.

TORTWORTH

Overlooking the village green stands the Church of St Leonard, which contains some fine 15th century stained glass and a pair of canopied tombs of the Throckmorton family, former owners of the Tortworth Park estate. In a field over the church wall are several interesting trees, including an American hickory, a huge silver-leafed linden and two Locust trees. Nearby, and the most famous of all, is the famous **Tortworth Chestnut**, a massive Spanish chestnut which the diarist John Evelyn called "the great chestnut of King Stephen's time". Certainly it was well established by Stephen's time (1130s), and a fence was put up to protect it in 1800. At that time a brass plaque was put up with this inscription:

> *"May man still guard thy venerable form*
> *From the rude blasts and tempestuous storms.*
> *Still mayest thou flourish through succeeding time*
> *And last long last the wonder of the clime."*

And last it has; its lower branches have bent to the ground and rooted in the soil, giving the impression of a small copse rather than a single tree.

ULEY

Calm and quiet now, Uley was once a busy centre of commerce, mainly in the cloth-making industry. The most distinguished house in the area is **Owlpen Manor**, a handsome Tudor country house set in formal Queen Anne terraced yew gardens. Inside, contrasting with the ancient polished flagstones and the putty-coloured plaster, are fine pieces of William Morris-inspired Arts and Crafts furniture; there's also a rare beadwork collection and some unique 17th-century wall hangings.

The village lies in the shadow of **Uley Bury**, a massive Iron Age hill fort which has thrown up evidence of habitation by a prosperous community of warrior farmers during the 1st century BC. Another prehistoric site, a mile along the ridge, is Uley Long Barrow, known locally as **Hetty Pegler's Tump**. This chambered long barrow, 180 feet in length, takes its name from Hester Pegler, who came from a family of local land-owners. Adventurous spirits can crawl into this Neolithic tomb on all fours, braving the dark and the dank smell to reach the burial chambers, where they will no longer be scared by the skeletons that terrified earlier visitors. The walls and ceilings of the chamber are made of huge stone slabs infilled with drystone material.

A little further north, at the popular picnic site of **Coaley Peak** with its adjoining National Trust nature reserve, is another spectacular chambered tomb, **Nympsfield Long Barrow**.

UPLEADON

The **Church of St Mary the Virgin** features some fine Norman and Tudor work but is best known for its unique tower, half-timbered from bottom to top; even the mullion windows are of wood. The church has a great treasure in its Bible, an early example of the Authorised Version printed by the King's printer Robert Barker. This was the unfortunate who later issued an edition with a small but rather important word missing. The so-called Wicked Bible of 1631 renders Exodus 20.14 as "Thou shalt commit adultery."

WESTBURY-ON-SEVERN

The village is best known for the National Trust's **Westbury Court Garden**, a formal Dutch water garden laid out between 1696 and 1705. Historic varieties of apple, pear and plum, along with many other species introduced to England before 1700, make this a must for any enthusiastic gardener. The house was long ago demolished, and the only building to survive is an elegant two-storey redbrick pavilion with a tower and weather vane.

Westbury Court Garden

Also worth a visit in Westbury is the Church of Saints Peter, Paul and Mary with its detached tower and wooden spire.

WESTONBIRT

Westonbirt Arboretum, three miles south of Tetbury, contains one of the finest collections of trees and shrubs in Europe - 18,000 of them spread over 600 acres of glorious Cotswold countryside. Wealthy landowner Robert Stayner Holford founded this tree wonderland by planting trees for his own interest and pleasure. His son, Sir George Holford, was equally enthusiastic about trees and continued his father's work until his death in 1926, when he was succeeded by his nephew, the 4th Earl of Morley. Opened to the public in 1956 and now managed by the Forestry Commission, the arboretum has something to offer all year round: a crisp white wonderland after winter snows, flowering shrubs and rhododendrons in spring, tranquil glades in summer, glorious reds and oranges and golds in the autumn. The grounds provide endless delightful walks, including 17 miles of footpaths, and there's a visitor centre, plant centre, café and picnic areas. Open all year.

WOODCHESTER

The mysteriously unfinished **Woodchester Mansion** is one of Britain's most intriguing Victorian country houses. It's like a Victorian building site caught in a time warp, having been started in 1854 and suddenly abandoned in 1868, three-quarters finished and with the scaffolding in place and the workmen's tools left behind. What stands now, as in 1868, is a vast shell with gargoyles and flying buttresses on the Gothic facade, and all the props and stays and tools exposed inside. This incomplete masterpiece is now used as a training ground for stonemasons.

WORTLEY

Wortley boasts some impressive Roman remains. Parts of a mosaic floor of a Roman villa were unearthed by chance in 1981, and further excavation revealed a large bath house, a 3rd century paved courtyard and some massive stone drain-blocks.

WOTTON-UNDER-EDGE

A hillside former wool town with a number of interesting buildings: Berkeley House with its stone Jacobean front; the terraced house that was the family home of Isaac Pitman and where he devised his renowned method of shorthand; the Perry and Dawes almshouses around a quadrangle with a small chapel; and Tolsey House,

166

an early brick structure that was once a tollhouse for the market. The Church of St Mary (13th to 15th centuries) contains memorials to Lord Berkeley, who fought at Agincourt, and his wife Margaret. In a converted fire station, the **Heritage Centre** incorporates a museum with an intriguing collection of artefacts from Wotton's crafts and industries.

Bailey Inn | **167**

Bailey Hill
Yorkley
Lydney
Gloucestershire
GL15 4RP
Tel: 01594 562670

Directions:

Leave the M5 at junction 11 and take the A40 towards Gloucester and beyond. Two miles beyond Gloucester turn onto the A48 Chepstow road. About 13 miles along this road you will find Blakeney from where the village of Yorkley will be signposted to the right.

The village of Yorkley lies on the edge of the Royal Forest of Dean, a place with a long and fascinating past. Throughout its history this ancient forest has been a Royal hunting ground, an important mining and industrial area and a naval timber reserve. There are a number of waymarked walks through the forest which are fully described in an excellent range of leaflets and guides. There is also a heritage centre at nearby Lower Soudley which is an interesting place to visit for all ages.

Conveniently situated on the main road through Yorkley, visitors will easily find **The Bailey Inn**. This typical Victorian establishment has hardly changed since it was built and retains a quiet, traditional feel. Catering to the local community this is a popular hostelry, though visitors are more than welcome. Behind the bar there is a fine selection of beers and lager and there is a choice of real ales. There is a range of bar snacks and sandwiches served each lunchtime and evenings and a traditional roast lunch is available on Sundays. In addition to a car park, there is a beer garden at the rear, and this is a most pleasant spot in which to enjoy a refreshing drink and a bite to eat in warm, summer months. There is live entertainment and a good choice of traditional pub games is offered with skittles, quoits, darts, pools and cards.

Opening Hours: Mon-Thur 12.00-15.00, 19.00-23.00 Fri-Sat 11.00-23.00; Sun 12.00-22.30.

Food: Bar meals and snacks, Traditional Sunday Lunch.

Credit Cards: All the major cards

Facilities: Beer garden, Car Park.

Local Places of Interest/Activities: Littledean Hall 10 miles, Westbury Court Garden 9 miles, Forest of Dean 2 miles, Clearwell Caves 6 miles, Symonds Yat 10 miles, Gloucester 18 miles, St Briavels Castle 7 miles.

168   The Black Dog Inn

47 Church Street
Newent
Gloucestershire
GL18 1AA
Tel: 01531 821012

Directions:

The town of Newent can be found at the intersection of the B4216 and the B4215, 4 miles from junction 3 of the M50. The Black Dog Inn can be found in the centre of the town on Church Street.

The centre of Newent hides some real gems for the tourist and first time visitor. There is an elegant church, a 17th century Market House and a selection of small shops. Tucked away, just off Church Street lies The Shambles, a jumble of cobbled streets, alleyways and squares, houses, cottages and shops, recreating a small Victorian town.

Not far from this unusual visitor attraction you can find **The Black Dog**, a long established locals' pub. It would appear that the pub is housed within what were originally farm buildings which were converted into a small pub and subsequently grew into the much larger establishment you see today. Recently taken over by new managers, at the time of writing the Black Dog is undergoing extensive refurbishment to bring the interior, which had been sadly neglected, up to scratch. The refurbishment will endeavour to recreate the character and charm of a country pub while remaining welcoming and comfortable for visitors. The outside retains its period charm with part of the building being timbered.

At present there is a small menu offering traditional pub fayre ranging from snacks to hot dishes. Food is available each lunch time and early evening. In due course the menus and serving times will be extended to provide a wider choice of meals and snacks. To enjoy with your meal the bar stocks the usual selections of beer, lager and soft drinks with real ale also being kept on tap.

Opening Hours: Mon-Sat 11.00-14.30, 18.00-23.00; Sun 12.00-14.30, 18.00-22.30.

Food: Bar meals and snacks.

Credit Cards: Visa, Access, Delta, Switch.

Facilities: Pool, Darts, Car Park.

Local Places of Interest/Activities: The Shambles, Newent, Butterfly Centre 1 mile, Gloucester 10 miles, Forest of Dean 7 miles.

The Cross Hands | 169

The Down
Alveston
Bristol BS35 3PH
Tel: 01454 412331

Directions:

From the M5 take junction 14 and pick up the A38 heading south. About five miles along this road the village of Alveston will be signposted on the right.

Just off the busy A38 you will find **The Cross Hands** in the village of Alveston. Built at the turn of the century this is a neatly presented pub, the interior is simple and traditional in its feel, with no pretensions to being something its not. Popular with the locals, the landlords have created a happy, relaxed and welcoming atmosphere here. If you would like a refreshing drink then there is a choice of draught beer, lager and cider. The food is very popular with everyone, with meals being served each lunch time and evening Monday to Saturday. The menu offers a surprisingly good choice of starters, grills, fish and vegetarian dishes with some tasty desserts and farm-made ice-cream to round things off.

Opening Hours: Mon-Sat 11.00-23.00; Sun 12.00-22.30.

Food: Bar meals and snacks, A la Carte, Traditional Sunday Lunch.

Credit Cards: Visa, Access, Delta, Switch.

Facilities: Beer garden, Car Park.

Local Places of Interest/Activities: Bristol 10 miles, Dyrham Park 15 miles, Little Sodbury Manor 11 miles, Clevedon Court 19 miles, Weston-super-Mare 29 miles, Thornbury 1 miles, Chepstow 8 miles.

170 The Crown

Bristol Road,
Hambrook,
Bristol
BS16 1RY
Tel: 0117 956 6701

Directions:

From Exit 19 of the M4, take the M32 towards Bristol. Take Exit 1 signposted to Hambrook and The Crown Inn is about ¾ of a mile along this road, on the left.

Built in Victorian times, **The Crown** is very popular these days, especially with local people, because of its wholesome food at value-for-money prices and its well-maintained ales. With its beamed ceilings and log fire, the inn has all the warm, cosy atmosphere and character one would expect of a traditional English hostelry.

Mine host, Andrew Lewis, offers his customers a full range of pub food, - main meals, steak pies, ploughman's, sandwiches and bar snacks. Vegetarian dishes are also available. Sunday lunch is definitely rather special, with a menu providing 3 different roasts and all the trimmings. The well-stocked bar offers a wide selection of beverages, including 2 real ales, Stella, Bass, Courage, Guinness and Blackthorn Cider. The Crown also has 4 guest bedrooms, one of them with en suite facilities, and all of them available throughout the year. The City of Bristol's many attractions are within easy reach and the nearby motorway means that the Cotswolds, Exmoor, South Wales and the historic city of Bath can all be enjoyed within the space of a day's outing.

Opening Hours: Mon-Fri: 11.30-14.30; 17.00-23.00 Sat: 11.00-23.00 Sun: 12.00-16.00; 19.00-22.30

Food: Full meals and bar snacks available every lunchtime & evening

Credit Cards: All major cards except Amex & Diners

Facilities: Small rear patio; some parking

Entertainment: Petanque

Accommodation: 4 rooms, 1 en suite

Local Places of Interest/Activities: Bristol Cathedral, John Cabot's House, Trinity Almshouses, City Museum & Art Gallery; Clifton Suspension Bridge, Avon Gorge Nature Reserve, all in Bristol City Centre

George Inn

171

High Street
Aylburton
Gloucestershire
GL15 6DE
Tel: 01594 842163

Directions:

Leave the M5 at junction 11 and take the A40 towards Gloucester and beyond. Two miles beyond Gloucester turn onto the A48 Chepstow road. The village of Aylburton can be found about 19 miles along this road.

In the heart of the village of Aylburton, on the busy A48, you will find the charming **George Inn**. This attractive, Victorian building is constructed of local dressed stone and is conveniently located for travellers. The existing structure will be greatly enhanced when the new, adjoining accommodation complex is completed in early 2001. The extension has been carefully designed to blend in with the rest of the main building and the addition of 14 en-suite rooms makes this one of the best pubs with accommodation in this area. Each of the rooms is comfortably furnished and provided with a TV and tea and coffee making facilities. Some rooms are also suitable for disabled or less mobile guests.

Improvement work has also been carried out in the bar area to extend and update the furnishings and facilities. The interior has retained its comfortable, cosy character while being roomy enough to accommodate the regulars and the many visitors to the area that stumble across The George. Everyone enjoys the selection of beer and lager that is available, with some well known names as well as guest real ales and a traditional brew. Food is also served in both the bar and the separate 30-seater Millingbrook Restaurant with the menu offering a select number of interesting dishes catering to a variety of tastes. All meals are freshly prepared to order and served in good sized portions. To while away a long evening there is a darts board and occasionally live entertainment is arranged.

Opening Hours: Mon-Fri 12.00-14.30, 17.00-23.00; Sat 12.00-23.00; Sun 12.00-22.30.

Food: Restaurant and Bar meals.

Credit Cards: None.

Accommodation: 14 en-suite rooms.

Facilities: Car Park.

Entertainment: Occasional live entertainment.

Local Places of Interest/Activities: Chepstow 7 miles, Dean Forest Railway Centre 2 miles, Forest of Dean 5 miles, Clearwell Caves 8 miles, Symonds Yat 13 miles, Gloucester 21 miles, St Briavels Castle 5 miles. Cheltenham 30 miles

172   The George Inn

Peter Street, Frocester,
nr Stonehouse,
Gloucestershire GL10 3TQ
Tel: 01453 822302
Fax: 01453 791612

Directions:

From Exit 13 of the M5, take the A419 towards Stroud. At the first roundabout (1 mile), follow the signs for Frocester (2.5 miles). As you enter the village you will see The George Inn on the right

The George Inn was first recorded in 1711 when it was a staging post where horses could rest before tackling the long, arduous climb up Frocester Hill. Almost 300 years later, the inn is still dispensing food, drink and copious hospitality but, most unusually, this welcoming hostelry is now owned by the local community with all its food coming from local farms. The interior has everything you would hope for in a traditional Cotswold inn, - open fires, ancient beams, gleaming brassware and walls adorned with horse tack and other memorabilia. The food here is truly outstanding, ranging from main dishes such as The George Platter of Frocester Fayre Ham or a 12oz Rump Steak, through Light Bites, jacket potatoes, sandwiches or freshly baked baguettes, vegetarian options and a Kiddies Corner. On Sunday lunchtimes there's a popular carvery. Don't miss out on the wonderful desserts, all of them prepared in the inn's kitchen and made up freshly to order. To accompany your meal, choose from the comprehensive wine list, sup one of the 4 real ales on tap, or select from the wide range of other alcoholic and soft drinks. There's a non-smoking area and in good weather you can enjoy your food and drink in the attractive beer garden. For special occasions, there's a function room capable of accommodation up to 80 guests and for larger parties the inn is happy to arrange a marquee function in the charming courtyard garden.

Opening Hours: Mon-Fri: 11.30-15.00; 17.00-23.00 Sat: 11.30-23.00 Sun: 12.00-22.30

Food: Available every lunchtime & evening

Credit Cards: All major cards except Amex & Diners

Facilities: Beer garden; games room; function room for 80; large car park

Entertainment: Boules; live music every 2-3 weeks on Fridays

Accommodation: 5 rooms, (3 en suite)

Local Places of Interest/Activities: Cotswold Way, 2 miles; canal & fishing, 3 miles; Owlpen Manor, 3.5 miles; horse riding, 4 miles; Slimbridge Wildfowl Trust, 4 miles; Berkeley Castle, 7 miles; golf - 5 courses within an 8 miles radius; Prinknash Abbey, 11 miles; Miserden Park Gardens, 14 miles; City of Gloucester, 14 miles

Internet/Website: www.georgeinn.co.uk

The Hedgehog Freehouse | 173

High Street, Bream,
Lydney,
Gloucestershire
GL15 6JS
Tel/Fax: 01594 562358

Directions:

From the A48 in Lydney, take the B4321 towards Monmouth. About 3 miles along this road, turn right on minor road to Bream (0.5 miles)

Bream village is located on the southern edge of the Forest of Dean where hundreds of miles of paths and bridleways criss-cross the woodlands. **The Hedgehog Freehouse** is conveniently situated at this "Gateway to the Forest", providing walkers, riders and other travellers with good food, real ales, and comfortable accommodation. Mine hosts, John and Evelyne Townson, bought the pub in the autumn of 2000, but John has more than a quarter of a century's experience in the hospitality business. This welcoming hostelry was originally built as a private house in the early 1900s and, with its real fire, still has a very homely atmosphere.

The pub is closed on Mondays, but from Tuesday to Saturday meals are served every lunchtime, - an appetising selection of main meals and snacks, jacket potatoes, freshly cut sandwiches and baguettes, and sweets. On Friday and Saturday evenings, a hearty 3-course meal is served between 7pm and 8.30pm, - bookings are essential. To complement your meal, there's a choice of 3 real ales, a fairly extensive wine list, and a wide range of other popular beverages. The Hedgehog also provides an excellent base for visitors to the Forest of Dean, with 2 guest bedrooms available, both doubles en suite, very well equipped and furnished to a high standard.

Opening Hours: Tue-Fri: 10.30-14.30; 18.30-23.00 Sat: 11.00-23.00 Sun: 11.00-22.30

Food: Bar meals, Tue-Sat lunchtimes; Dinner: Fri-Sat

Credit Cards: All major cards except Amex & Diners

Facilities: Children welcome; beer garden; large car park

Entertainment: Darts; quoits; monthly entertainment

Accommodation: 2 double rooms, both en suite

Local Places of Interest/Activities: Forest of Dean, 1 mile; Dean Forest Railway, Parkend, 2 miles; Lydney Park Gardens, Lydney, 3.5 miles

Internet/Website: hedgehogfreehouse@btinternet.com

174 The Old Crown Inn

Uley, Dursley
Gloucestershire
GL11 5SN
Tel: 01453 860502

Directions:

Leave the M5 at junction 13 and take the A419 east towards Stroud. As you come into Stroud take the B4066 signposted for Dursley. About 6 miles along this road will bring you to the village of Uley.

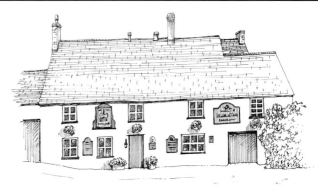

The peaceful village of Uley lies in the shadow of the massive Uley Bury Iron Age hill fort. The 32-acre construction is largely unexcavated however in recent years some evidence of the wealthy community who inhabited the fort in the first century BC has been uncovered with the items found including bronze, glass jewellery, gold coins and ingots. About a mile from the hill fort lies Uley Tumulus which is better known as Hetty Pegler's Tump. This 180-foot long Neolithic barrow, which contains four burial chambers, takes its name from Hester Pegler, the wife of a landowner who lived nearby in the 17th century.

Back in the village, **The Old Crown Inn** is a charming 17th century building of Cotswold stone. Originally a row of cottages this is now a cosy village pub with an interior featuring exposed wooden beams and an open fire. This is a popular establishment with the locals from Uley and the surrounding area, and is also well liked by tourists. The Old Crown stocks a wide range of real ales, with six usually on offer, including the renowned, locally brewed Uley Bitter. It is not surprising to learn that this is a CAMRA establishment with all the beer being kept in tip top condition. Meals are available every day at lunch time and each evening with all credit cards welcome. The wide ranging menu includes a fine selection of hot dishes, salads, jacket potatoes and desserts and there are some classic choices as well as some more unusual options. All the meals are home cooked, freshly prepared to order and served in an efficient and friendly manner to your table. In addition to fine food and drink there are three en-suite rooms available for bed and breakfast accommodation. Comfortably furnished the rooms are of varying sizes and each is provided with a TV and tea and coffee making facilities.

Opening Hours: Mon-Sat 11.00-15.00, 17.00-23.00; Sun 12.00-15.00, 18.00-22.30.

Food: Bar meals and snacks.

Credit Cards: Visa, Access, Delta, Switch.

Accommodation: 3 en-suite rooms.

Facilities: Pool table/games room, Beer garden.

Local Places of Interest/Activities: Slimbridge Wildfowl Trust 8 miles, Owlpen Manor 1 mile, Berkeley Castle 8 miles, Miserden Park Gardens 15 miles, Prinknash Abbey 12 miles.

The Stagecoach Inn 175

Newport, Berkeley,
Gloucestershire
GL13 9PY
Tel: 01453 810385
Fax: 01453 819128

Directions:

From the M5 take Exit 14 and then go north on the A38 towards Gloucester. About 3.5 miles along this road you will come to Newport and you will see The Stagecoach Inn on your left

As its name suggests, **The Stagecoach Inn** was built in the romantic era of stagecoach travel although, oddly, it was then called The White Hart and only assumed its present name in 1940. The inn still exudes a wonderful olde-worlde atmosphere with its open fire, ancient beams and with its brass items and other collectibles hanging on the walls.

This welcoming Free House has acquired county-wide fame for one of the dishes featured on its very extensive menu. "The One and Only Original & Infamous Dragon Pie" is made to a closely guarded secret recipe but mine hosts, David and Lynn Heenan, are prepared to reveal that it is made of prime beef, ("dragons being out of season"), steeped in red wine and lots of hot things, including hot chillies. The really brave can order a Double Dragon, - "twice the size, not twice as hot!" For those with regular appetites, the menu offers a huge choice of traditional pub food, starters, healthy salads and snacks, as well as a selection of Smaller Portions for Small Appetites. Whatever your choice, enjoy it either in the spacious bar or in the non-smoking area, accompanied perhaps by one of the 3 real ales on tap, a selection from the wine list or from David's own personal favourite wines listed on the blackboard behind the bar.

Opening Hours: Mon-Sat: 11.00-15.00; 17.30-23.00 Sun: 12.00-22.30

Food: Main meals & bar snacks available every lunchtime, evening and all day Sunday

Credit Cards: All major cards accepted

Facilities: Large beer garden; barbecue area; 2 large car parks

Entertainment: Pétanque piste; occasional live music

Local Places of Interest/Activities:
Berkeley Castle, 2.5 miles; Slimbridge Wildfowl Trust, 7 miles; Owlpen Manor, 8 miles; Woodchester Park Gardens (NT), 10 miles; City of Bristol, 15 miles; City of Gloucester, 15 miles

Internet/Website:
e-mail: stagecoach@newportglos.fsnet.co.uk

176 Vine Tree Inn

Randwick, Stroud,
Gloucestershire
GL6 6JA
Tel: 01453 763748

Directions:

From Exit 13 of the M5, take the A419 towards Stroud & Cirencester. After 4½ miles you will see a signpost to Cashergreen. Follow this road and after another mile there is a signpost to Randwick. Take this turning and The Vine Tree Inn is on the right, just after the church

Originally an ale house and two cottages, the **Vine Tree Inn** has a history going back to the 1600s and it's reputed that one of its earliest customers was no less a luminary than Oliver Cromwell himself. Although the inn has been altered over the years, the interior with its exposed stone walls, ancient beams and vintage brasses, has all the character and charm you would expect of such a venerable building. A wood-burning fire, a collection of old plates and another of wind chimes all add to the relaxing atmosphere.

Mine hosts at the Vine Tree are Loretta and Scott Miles who took over here in the autumn of 2000 and offer their customers an appetising choice of home cooked food, freshly prepared and served every lunchtime and evening except Monday lunchtimes. Real Ale fans will find a choice of 3 ever-changing brews, wine lovers are offered a small selection of quality wines, and the inn stocks a very wide range of non-alcoholic drinks. The spacious bar is divided into 3 areas, one of them non-smoking, and in good weather customers can also enjoy the wholesome fare on the beer patio. Children are welcome and there's a Wendy House and pets' corner to help keep them entertained. Other entertainment includes darts, crib and dominoes, and live music every 6 weeks or so.

Opening Hours: Mon: 18.30-23.00 Tue-Fri: 12.00-15.00; 18.30-23.00 Sat: 11.00-23.00 Sun: 12.00-22.30

Food: Home cooked food available lunchtimes, Tue-Sun, and every evening

Credit Cards: All major cards except Amex & Diners

Facilities: Beer patio; Wendy House; pets corner; large car park

Entertainment: Darts, crib, dominoes; live music every 6 weeks

Local Places of Interest/Activities: Selsey Herb Farm, 4 miles; Woodchester Mansion (NT), 6 miles; Slimbridge Wildfowl and Wetlands Trust, 9 miles; Gloucester Cathedral, Gloucester Docks, Robert Opie Collection, Transport Museum, Folk Museum, Jet Age Museum, all at Gloucester, 10 miles

The White Hart Inn   177

The Street,
Leonard Stanley,
Gloucestershire
GL10 3NR
Tel: 01453 822702

Directions:

Leave the M5 at Exit 13 and take the A419 east towards Stroud. About 2 miles from the motorway, the village of Leonard Stanley is signposted to the right

As you walk down towards Leonard Stanley, the Vale of Severn is spread before you and the famous river cuts through the landscape like a silver ribbon in the far distance. In the heart of this peaceful and picturesque village, **The White Hart** stands with the magnificent church of St Swithin's on one side and several old timber-framed cottages meandering up the quiet street on the other. Mine hosts at this traditional coaching inn dating from the early 18th century are Steve and Julie Price who offer a warm welcome with a selection of fine ales, cider and wines, along with a tasty selection of home cooked country fayre.

The White Hart has been recently renovated and retains its open log fires, exposed beams and a warm and friendly atmosphere. There is a small garden and, for those of a more sporting nature, a fine pool room. For those interested in the Arts, there is a rare treat, - The White Hart was home to the artist Stanley Spencer during the years 1941-43 when, because of the war, he left his beloved Cookham to live and work in Leonard Stanley. In an upstairs room he painted some of his most famous canvasses. Reproductions of these works around the bar give rise to the odd chuckle from older locals who remember Stanley, or "Sir Stanley" as they will remind you, drawing them as children while they went about their business. They in their turn were amused at the sometimes odd behaviour of the artist and his special women friends.

Opening Hours: Mon-Sun: 12.00-16.00; 18.00-23.00

Food: Bar meals and snacks

Credit Cards: Not accepted

Facilities: Beer garden

Entertainment: Pool table; games room

Local Places of Interest/Activities:
Owlpen Manor, 4 miles; Slimbridge Wildfowl Trust, 6 miles; Berkeley Castle, 9 miles; Prinknash Abbey, 10 miles; Miserden Park Gardens, 13 miles; City of Gloucester, 13 miles

178   The White Hart Inn

Broadoak
Newnham on Severn
Gloucestershire
GL14 1JB
Tel: 01594 516319

Directions:

Leave the M5 at junction 11 and take the A40 towards Gloucester. Two miles beyond Gloucester turn onto the A48 Chepstow road. The village of Broadoak can be found about 9 miles along this road, just before you reach Newnham.

The villages of Newnham and Broadoak are said to be two of the best places from which to see the famous Severn Bore, the natural wave formation which is created when the incoming tide from the Bristol Channel meets the water flowing seawards from the Severn. Here the river is quite narrow and the main road passes quite close to its banks, making viewing a very dramatic affair.

The White Hart Inn is a large comfortable pub located on the main A48 overlooking the River Severn and an ideal spot for viewing a 'bore'. In warm summer weather the beautiful patio garden is also popular with customers who want to catch a little sunshine while enjoying a drink and a bite to eat. The large interior is cosy and welcoming, the open fire that is lit in winter makes it even more inviting, and the decor has a navel theme throughout. The inn is popular with locals and is very conveniently located for travellers along the busy Gloucester-Chepstow road. The restaurant is exceedingly popular and bookings are to be recommended at weekends throughout the year. The menu offers an excellent choice of delicious, freshly prepared dishes featuring fish, meat and vegetarian options. The quality of the meals is excellent and everyone is sure to find something on the menu to suit their taste. Traditional Sunday Lunches are served and there is also a bar menu of specials and snacks. Behind the bar there is stocked a good selection of real ales, beer and lager together with the usual range of wine, spirits and soft drinks. At present no accommodation is available although a Travel Lodge is planned.

Opening Hours: Mon-Sun 12.00-15.00, 18.30-23.00.

Food: Bar meals and snacks, A la Carte, Traditional Sunday Lunch.

Credit Cards: None.

Facilities: Pool table/games room, Patio garden, Car Park.

Entertainment: Regular Live Music.

Local Places of Interest/Activities: Littledean Hall 3 miles, Westbury Court Garden 2 miles, Forest of Dean 4 miles, Clearwell Caves 9 miles, Symonds Yat 15 miles, Gloucester 11 miles, St Briavels Castle 15 miles.

The Yew Tree | 179

Clifford's Mesne
nr Mayhill
Gloucestershire
GL18 1JS
Tel: 01531 820719

Directions:

From Ross-on-Wye follow the A40 towards Gloucester. After 5 miles turn left onto the B4222 and then after two miles turn right for Clifford's Mesne. After about a mile a turning on the right will lead to the village of May Hill.

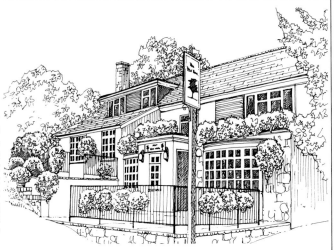

The delightful village of Clifford's Mesne, near to May Hill, is the location of the charming establishment of **The Yew Tree**. The attractive building in which this country inn and restaurant is housed is set slightly back from the road and was originally a cider press. Over the years the building has been enlarged in stages resulting in the sprawling, spacious building we see today. The interior is well furnished throughout in a modern style while still retaining many original features. The bar area is a pleasant place in which to enjoy a refreshing drink or light snack, and there is also a delightful dining room. Food is served from a blackboard menu in the bar, or from a more extensive menu in the restaurant, both of which regularly feature fresh fish from Brixham and home-made bread. The wide choice of superb food, which is cooked to perfection, is due in no small part to the owner Paul, who trained with the Roux brothers. In addition to planning the seasonal menus, Paul also arranges regular gourmet evenings. These evenings prove to be very popular and these, in addition to the Sunday lunches, should be booked in advance. To accompany your meal the bar serves a good range of beers, ales and cider with some local brews being featured. If you are in need to a comfortable place to stay then you need look no further than The Yew Tree. Here they have two double en-suite rooms furnished to an exceptional standard.

Opening Hours: Tues-Sat 12.00-15.00, 18.30-23.00; Sun 12.00-15.00, 18.30-22.30.

Food: Bar meals and snacks, Traditional Sunday Lunch, also à la carte restaurant and regular Gourmet Evenings.

Credit Cards: Visa, Access, Delta, Switch, Diners.

Accommodation: Two double en-suite rooms.

Facilities: Patio, Car Parking.

Local Places of Interest/Activities: Ross-on-Wye 5 miles, Forest of Dean 6 miles, Goodrich Castle 10 miles, Symonds Yat 15 miles.

Internet/website:
www.yewtreeinnuk/cliffordmesne.co.uk

The Hidden Inns of the Welsh Borders

ALPHABETIC LIST OF INNS   181

A

The Acton Arms	Morville, Shropshire	33
The Admiral Duncan	Baschurch, Shropshire	10
The Admiral Rodney	Criggion, Powys	11
The Albion	Worcester, Worcestershire	97
Alma Inn	Linton, Herefordshire	78

B

The Bailey Inn	Yorkley, Gloucestershire	167
The Baron of Beef	Bucknell, Shropshire	34
The Bell Inn	Moreton-in-Marsh, Gloucestershire	139
The Bell	Pensax, Worcestershire	98
The Black Bear Inn	Moreton-in-Marsh, Gloucestershire	140
The Black Bear	Whitchurch, Shropshire	12
The Black Dog	Newent, Gloucestershire	168
The Black Horse Inn	Maesbrook, Shropshire	13
The Black Lion	Hereford, Herefordshire	79
The Black Swan Inn	Gloucester, Gloucestershire	141
The Boat Inn	Whitney on Wye, Herefordshire	80
The Boot Inn	Flyford Flavell, Worcestershire	117
The Bradford Arms	Knockin, Shropshire	14
The Bradford Arms	Llanymynech, Shropshire	15
The Brewers Arms	Lower Dingle, Worcestershire	118
The Bridge Inn	Stourport-on-Severn, Worcestershire	99
The Bridge Inn	Tibberton, Worcestershire	100
The Butchers Arms	Stoke Prior, Worcestershire	101

C

The Chase Inn	Bishop's Frome, Herefordshire	55
The Chequers Inn	Fladbury, Worcestershire	119
The Church Inn	Ludlow, Shropshire	35
The Cleveland Arms	High Ercall, Shropshire	16
The Cliffe Arms	Mathon, Herefordshire	56
The Cross Hands	Alveston, Bristol	169
The Crown Inn	Longtown, Herefordshire	81
The Crown Inn	Clunton, Shropshire	36
The Crown Inn	Evesham, Worcestershire	120
The Crown Inn	Wentnor, Shropshire	37
The Crown Inn	Worcester, Worcestershire	102
The Crown	Hambrook, Bristol	170

E

England's Gate Inn	Bodenham, Herefordshire	57

F

The Fountain Inn	St. Michaels, Worcestershire	103

ALPHABETIC LIST OF INNS

G

The George Inn	Aylburton, Gloucestershire	171
The George Inn	Frocester, Gloucestershire	172
The Green Dragon	Little Stretton, Shropshire	38

H

The Hedgehog	Bream, Gloucestershire	173
The Hollow Bottom	Guiting Power, Gloucestershire	142
The Hop Pole Inn	Leominster, Herefordshire	58
The Horn and Trumpet	Bewdley, Worcestershire	104
The Horse & Groom	South Cerney, Gloucestershire	143
The Horse and Jockey	Whitchurch, Shropshire	17
The Horseshoes	Tilstock, Shropshire	18

K

The Kings Head Inn	Bledington, Gloucestershire	144
The Kings Head's	Upton-upon-Severn, Worcestershire	121
The Kingsholm Inn	Gloucester, Gloucestershire	145
The Kynnersley Arms	Leighton, Shropshire	39

L

The Lamb Inn	Stoke Prior, Herefordshire	59

M

The Maidenhead Inn	Orleton, Herefordshire	60
The Malvern Hills Hotel	Malvern, Herefordshire	61
The Marshpools Country Inn	Ledgemoor, Herefordshire	62

N

The Nags Head Inn	Canon Pyon, Herefordshire	63
The Narrowboat Inn	Whittington, Shropshire	19

O

The Old Crown Inn	Uley, Gloucestershire	174

P

The Penrhos Arms	Whittington, Shropshire	20
The Plaisterers Arms	Winchcombe, Gloucestershire	146
The Plough and Harrow	Guarlford, Worcestershire	122
The Plough Inn	Lower Broadheath, Worcestershire	105
The Plough Inn	Stratton, Gloucestershire	147
The Plume of Feathers	Castlemorton Common, Worcestershire	123

R

The Red Lion Inn	Kilpeck, Herefordshire	82
The Red Lion Inn	Madley, Herefordshire	83
The Red Lion Inn	Pembridge, Herefordshire	64
The Red Lion	Bradley Green, Worcestershire	106

ALPHABETIC LIST OF INNS

The Rising Sun	Stourport-on-Severn, Worcestershire	107
Riverside Lechlade Ltd	Lechlade, Gloucestershire	148
Roebuck Inn	Brimfield, Herefordshire	65
The Rose & Crown	Ludlow, Shropshire	40

S

The Seven Stars	Beckbury, Shropshire	41
The Snowshill Arms	Snowshill, Gloucestershire	149
The Stable Tavern	Cleobury Mortimer, Shropshire	42
The Stagecoach Inn	Newport, Gloucestershire	175
The Stokesay Castle Inn	Craven Arms, Shropshire	43
The Swan Inn	Moreton-in-Marsh, Gloucestershire	150
The Swan	Dorrington, Shropshire	44

T

The Talbot Inn	Much Wenlock, Shropshire	45
The Talbot	Pershore, Worcestershire	124
The Temple Bar	Ewyas Harold, Herefordshire	84
The Three Horseshoes	Alveley, Shropshire	46
The Travellers Rest	Stretton Sugwas, Herefordshire	85

V

The Vernon Arms	Hanbury, Worcestershire	108
The Vine Tree Inn	Randwick, Gloucestershire	176

W

The Wheatsheaf Inn	Fromes Hill, Herefordshire	66
The White Hart Inn	Newnham on Severn, Gloucestershire	178
The White Hart	Leonard Stanley, Gloucestershire	177

Y

Ye Olde Ferrie Inne	Symonds Yat West, Herefordshire	86
The Yew Tree	Clifford's Mesne, Gloucestershire	179

SHREWSBURY AND NORTH SHROPSHIRE

| The Bradford Arms | Llanymynech, Shropshire | 15 |

BRIDGNORTH AND SOUTH SHROPSHIRE

The Acton Arms	Morville, Shropshire	33
The Church Inn	Ludlow, Shropshire	35
The Crown Inn	Wentnor, Shropshire	37
The Kynnersley Arms	Leighton, Shropshire	39
The Rose & Crown	Ludlow, Shropshire	40
The Stokesay Castle Inn	Craven Arms, Shropshire	43
The Talbot Inn	Much Wenlock, Shropshire	45

LEOMINSTER AND NORTH HEREFORDSHIRE

The Chase Inn	Bishop's Frome, Herefordshire	55
The Malvern Hills Hotel	Malvern, Herefordshire	61
The Marshpools Country Inn	Ledgemoor, Herefordshire	62
The Nags Head Inn	Canon Pyon, Herefordshire	63
Roebuck Inn	Brimfield, Herefordshire	65
The Wheatsheaf Inn	Fromes Hill, Herefordshire	66

HEREFORD AND SOUTH HEREFORDSHIRE

Alma Inn	Linton, Herefordshire	78
The Boat Inn	Whitney on Wye, Herefordshire	80
The Red Lion Inn	Madley, Herefordshire	83
Ye Olde Ferrie Inne	Symonds Yat West, Herefordshire	86

WORCESTER AND NORTH WORCESTERSHIRE

| The Horn and Trumpet | Bewdley, Worcestershire | 104 |

SOUTH WORCESTERSHIRE

The Boot Inn	Flyford Flavell, Worcestershire	117
The Chequers Inn	Fladbury, Worcestershire	119
The Crown Inn	Evesham, Worcestershire	120

ACCOMMODATION

GLOUCESTER AND EAST GLOUCESTERSHIRE

The Bell Inn	Moreton-in-Marsh, Gloucestershire	139
The Black Bear Inn	Moreton-in-Marsh, Gloucestershire	140
The Black Swan Inn	Gloucester, Gloucestershire	141
The Hollow Bottom	Guiting Power, Gloucestershire	142
The Horse & Groom	South Cerney, Gloucestershire	143
The Kings Head Inn	Bledington, Gloucestershire	144
The Kingsholm Inn	Gloucester, Gloucestershire	145
The Plaisterers Arms	Winchcombe, Gloucestershire	146
The Plough Inn	Stratton, Gloucestershire	147
Riverside Lechlade Ltd	Lechlade, Gloucestershire	148
The Swan Inn	Moreton-in-Marsh, Gloucestershire	150

SOUTH AND WEST GLOUCESTERSHIRE

The Crown	Hambrook, Bristol	170
The George Inn	Aylburton, Gloucestershire	171
The George Inn	Frocester, Gloucestershire	172
The Hedgehog	Bream, Gloucestershire	173
The Old Crown Inn	Uley, Gloucestershire	174
The Yew Tree	Clifford's Mesne, Gloucestershire	179

186   *ALL DAY OPENING*

SHREWSBURY AND NORTH SHROPSHIRE

The Black Bear	Whitchurch, Shropshire	12
The Cleveland Arms	High Ercall, Shropshire	16
The Horseshoes	Tilstock, Shropshire	18
The Penrhos Arms	Whittington, Shropshire	20

BRIDGNORTH AND SOUTH SHROPSHIRE

The Church Inn	Ludlow, Shropshire	35
The Crown Inn	Clunton, Shropshire	36
The Rose & Crown	Ludlow, Shropshire	40
The Stable Tavern	Cleobury Mortimer, Shropshire	42
The Stokesay Castle Inn	Craven Arms, Shropshire	43

LEOMINSTER AND NORTH HEREFORDSHIRE

England's Gate Inn	Bodenham, Herefordshire	57
The Hop Pole Inn	Leominster, Herefordshire	58
The Malvern Hills Hotel	Malvern, Herefordshire	61
The Wheatsheaf Inn	Fromes Hill, Herefordshire	66

HEREFORD AND SOUTH HEREFORDSHIRE

The Black Lion	Hereford, Herefordshire	79
The Boat Inn	Whitney on Wye, Herefordshire	80
Ye Olde Ferrie Inne	Symonds Yat West, Herefordshire	86

WORCESTER AND NORTH WORCESTERSHIRE

The Bridge Inn	Stourport-on-Severn, Worcestershire	99
The Butchers Arms	Stoke Prior, Worcestershire	101
The Fountain Inn	St. Michaels, Worcestershire	103
The Horn and Trumpet	Bewdley, Worcestershire	104
The Rising Sun	Stourport-on-Severn, Worcestershire	107

SOUTH WORCESTERSHIRE

The Kings Head's	Upton-upon-Severn, Worcestershire	121
The Plume of Feathers	Castlemorton Common, Worcestershire	123

ALL DAY OPENING

GLOUCESTER AND EAST GLOUCESTERSHIRE

The Bell Inn	Moreton-in-Marsh, Gloucestershire	139
The Black Bear Inn	Moreton-in-Marsh, Gloucestershire	140
The Black Swan Inn	Gloucester, Gloucestershire	141
The Hollow Bottom	Guiting Power, Gloucestershire	142
The Horse & Groom	South Cerney, Gloucestershire	143
Riverside Lechlade Ltd	Lechlade, Gloucestershire	148
The Swan Inn	Moreton-in-Marsh, Gloucestershire	150

SOUTH AND WEST GLOUCESTERSHIRE

The Cross Hands	Alveston, Bristol	169

188 *CHILDRENS FACILITIES*

SHREWSBURY AND NORTH SHROPSHIRE

The Admiral Rodney	Criggion, Powys	11
The Cleveland Arms	High Ercall, Shropshire	16
The Horseshoes	Tilstock, Shropshire	18
The Penrhos Arms	Whittington, Shropshire	20

BRIDGNORTH AND SOUTH SHROPSHIRE

The Acton Arms	Morville, Shropshire	33
The Baron of Beef	Bucknell, Shropshire	34
The Seven Stars	Beckbury, Shropshire	41
The Stokesay Castle Inn	Craven Arms, Shropshire	43
The Three Horseshoes	Alveley, Shropshire	46

LEOMINSTER AND NORTH HEREFORDSHIRE

The Maidenhead Inn	Orleton, Herefordshire	60
The Malvern Hills Hotel	Malvern, Herefordshire	61
The Marshpools Country Inn	Ledgemoor, Herefordshire	62
The Nags Head Inn	Canon Pyon, Herefordshire	63
The Wheatsheaf Inn	Fromes Hill, Herefordshire	66

HEREFORD AND SOUTH HEREFORDSHIRE

The Temple Bar	Ewyas Harold, Herefordshire	84
The Travellers Rest	Stretton Sugwas, Herefordshire	85

WORCESTER AND NORTH WORCESTERSHIRE

The Butchers Arms	Stoke Prior, Worcestershire	101
The Fountain Inn	St. Michaels, Worcestershire	103
The Plough Inn	Lower Broadheath, Worcestershire	105
The Red Lion	Bradley Green, Worcestershire	106
The Vernon Arms	Hanbury, Worcestershire	108

SOUTH WORCESTERSHIRE

The Crown Inn	Evesham, Worcestershire	120
The Plough and Harrow	Guarlford, Worcestershire	122
The Plume of Feathers	Castlemorton Common, Worcestershire	123

GLOUCESTER AND EAST GLOUCESTERSHIRE

The Bell Inn	Moreton-in-Marsh, Gloucestershire	139
The Plough Inn	Stratton, Gloucestershire	147
The Snowshill Arms	Snowshill, Gloucestershire	149

SOUTH AND WEST GLOUCESTERSHIRE

The Vine Tree Inn	Randwick, Gloucestershire	176

CREDIT CARDS ACCEPTED

SHREWSBURY AND NORTH SHROPSHIRE

The Admiral Duncan	Baschurch, Shropshire	10
The Admiral Rodney	Criggion, Powys	11
The Black Horse Inn	Maesbrook, Shropshire	13
The Bradford Arms	Llanymynech, Shropshire	15
The Bradford Arms	Knockin, Shropshire	14
The Cleveland Arms	High Ercall, Shropshire	16
The Horse and Jockey	Whitchurch, Shropshire	17
The Narrowboat Inn	Whittington, Shropshire	19
The Penrhos Arms	Whittington, Shropshire	20

BRIDGNORTH AND SOUTH SHROPSHIRE

The Acton Arms	Morville, Shropshire	33
The Baron of Beef	Bucknell, Shropshire	34
The Church Inn	Ludlow, Shropshire	35
The Crown Inn	Wentnor, Shropshire	37
The Seven Stars	Beckbury, Shropshire	41
The Stable Tavern	Cleobury Mortimer, Shropshire	42
The Stokesay Castle Inn	Craven Arms, Shropshire	43
The Talbot Inn	Much Wenlock, Shropshire	45
The Three Horseshoes	Alveley, Shropshire	46

LEOMINSTER AND NORTH HEREFORDSHIRE

The Chase Inn	Bishop's Frome, Herefordshire	55
The Cliffe Arms	Mathon, Herefordshire	56
England's Gate Inn	Bodenham, Herefordshire	57
The Hop Pole Inn	Leominster, Herefordshire	58
The Maidenhead Inn	Orleton, Herefordshire	60
The Malvern Hills Hotel	Malvern, Herefordshire	61
The Marshpools Country Inn	Ledgemoor, Herefordshire	62
The Nags Head Inn	Canon Pyon, Herefordshire	63
Roebuck Inn	Brimfield, Herefordshire	65
The Wheatsheaf Inn	Fromes Hill, Herefordshire	66

HEREFORD AND SOUTH HEREFORDSHIRE

The Black Lion	Hereford, Herefordshire	79
The Boat Inn	Whitney on Wye, Herefordshire	80
The Red Lion Inn	Madley, Herefordshire	83
The Temple Bar	Ewyas Harold, Herefordshire	84
Ye Olde Ferrie Inne	Symonds Yat West, Herefordshire	86

WORCESTER AND NORTH WORCESTERSHIRE

The Bell	Pensax, Worcestershire	98
The Bridge Inn	Stourport-on-Severn, Worcestershire	99
The Bridge Inn	Tibberton, Worcestershire	100

WORCESTER AND NORTH WORCESTERSHIRE (CONT.)

The Fountain Inn	St. Michaels, Worcestershire	103
The Plough Inn	Lower Broadheath, Worcestershire	105
The Red Lion	Bradley Green, Worcestershire	106
The Vernon Arms	Hanbury, Worcestershire	108

SOUTH WORCESTERSHIRE

The Boot Inn	Flyford Flavell, Worcestershire	117
The Chequers Inn	Fladbury, Worcestershire	119
The Crown Inn	Evesham, Worcestershire	120
The Kings Head's	Upton-upon-Severn, Worcestershire	121
The Plough and Harrow	Guarlford, Worcestershire	122

GLOUCESTER AND EAST GLOUCESTERSHIRE

The Bell Inn	Moreton-in-Marsh, Gloucestershire	139
The Black Bear Inn	Moreton-in-Marsh, Gloucestershire	140
The Black Swan Inn	Gloucester, Gloucestershire	141
The Hollow Bottom	Guiting Power, Gloucestershire	142
The Horse & Groom	South Cerney, Gloucestershire	143
The Kings Head Inn	Bledington, Gloucestershire	144
The Plaisterers Arms	Winchcombe, Gloucestershire	146
The Plough Inn	Stratton, Gloucestershire	147
Riverside Lechlade Ltd	Lechlade, Gloucestershire	148
The Swan Inn	Moreton-in-Marsh, Gloucestershire	150

SOUTH AND WEST GLOUCESTERSHIRE

The Bailey Inn	Yorkley, Gloucestershire	167
The Black Dog	Newent, Gloucestershire	168
The Cross Hands	Alveston, Bristol	169
The Crown	Hambrook, Bristol	170
The George Inn	Frocester, Gloucestershire	172
The Hedgehog	Bream, Gloucestershire	173
The Old Crown Inn	Uley, Gloucestershire	174
The Stagecoach Inn	Newport, Gloucestershire	175
The Vine Tree Inn	Randwick, Gloucestershire	176
The Yew Tree	Clifford's Mesne, Gloucestershire	179

GARDEN, PATIO OR TERRACE | 191

SHREWSBURY AND NORTH SHROPSHIRE

The Admiral Rodney	Criggion, Powys	11
The Black Bear	Whitchurch, Shropshire	12
The Bradford Arms	Knockin, Shropshire	14
The Cleveland Arms	High Ercall, Shropshire	16
The Horse and Jockey	Whitchurch, Shropshire	17
The Horseshoes	Tilstock, Shropshire	18
The Narrowboat Inn	Whittington, Shropshire	19
The Penrhos Arms	Whittington, Shropshire	20

BRIDGNORTH AND SOUTH SHROPSHIRE

The Acton Arms	Morville, Shropshire	33
The Baron of Beef	Bucknell, Shropshire	34
The Crown Inn	Clunton, Shropshire	36
The Green Dragon	Little Stretton, Shropshire	38
The Rose & Crown	Ludlow, Shropshire	40
The Seven Stars	Beckbury, Shropshire	41
The Stokesay Castle Inn	Craven Arms, Shropshire	43
The Swan	Dorrington, Shropshire	44
The Three Horseshoes	Alveley, Shropshire	46

LEOMINSTER AND NORTH HEREFORDSHIRE

The Cliffe Arms	Mathon, Herefordshire	56
England's Gate Inn	Bodenham, Herefordshire	57
The Hop Pole Inn	Leominster, Herefordshire	58
The Lamb Inn	Stoke Prior, Herefordshire	59
The Maidenhead Inn	Orleton, Herefordshire	60
The Malvern Hills Hotel	Malvern, Herefordshire	61
The Marshpools Country Inn	Ledgemoor, Herefordshire	62
The Nags Head Inn	Canon Pyon, Herefordshire	63
The Wheatsheaf Inn	Fromes Hill, Herefordshire	66

HEREFORD AND SOUTH HEREFORDSHIRE

Alma Inn	Linton, Herefordshire	78
The Boat Inn	Whitney on Wye, Herefordshire	80
The Red Lion Inn	Kilpeck, Herefordshire	82
The Temple Bar	Ewyas Harold, Herefordshire	84
The Travellers Rest	Stretton Sugwas, Herefordshire	85
Ye Olde Ferrie Inne	Symonds Yat West, Herefordshire	86

WORCESTER AND NORTH WORCESTERSHIRE

The Albion	Worcester, Worcestershire	97
The Bell	Pensax, Worcestershire	98
The Bridge Inn	Stourport-on-Severn, Worcestershire	99
The Bridge Inn	Tibberton, Worcestershire	100
The Butchers Arms	Stoke Prior, Worcestershire	101

192 · *GARDEN, PATIO OR TERRACE*

WORCESTER AND NORTH WORCESTERSHIRE (CONT.)

The Crown Inn	Worcester, Worcestershire	102
The Fountain Inn	St. Michaels, Worcestershire	103
The Plough Inn	Lower Broadheath, Worcestershire	105
The Red Lion	Bradley Green, Worcestershire	106
The Vernon Arms	Hanbury, Worcestershire	108

SOUTH WORCESTERSHIRE

The Boot Inn	Flyford Flavell, Worcestershire	117
The Crown Inn	Evesham, Worcestershire	120
The Kings Head's	Upton-upon-Severn, Worcestershire	121
The Plough and Harrow	Guarlford, Worcestershire	122
The Plume of Feathers	Castlemorton Common, Worcestershire	123
The Talbot	Pershore, Worcestershire	124

GLOUCESTER AND EAST GLOUCESTERSHIRE

The Bell Inn	Moreton-in-Marsh, Gloucestershire	139
The Black Bear Inn	Moreton-in-Marsh, Gloucestershire	140
The Hollow Bottom	Guiting Power, Gloucestershire	142
The Horse & Groom	South Cerney, Gloucestershire	143
The Kingsholm Inn	Gloucester, Gloucestershire	145
The Plaisterers Arms	Winchcombe, Gloucestershire	146
The Plough Inn	Stratton, Gloucestershire	147
Riverside Lechlade Ltd	Lechlade, Gloucestershire	148
The Snowshill Arms	Snowshill, Gloucestershire	149
The Swan Inn	Moreton-in-Marsh, Gloucestershire	150

SOUTH AND WEST GLOUCESTERSHIRE

The Bailey Inn	Yorkley, Gloucestershire	167
The Cross Hands	Alveston, Bristol	169
The Crown	Hambrook, Bristol	170
The George Inn	Frocester, Gloucestershire	172
The Hedgehog	Bream, Gloucestershire	173
The Old Crown Inn	Uley, Gloucestershire	174
The Stagecoach Inn	Newport, Gloucestershire	175
The Vine Tree Inn	Randwick, Gloucestershire	176
The White Hart	Leonard Stanley, Gloucestershire	177
The White Hart Inn	Newnham on Severn, Gloucestershire	178
The Yew Tree	Clifford's Mesne, Gloucestershire	179

Live Entertainment

Shrewsbury and North Shropshire

The Admiral Duncan	Baschurch, Shropshire	10
The Admiral Rodney	Criggion, Powys	11
The Black Horse Inn	Maesbrook, Shropshire	13
The Bradford Arms	Knockin, Shropshire	14

Bridgnorth and South Shropshire

The Acton Arms	Morville, Shropshire	33
The Baron of Beef	Bucknell, Shropshire	34
The Crown Inn	Clunton, Shropshire	36
The Green Dragon	Little Stretton, Shropshire	38

Leominster and North Herefordshire

England's Gate Inn	Bodenham, Herefordshire	57
The Malvern Hills Hotel	Malvern, Herefordshire	61
The Wheatsheaf Inn	Fromes Hill, Herefordshire	66

Hereford and South Herefordshire

The Red Lion Inn	Kilpeck, Herefordshire	82
The Red Lion Inn	Madley, Herefordshire	83
The Temple Bar	Ewyas Harold, Herefordshire	84

Worcester and North Worcestershire

The Albion	Worcester, Worcestershire	97
The Bridge Inn	Stourport-on-Severn, Worcestershire	99
The Butchers Arms	Stoke Prior, Worcestershire	101
The Crown Inn	Worcester, Worcestershire	102
The Plough Inn	Lower Broadheath, Worcestershire	105
The Rising Sun	Stourport-on-Severn, Worcestershire	107
The Vernon Arms	Hanbury, Worcestershire	108

South Worcestershire

The Brewers Arms	Lower Dingle, Worcestershire	118
The Crown Inn	Evesham, Worcestershire	120
The Kings Head's	Upton-upon-Severn, Worcestershire	121
The Plough and Harrow	Guarlford, Worcestershire	122
The Plume of Feathers	Castlemorton Common, Worcestershire	123
The Talbot	Pershore, Worcestershire	124

194 LIVE ENTERTAINMENT

GLOUCESTER AND EAST GLOUCESTERSHIRE

The Bell Inn	Moreton-in-Marsh, Gloucestershire	139
The Black Swan Inn	Gloucester, Gloucestershire	141
The Plough Inn	Stratton, Gloucestershire	147
Riverside Lechlade Ltd	Lechlade, Gloucestershire	148

SOUTH AND WEST GLOUCESTERSHIRE

The Bailey Inn	Yorkley, Gloucestershire	167
The George Inn	Frocester, Gloucestershire	172
The George Inn	Aylburton, Gloucestershire	171
The Hedgehog	Bream, Gloucestershire	173
The Stagecoach Inn	Newport, Gloucestershire	175
The Vine Tree Inn	Randwick, Gloucestershire	176
The White Hart	Leonard Stanley, Gloucestershire	177

RESTAURANT/DINING AREA 195

SHREWSBURY AND NORTH SHROPSHIRE

The Admiral Duncan	Baschurch, Shropshire	10
The Bradford Arms	Knockin, Shropshire	14
The Bradford Arms	Llanymynech, Shropshire	15
The Cleveland Arms	High Ercall, Shropshire	16
The Horse and Jockey	Whitchurch, Shropshire	17
The Narrowboat Inn	Whittington, Shropshire	19

BRIDGNORTH AND SOUTH SHROPSHIRE

The Acton Arms	Morville, Shropshire	33
The Baron of Beef	Bucknell, Shropshire	34
The Church Inn	Ludlow, Shropshire	35
The Crown Inn	Clunton, Shropshire	36
The Crown Inn	Wentnor, Shropshire	37
The Green Dragon	Little Stretton, Shropshire	38
The Kynnersley Arms	Leighton, Shropshire	39
The Seven Stars	Beckbury, Shropshire	41
The Stokesay Castle Inn	Craven Arms, Shropshire	43
The Swan	Dorrington, Shropshire	44
The Talbot Inn	Much Wenlock, Shropshire	45

LEOMINSTER AND NORTH HEREFORDSHIRE

The Chase Inn	Bishop's Frome, Herefordshire	55
England's Gate Inn	Bodenham, Herefordshire	57
The Hop Pole Inn	Leominster, Herefordshire	58
The Lamb Inn	Stoke Prior, Herefordshire	59
The Maidenhead Inn	Orleton, Herefordshire	60
The Malvern Hills Hotel	Malvern, Herefordshire	61
The Nags Head Inn	Canon Pyon, Herefordshire	63
The Red Lion Inn	Pembridge, Herefordshire	64
Roebuck Inn	Brimfield, Herefordshire	65
The Wheatsheaf Inn	Fromes Hill, Herefordshire	66

HEREFORD AND SOUTH HEREFORDSHIRE

The Red Lion Inn	Madley, Herefordshire	83
The Temple Bar	Ewyas Harold, Herefordshire	84
The Travellers Rest	Stretton Sugwas, Herefordshire	85
Ye Olde Ferrie Inne	Symonds Yat West, Herefordshire	86

196   *RESTAURANT/DINING AREA*

WORCESTER AND NORTH WORCESTERSHIRE

The Albion	Worcester, Worcestershire	97
The Bell	Pensax, Worcestershire	98
The Fountain Inn	St. Michaels, Worcestershire	103
The Red Lion	Bradley Green, Worcestershire	106
The Vernon Arms	Hanbury, Worcestershire	108

SOUTH WORCESTERSHIRE

The Boot Inn	Flyford Flavell, Worcestershire	117
The Chequers Inn	Fladbury, Worcestershire	119
The Crown Inn	Evesham, Worcestershire	120
The Kings Head's	Upton-upon-Severn, Worcestershire	121
The Plough and Harrow	Guarlford, Worcestershire	122
The Plume of Feathers	Castlemorton Common, Worcestershire	123

GLOUCESTER AND EAST GLOUCESTERSHIRE

The Bell Inn	Moreton-in-Marsh, Gloucestershire	139
The Black Bear Inn	Moreton-in-Marsh, Gloucestershire	140
The Hollow Bottom	Guiting Power, Gloucestershire	142
The Horse & Groom	South Cerney, Gloucestershire	143
The Kings Head Inn	Bledington, Gloucestershire	144
The Kingsholm Inn	Gloucester, Gloucestershire	145
The Plough Inn	Stratton, Gloucestershire	147
Riverside Lechlade Ltd	Lechlade, Gloucestershire	148

SOUTH AND WEST GLOUCESTERSHIRE

The George Inn	Aylburton, Gloucestershire	171
The White Hart	Leonard Stanley, Gloucestershire	177
The Yew Tree	Clifford's Mesne, Gloucestershire	179

A

Abbey Dore 70
Acton Scott 23
Alfrick 89
Almeley 49
Ashton 49
Aston-under-Clun 23
Atcham 23

B

Badminton 154
Belbroughton 89
Berkeley 154
Bewdley 89
Bibury 127
Billingsley 24
Bishop's Castle 24
Bisley 155
Blakeney 156
Blockley 127
Boscobel 3
Bourton-on-the-Water 127
Brampton Bryan 49
Bredon 111
Bretforton 111
Bridgnorth 24
Broadway 111
Brockhampton 70
Bromfield 25
Bromsgrove 90
Bromyard 49
Broseley 25

C

Callow Hill 91
Cannop 156
Cheltenham 128
Childswickham 112
Chipping Campden 129
Chipping Sodbury 156
Church Stretton 25
Cirencester 129
Cleeve Hill 130
Cleobury Mortimer 26
Clifton 91
Clun 26
Coleford 156
Colehurst 3
Colwall 112
Craven Arms 27

D

Deerhurst 130
Dilwyn 50
Dorstone 70
Droitwich 91
Drybrook 157
Dursley 157
Dymock 158

E

Eardisland 50
Eardisley 50
Earls Croome 112
Edge 130
Ellesmere 3
Elmley Castle 112
English Bicknormap 158
Evesham 113

F

Fairford 130
Forthampton 130
Frampton-on-Severn 158
Frocester 159

G

Garway 71
Gloucester 130
Goodrich 71
Great Malvern 113
Great Witley 92
Grosmont 71

H

Hagley 92
Hanbury 92
Hartlebury 92
Hartpury 132
Harvington 93
Hay-on-Wye 71
Hereford 71
Hoarwithy 73
Hodnet 4
Holme Lacy 73
Honeybourne 114
Hope under Dinmore 50
Horton 159
How Caple 73

I

Inkberrow 93
Ironbridge 27

K

Kempley 159
Kidderminster 93
Kilpeck 73
Kimbolton 51
Kington 51
Kinnersley 52

L

Lechlade 132
Ledbury 73
Leigh 93
Leominster 52
Little Malvern 114
Little Stretton 28
Littledean 159
Llanymynech 4

198 INDEX OF PLACES OF INTEREST

Lower Broadheath 94
Ludlow 28
Lydney 159
Lyonshall 52

M

Madley 74
Maesbury 4
Marchamley 4
Market Drayton 4
Marshfield 160
Melverley 5
Middle Littleton 114
Minchinhampton 160
Moccas 75
Monnington-on-Wye 75
Montford 5
Moreton Corbet 5
Moreton Jeffries 52
Moreton-in-Marsh 133
Mortimer's Cross 52
Morville 29
Much Marcle 75
Much Wenlock 29

N

Nailsworth 161
Nesscliffe 5
Newent 161
Newland 161
Newport 5
North Nibley 161
Northleach 133

O

Onibury 30
Orleton 52
Oswestry 6
Ozleworth 162

P

Painswick 133
Parkend 162
Pauntley 134
Pembridge 53
Pershore 115
Peterstow 75
Prestbury 134

Q

Quatt 30

R

Redditch 94
Ross-on-Wye 75
Rous Lench 115
Ruardean 162

S

Sellack 76
Selsley 163
Shatterford 94

Shifnal 30
Shobdon 53
Shrewsbury 6
Skenfrith 76
Slad 135
Slimbridge 163
Spetchley 94
St Briavels 162
Stanton 135
Stanway 135
Staunton 163
Stinchcombe 163
Stokesay 30
Stourport-on-Severn 94
Stow-on-the-Wold 135
Stroud 163
Sudeley 136
Sutton St Nicholas 53
Swainshill 76
Symonds Yat 76

T

Telford 31
Tetbury 163
Tewkesbury 136
Toddington 137
Tong 8
Tortworth 164
Twigworth 137

U

Uley 164
Upleadon 165
Upton-on-Severn 116

W

Wellington 31
Welsh Newton 77
Wem 8
Wenlock Edge 31
Weobley 53
Westbury-on-Severn 165
Weston-under-Lizard 8
Weston-under-Penyard 77
Westonbirt 165
Whitchurch 8, 77
Whittington 9
Wichenford 94
Wigmore 54
Wilton 77
Winchcombe 137
Wollaston 9
Woodchester 165
Worcester 95
Wortley 166
Wotton-under-Edge 165
Wroxeter 32
Wythall 96

Y

Yarpole 54

Hidden Inns Reader Reaction

The *Hidden Inns* research team would like to receive reader's comments on any visitor attractions or places reviewed in the book and also recommendations for suitable entries to be included in the next edition. This will help ensure that the *Hidden Inns* series continues to provide its readers with useful information on the more interesting, unusual or unique features of each attraction or place ensuring that their stay in the local area is an enjoyable and stimulating experience.

To provide your comments or recommendations would you please complete the forms below and overleaf as indicated and send to:

The Research Department, Travel Publishing Ltd,
7a Apollo House, Calleva Park, Aldermaston, Reading, RG7 8TN.

Your Name:

Your Address:

Your Telephone Number:

Please tick as appropriate: Comments ☐   Recommendation ☐

Name of *"Hidden Place"*:

Address:

Telephone Number:

Name of Contact:

Hidden Inns Reader Reaction

Comment or Reason for Recommendation:

....

....

....

....

....

....

....

....

....

....

....

....